Living Together Across Borders

OXFORD STUDIES IN THE ANTHROPOLOGY OF LANGUAGE

Series editor: Alessandro Duranti, University of California at Los Angeles

This series is devoted to works from a wide array of scholarly traditions that treat linguistic practices as forms of social action.

Editorial Board

Patricia Baquedano-López, University of California, Berkeley

Donald Brenneis, University of California at Santa Cruz

Paul B. Garrett, Temple University

Janet McIntosh, Brandeis University

Justin Richland, The University of Chicago

Thank You for Dying for Our Country: Commemorative Texts and Performances in Jerusalem
Chaim Noy

Singular and Plural: Ideologies of Linguistic Authority in 21st Century Catalonia
Kathryn A. Woolard

Linguistic Rivalries: Tamil Migrants and Anglo-Franco Conflicts
Sonia Neela Das

The Monologic Imagination
Edited by Matt Tomlinson and Julian Millie

Looking like a Language, Sounding like a Race: Raciolinguistic Ideologies and the Learning of Latinidad
Jonathan Rosa

Talking Like Children: Language and the Production of Age in the Marshall Islands
Elise Berman

The Struggle for a Multilingual Future: Youth and Education in Sri Lanka
Christina P. Davis

The Last Language on Earth: Linguistic Utopianism in the Philippines
Piers Kelly

Rethinking Politeness with Henri Bergson
Edited by Alessandro Duranti

Other Indonesians: Nationalism in an Unnative Language
Joseph Errington

Living Together Across Borders

Communicative Care in Transnational Salvadoran Families

Lynnette Arnold

OXFORD
UNIVERSITY PRESS

Oxford University Press is a department of the University of Oxford. It furthers
the University's objective of excellence in research, scholarship, and education
by publishing worldwide. Oxford is a registered trade mark of Oxford University
Press in the UK and certain other countries.

Published in the United States of America by Oxford University Press
198 Madison Avenue, New York, NY 10016, United States of America.

© Oxford University Press 2024

All rights reserved. No part of this publication may be reproduced, stored in
a retrieval system, or transmitted, in any form or by any means, without the
prior permission in writing of Oxford University Press, or as expressly permitted
by law, by license, or under terms agreed with the appropriate reproduction
rights organization. Inquiries concerning reproduction outside the scope of the
above should be sent to the Rights Department, Oxford University Press, at the
address above.

You must not circulate this work in any other form
and you must impose this same condition on any acquirer.

Library of Congress Cataloging-in-Publication Data
Names: Arnold, Lynnette, author.
Title: Living together across borders : communicative care in transnational
Salvadoran families / Lynnette Arnold.
Description: New York, NY : Oxford University Press, 2024. |
Series: Oxford studies anthropology lang series |
Includes bibliographical references and index.
Identifiers: LCCN 2024009106 (print) | LCCN 2024009107 (ebook) |
ISBN 9780197755730 (hardback) | ISBN 9780197755747 (paperback) |
ISBN 9780197755761 (epub)
Subjects: LCSH: Transnationalism. | Salvadorans—United States—Social conditions. |
Communication in families—El Salvador. | Salvadorans—United States—Communication. |
Emigration and immigration—Economic aspects. | El Salvador—Foreign relations—United States. |
United States—Foreign relations—El Salvador.
Classification: LCC JZ1320 .A76 2024 (print) | LCC JZ1320 (ebook) |
DDC 305.868/7284073—dc23/eng/20240316
LC record available at https://lccn.loc.gov/2024009106
LC ebook record available at https://lccn.loc.gov/2024009107

DOI: 10.1093/oso/9780197755730.001.0001

A mi querida comadre. Sin vos este libro no existiría. Gracias por tu amistad y tu apoyo, por tu cariño, tus consejos, y tu compañía en este camino de la vida.

Contents

Acknowledgments	ix
Transcription Conventions	xv
About the Companion Website	xvii
Prologue: Why I Wrote This Book	xix

Introduction: Communication and Care-at-a-Distance	**1**
Communicative *Convivencia* (Living-Together)	1
Navigating Family Separation through Communication	4
Migration and Family Care in Rural El Salvador	8
What Is Care?	14
Care and Kinship across Borders	16
Communicative Care	19
Methods for Studying Cross-Border Communication	24
Organization of the Book	27

1 . Making Family Care Political: State-Endorsed Migration Discourse in El Salvador	**30**
Hermano Lejano ¡Bienvenido! (Distant Brother, Welcome!)	30
Ustedes Son Embajadores Laborales (You Are Working Ambassadors)	30
State-Endorsed Migration Discourse	31
Contrastive Migrant Personhood: Heroes or Dangerous Failures?	33
The Heroic Migrant as Economic Provider	35
Failed Migrants as Scapegoats in Transnational Moral Panics	44
The Selfish Migrant: Family Disintegration as a National Threat	46
Conclusion	54

2 . Transnational Care in Multigenerational Households: Asymmetrical Practices and Moral Meanings	**57**
Quinceañera	57
Signifying and Enacting Obligations with Relational Grammars	60
Care in Multigenerational Extended Households	64
Envisioning Asymmetry and Reciprocity	68
Communication Technologies and Affordances	74
Contesting Asymmetries through Interwoven Conversations	79
Conclusion	83

3 . "*Les Mando Saludos*": Sending Greetings, Envisioning Family, and Grappling with Inequality	**86**
Communicative Emissaries	86

viii Contents

How Greetings Matter	89
Sending Greetings in Latin America	90
Mandar Saludos as a Genre of Communicative Care	92
Envisioning Kin Care through Reference Patterns	95
Learning to Send Greetings and Family Futures	99
Resignifying and Reproducing Care Asymmetries	106
Conclusion	110

4 Talking Remittances: The Conversational Temporalities of Intergenerational Care — **112**

Consequential Conversational Temporalities	112
Communicative Labor in Remittance Conversations	114
A Birthday to Remember	116
The Interactive Temporality of Requests	121
Making Indirect Requests through Complaints	123
Intensifying Complaints with Reported Speech	126
Creating and Breaking Communicative Norms	129
Conclusion	135

5 Communicative Memory: Defying Institutional Forgetting through Remembering as Care — **138**

¿Se Acuerda Cuando . . . ? (Do You Remember When . . . ?)	138
Institutional Forgetting and the Struggle for Memory	140
Naming the Dead to Preserve *Memoria Histórica*	142
Making Meaning in *Día de los Difuntos* Rituals	146
Remembering Together across Borders	149
Connecting Past and Present through Stance Alignment	150
Motivations for Remembering	152
Dialogic *Convivencia* and Imagined Togetherness	155
The Future of the Past	157
Conclusion	159

Conclusion: Social Change through Communicative Care — **161**

A Miracle?	161
Thinking Communication and Care Together	163
A Call to Accompany as Accomplices	169

Notes	175
References	183
Index	213

Acknowledgments

I owe an overwhelming debt of gratitude to the many people who accompanied me in the journey of researching and writing this book: first and foremost, the transnational Salvadoran families I worked with, without whom none of this would have been possible. They have continually welcomed me into their homes and into their lives, sharing the joys and sorrows, the struggles and the successes, of cross-border family. The opportunity to accompany them over the past two decades has taught me so much and has quite literally changed my life. I will be forever indebted to them for their generosity, patience, and kindness, and for the many ways they have cared for me, not least by participating in this research. *Mil gracias por todo. Las palabras no son suficientes para expresar la deuda enorme que tengo con ustedes. Por esto les dejo mi firme compromiso de seguir con el trabajo solidario hasta donde la vida me lo permita.*

I have experienced deep academic accompaniment from a wonderful series of mentors and colleagues. My journey began with my undergraduate advisor Judith Bishop who was the first person to connect me to the field of linguistics. As an undergraduate, I was fortunate to take several courses with Robin Lakoff, and her interest in my own fledgling research boosted my intellectual self-confidence. It was in one of her courses that I first met Mary Bucholtz when she came to give a guest lecture. Mary went on to become my advisor in graduate school, and I am deeply grateful to her for all the support over the years. I would not be the scholar I am today without that formative graduate school experience: thank you Mary for continually modeling what it means to be an academic dedicated to systems change for racial and social justice. My gratitude also to the other members of my dissertation committee—Jack Du Bois, Candy Goodwin, and Hilary Parsons Dick—for their support of the research that this book is based on. Since I received my PhD, Hilary has become a close colleague, a confidante, and a friend. Deepest gratitude to you, Hilary, for your staunch support over the years and for your intellectual work on language and migration that has been so foundational to my own thinking.

This book builds on the groundwork laid by many other interdisciplinary scholars. In particular, the scholarship of Leisy Abrego and Cecilia Menjívar has deeply shaped my thinking about Salvadoran migration and how it is experienced in families and communities. During my two years as a post-doc at Brown University, I was fortunate to learn so much about migration and

x Acknowledgments

family from conversations with Paja Faudree, Jessa Leinaweaver, Almita Miranda, and Gail Mummert. My understanding of language in the world has been endlessly enriched through ongoing exchanges with colleagues in my field, including Diego Arispé-Bazan, Emily Avera, Steven Black, Anna Corwin, Mariam Durrani, Jennifer Guzmán, Kristine Køhler Mortensen, Adrienne Lo, Catherine Rhodes, and Jonathan Rosa, and others too numerous to name. I am especially indebted to all those who have participated in the Language and Social Justice Committee of the Society for Linguistic Anthropology—and to Janie Lee for introducing me to this group—for continually inspiring me to attend to the inescapable politics of language.

I have benefited from the intellectual community of many other interdisciplinary spaces I have participated in over the years. I have learned a great deal from colleagues in two migration working groups and am deeply grateful to the organizers for creating these spaces: Andrea Flores and Kevin Escudero (at Brown University) and Rebecca Hamlin, Scott Blinder, and Tania DoCarmo (at the University of Massachusetts, Amherst). Heartfelt appreciation also to the team of the Demystifying Language Project—especially Ayala Fader—for the energizing collaboration that has inspired me to think about academic writing and knowledge production in new ways. In graduate school, I benefited greatly from my participation in the sister conferences CLIC (Center for Language, Interaction and Culture) and LISO (Language, Interaction, and Social Organization) at University of California Los Angeles and University of California Santa Barbara, respectively. I participated in meaningful sessions at the International Gender and Language Association Conference, the Latin American Studies Association Conference, and have especially warm memories of conversations at the 2013 Conference on Family Life in the Age of Migration and Mobility at Norrköping University in Sweden, the 2018 Symposium on the Politics of Participation at the Helsinki Collegium for Advanced Studies in Finland, and the 2023 Global Carework Summit at the University of Costa Rica in San José. I have participated in too many sessions to name at the American Anthropological Association's annual conferences, where I have particularly benefited from the opportunity to connect with Tanya Ahlin, Loretta Baldassar, Elana Buch, Cati Coe, Caitlin Fouratt, and Kristin Yarris, among many others.

This book has also been improved by the engagement of many students. Undergraduate research assistants have worked alongside me over the years. At University of California Santa Barbara, thanks to Mayra Alvarado, Daniel Alvarenga, Andy Amaya, Jessica Baumgardner Cortés, Christina Chilín, Douglas Linares, and Yashua Ovando for help with data transcription. Thanks also to David Wiegn (at Brown University) and to Magnus Popov, Ligia

Nuñez, and Laila Gold (at University of Massachusetts, Amherst). Students in several of my courses gave feedback on early drafts of the chapters, and these insights have strengthened my arguments and clarified my prose, I hope. Conversations with many graduate students over the years have been sources of intellectual stimulation and inspiration in my work, including Fu-Yu Chang, Kathleen Crotty, Claudia Morales Ramirez, Daniela Narvaez Burbano, Lara Sabra, and Cat Tebaldi.

The research on which this book was based was funded by the Jacob K. Javits Fellowship Program and the University of California Institute for Mexico and the United States. At University of California Santa Barbara, I received support from the Chicano Studies Institute, the Broom Center for Demography, the Interdisciplinary Humanities Center, and the Humanities and Social Science Dissertation Research Grant. At University of Massachusetts, Amherst, I have received annual small research grants from my union, the Massachusetts Society of Professors.

Limited portions of this book have appeared in *American Anthropologist*, *Gender and Language*, *Language and Linguistics Compass*, and *Pragmatics*. Parts of Chapter 1 appear in "National Heroes or Dangerous Failures" (Arnold 2023). Portions of Chapters 3 were published in "Communication as Care across Borders" (Arnold 2021), as well as in "Language Socialization across Borders" (Arnold 2019a). Finally, portions of the Conclusion appeared in "Accompanying as Accomplices" (Arnold 2019b).

This book has benefited from generous editorial and developmental support from many individuals. Thanks to Anitra Grisales for her work as a developmental editor that was instrumental in completing the first draft of this manuscript. The series editor, Sandro Duranti, and Oxford acquisitions editor Meredith Keffer found me two excellent readers whose feedback greatly improved the book. I am particularly indebted to one of the anonymous peer reviewers and to Sandro himself, both of whom generously provided detailed comments throughout the manuscript that I hope to have done justice to in my revisions. I was also fortunate to work with Lacey Harvey and Dharuman Bheeman and am grateful for their responsiveness and support through this process. Thanks to Lori Jacobs for the detailed copyediting work. A wonderful team of Spanish-language copy editors from Polífona Co-op (www.polif ona.com) checked the Spanish usage and translations throughout the book. Muchísimas gracias por sus valiosos aportes. Finally, deepest appreciation to my good friend Allison Adelman for producing such a thorough index!

The actual writing of this book was probably the hardest part of the process for me. Thanks to Rebecca Barret-Fox and the Any Good Thing writing community for inspiring me to write four hundred words a day. I am also

xii Acknowledgments

deeply grateful to those who accompanied me through different remote writing accountability groups. Deepest gratitude to the three amazing women of my Faculty Success Program group with the National Center for Faculty Development and Diversity—Andra Chastain, Amanda Doxtater, and Danielle Filipiak—for all the daily writing solidarity since 2019. Thanks to the Mutually Mentoring Moms group at University of Massachusetts, Amherst, especially Sade Bonilla, whose presence on the other side of the screen made me feel less alone during the most isolating phases of the pandemic. Appreciation for my University of Massachusetts, Amherst colleagues in the writing group led by Felicity Aulino. Thanks also Felicity for being an amazing colleague and co-conspirator: you always help me to think more deeply. And gratitude to my colleagues in the Department of Anthropology at University of Massachusetts, Amherst, who have supported my research as a junior scholar in numerous ways. Thanks especially to Julie Hemment, Betsy Krause, Amanda Johnson, Jen Sandler, Boone Shear, and Jackie Urla for helping me find a home here.

This book would never have been written if not for the many community and activist organizations that helped me connect to El Salvador and maintain that connection over the years. I must begin by acknowledging Barbara and Jorge, and their son Jonas, for introducing me to El Salvador. Your passion and drive to support the Salvadoran people inspired the same in me. Thanks to Building New Hope and Voices on the Border, the two organizations brave enough to take an eighteen-year-old to El Salvador on my first trip there, and especially to Wes Calendar and Geoff Herzog for your support of my naïve and incredibly sheltered teenage self. Gratitude to CRISPAZ (Christians for Peace in El Salvador), who agreed to take me on as a long-term volunteer when I had just turned twenty. Jeanne Rikkers, Rosa Anaya, Cory Henrickson, Elizabeth Hernandez, and of course the late and beloved Sister Mary Jane all taught me so much about how to be a strong woman out in the world beyond the gates of the community in which I was raised. I am also grateful for over two decades of connection to Miranda Cady Hallet, who coordinated the volunteer program I participated in with CRISPAZ, and has gone on to become a colleague, a fellow anthropologist from whom I have continued to learn so much about what it means to accompany migrant communities as an academic. Since moving to Massachusetts, I have been deeply touched and forever changed by my ongoing involvement with the Trans Asylum Seeker Support Network (TASSN). Thanks to all my TASSN comrades for your radical commitment to abolition and care. To those named here and to the many other activists and change-makers I have met in so many different spaces over the year: I am profoundly grateful to you for your tireless work to create *otro mundo posible* (another possible world). I hope to keep adding my *granito de arena* (grain of sand) to these ongoing struggles for justice.

I have made my own way in the world as an adult largely separate from my family of origin. In these acknowledgments, I have tried to list the many members of my found family who have supported me in so many different ways over the years. I have been supported by more people than I could ever name or acknowledge, and I deeply appreciate you all!

I cannot end without extending thanks to my grandparents—especially Grandpa Derek—for the many stories that enriched my childhood world and to my parents for raising me to be responsible to something bigger than myself. Gratitude to my brothers Hillel, Chris, and Alvin, and to their spouses Azra, Katie, and Lisa for your love. Thanks for hanging in there as we continue to work out how we want to be a family together. Thanks to my in-laws John and Caroline and to John Jr., Jenny, and Greg for your acceptance, kindness, and generosity. And last but very definitely not least, thanks from the bottom of my heart to my husband, Pat, for sticking with me through thick and thin and for the encouragement and laughter when the going gets rough. And endless gratitude to the universe for the gift of my daughter, Sophie, who continues to light up my life every day.

Transcription Conventions

In the text, Spanish direct excerpts from conversations are in Spanish enclosed in quote marks and roman type; Spanish terms and phrases appear without quote marks and in italics. All translations follow in parentheses in roman type. I use a simplified version of discourse transcription to present excerpts of spoken speech in tables. Spanish as spoken appears on the left and my English translation appears on the right in parentheses.

- . final falling intonation
- , continuing intonation
- ? rising intonation
- - truncated intonation
- [] overlapping speech
- @ one pulse of laughter

About the Companion Website

www.oup.com/us/livingtogetheracrossborders

Oxford has created a website to accompany *Living Together Across Borders: Communicative Care in Transnational Salvadoran Families*. Material that cannot be made available in a book, namely a teaching guide, is provided here. The reader is encouraged to consult this resource in conjunction the chapter[s].

Prologue

Why I Wrote This Book

I was cleaning my apartment in Oakland, California, when my cellphone rang. It was a rare call from my father. He told me that Grandpa Derek—my maternal grandfather—had passed away the night before. I was shocked. Grandpa Derek was the youngest of my grandparents: he went for hikes almost every day and had been in excellent health. I had never expected him to be the first grandparent I would lose. His letters were the most regular contact I had with my family, and they were always full of interesting details of new things he was learning about the world. I trace my love of stories and languages to him; he had worked as an interpreter and translator for most of his life and had started to learn Spanish in his seventies when I first traveled to El Salvador six years earlier. He was my favorite grandparent, and I hadn't been there when he died, nor would I be able to attend his funeral, which was scheduled for the next day. Alone on the other side of the country, I had no one to live this experience of grief with: no hugs, no shared mourning, no way to participate in collective work to organize the funeral or the memorial.

At the age of seventeen, I had left the Christian community in which I had been raised, leaving behind my family and my culture of origin to find a life less constrained by strict gender roles. I have not been present for any of my grandparents' deaths or funerals. I have missed my siblings' weddings and am aunt to over a dozen nieces and nephews whom I barely know. I graduated from college, and later from graduate school, with no family members in attendance. My parents were not at my wedding and my mother was not present as I made my own transition into motherhood with the birth of my daughter.

These experiences are an important personal starting point in my study of long-term family separation. My own family situation is of course significantly different from that of the transnational Salvadoran families whose stories are told in this book. My separation from my family is in some ways more voluntary, and our distant ties do not bear the same economic pressure to maintain collective survival. I am able to visit my family from time to time and cherish these opportunities to maintain connection despite divergent life paths. There are no government policies or hateful rhetoric targeting my attempts to maintain these ties to my family and community of origin.

xx Prologue

Nevertheless, it is my own lived experience that gave rise to my questions about how to enact family across space and time and different life experiences, questions that are at the heart of this book. I share these experiences because it feels only fair to begin this book about intimate family life by making myself vulnerable in this way. This personal narrative might be read as an authorizing move, an attempt on the part of a white author to gain greater credibility in writing about the experiences of separated Salvadoran families. While I cannot control how my words are read, I want to be clear that this is not my intention. Rather, I share my story because, as feminists have long argued, there is no view from nowhere. We experience the world and live our lives in ways that are profoundly shaped by who we are, by the bodies we inhabit, by the intersectional identities we carry, and by the past experiences we have had. This book is no exception. I have encountered the transnational families whose stories are told here from a particular positionality. I have accompanied them through the years, learned from them, and written about what I have learned, all as a white woman, an English-speaking US citizen with the legal and financial means to traverse borders at will. In addition to these more public identities, this book has been deeply shaped by my experiences as a daughter, a sister, an aunt, and a mother, in living apart from my family of origin.

I hope that by sharing vulnerably about my experiences I can encourage my readers to see that I—like all language users—have made both conscious and unconscious choices in writing this book. Perhaps knowing about my family background will help my readers understand more about why I made these particular choices. By writing about my own positionality, I ultimately hope to inspire readers to engage in this same reflexivity. So I ask you, my reader, to think about where you are encountering this book from: what experiences and identities inform how you read these words and shape the meanings you will make from them.

As a writer, I have thought deeply about how this book will go on to do work in the world that I cannot fully control. These considerations have led me to bring a deeper sensitivity to the process of writing, which I became particularly aware of in drafting this prologue. In writing about my own life, I am acutely aware of what my readers will bring to these words. For my relatives, this may include their own divergent perspectives on our shared family experiences. For others, widespread discourses about separatist religious communities may be brought to bear. This awareness led me to make careful choices about what I included here and how I wrote about it. I have striven to bring this same care to the book as a whole and have thought deeply about which aspects of transnational family life to emphasize. Of particular relevance have been the negative discourses in media and political rhetoric in the United States that increasingly criminalize Central American migrants and their transnational ties. I have striven to write this book in ways that counteract such narratives, aiming to highlight the creativity and resilience of transnational families in ways that underscore shared humanity.

* * *

My ongoing relationships with transnational Salvadoran families emerged directly from the experience of leaving my birth family. When I graduated from high school, my community of origin had instituted a policy in which all high school graduates spent one year living out in "the world" before they could request lifelong membership, a "year away" similar to the Amish practice of Rumspringa. The day I graduated from high school, I had my picture taken in my cap and gown, and then celebrated with other young women from the community. The next day, my father drove me and one bag of belongings to a nearby city, where the community had arranged for me to work at a child-care center while living with a family as a part-time nanny. At the child-care center I met a family—a Salvadoran father and an American mother—who had a long history of involvement with El Salvador and had founded a sister-city project with a rural village there. As my year at the child-care center came to its end, I realized I was not ready to go back to my home community. I knew next to nothing about El Salvador, but its distance seemed like an asset that would help me figure out the next steps in my life. The sister-city project helped me raise money, and in September 2000, I traveled to El Salvador for the first time. I was eighteen years old.

After two weeks of one-on-one Spanish lessons in the capital city, San Salvador, I traveled to a rural village set alongside the delta of the Lempa River, the largest river in the country. I lived with a family that patiently put up with my rudimentary Spanish and helped me learn more, so that by the end of my four-month stay, I was conversant in rural Salvadoran Spanish. During the days, I assisted the English teacher at the local high school, which was attended by students from around the area, including Cantón El Río (a pseudonym), the village that would ultimately become the hub of the research discussed in this book.

I was a complete anomaly. With my long skirts and head covering, I looked like a Catholic nun, but I wasn't, nor did I belong to any of the increasingly common evangelical sects in El Salvador, churches in which women often dressed like I did. I didn't fit the stereotype of the "loose" White American woman who appeared in movies and on TV, and yet I was undeniably a

xxii Prologue

young White American woman. Despite my strangeness, I was adopted by the five students from Cantón El Río, a tight-knit and particularly outgoing group who were willing to forge friendship with me. They took me to visit their village, planting a seed that would eventually grow into a long-term connection with families from the village, the relationships that form the basis of this book.

In September 2001, I returned to El Salvador—and Cantón El Río—as a volunteer with the only organization that would take on someone as young as myself. For a year, I lived in a small house in the village and was assigned to work with a new sewing cooperative being started by the women of the community as a source of income. I also assisted the English teacher at the village school, spent time with children at the child-care center, sang in the small women's choir at masses, played on the women's soccer team, and generally built relationships with a cohort of other young women in the village, and by extension their families. Eventually I found work with the same organization in San Salvador, first as a part-time interpreter for US delegations, and then as the coordinator of the volunteer program. This work allowed me to stay in El Salvador for three more years, and I maintained strong ties to Cantón El Río, visiting almost every weekend and spending most holidays with loved ones there.

At the same time, distance attenuated my ties with my family and community of origin. We maintained connection primarily through letters and the occasional email or phone call. The distance also gave me space to grow and change. I stopped wearing head coverings and long skirts. I started drinking the occasional beer, going to dances, and dating. These changes brought often painful conflict into my relationship with my parents and community of origin, who feared that I would be corrupted by the influence of the world and would forget the values I had been raised with.

When we are separated from loved ones, we worry that they will change, that distance will sever the ties that once bound us together. Through the process of writing this book, I learned that this is a common human fear. Transnational Salvadoran families likewise worry that materialism and individualism in the United States will make their migrant relatives forget their obligations to those back home. However, for cross-border Salvadoran families, these fears are amplified by media and governmental rhetoric that make family disintegration seem like an inevitable outcome of migration. These public discourses play on families' fears, heightening them to a moral panic: if transnational families fall apart, then the nation itself is under threat.

But accompanying transnational families for the past two decades has taught me that distance does not inevitably lead to loss of connection. In 2005,

I left El Salvador to belatedly begin college in the United States at the age of twenty-four. My Salvadoran boyfriend and his family brought me to the airport, and tears streamed down my face as I said my farewells, went through security, boarded the plane, and took off. I knew that I wasn't primarily crying for him, but for the many dear friends I was leaving behind. I wept for what felt like a familiar grief, for another loss of a community I had come to love.

But although I left, I did not lose this new community. The people I met in El Salvador had touched me deeply. This book is testament to the profound effects they have continued to have on my life. In college and later in graduate school, I continued to visit Cantón El Río each summer. There was only one phone in the village at that time, but I would call my friends each month. At the same time, members of my friends' families began to migrate to the United States, risking dangerous unauthorized journeys in search of work to provide for their families. Before I knew it, I was part of a transnational network of communication, speaking to relatives in both countries. We shared updates from our lives and at times I was asked not to tell the relative in the other country some piece of news, so as not to worry them. As I participated in these transnational relationships, I couldn't help but think through the lens of my own family. I had personally experienced the importance of communication with distant kin, but these transnational families used cross-border conversations to sustain family life across decades of separation unpunctuated by visits. Year after year, through conversations, they worked together to meet daily needs, maintain relationships, care for elders, and raise the next generation of children. I was then—and am still—in awe of the persistence, skill, creativity, and resilience of their ongoing communication.

As I continue to live with my own family separation and its shifting character across the years, I have brought a deeply personal motivation to this research, a search for knowledge and strategies through which I might be better able to build family relationships despite intervening distance and divergent life trajectories. I have striven to implement in my own life the lessons that transnational families have taught me, especially about the power of everyday conversations. I have no doubt that their insights have helped me sustain relationships despite distance with my family of origin and with my found family in El Salvador. This book is my attempt to share what I have learned, and it is written with my deepest respect for the profound strength and wisdom through which transnational families forge collective living in the face of overwhelming global forces that seek to tear them apart.

Introduction

Communication and Care-at-a-Distance

Communicative *Convivencia* (Living-Together)

For the past two months since he arrived in the United States after fleeing violence in his native El Salvador, eighteen-year-old Beto[1] calls his family back home every weekend. He always speaks to his grandfather David, who has been a surrogate father to him since he was seven, when his own father migrated to the United States. Their conversations follow a well-established pattern. Beto begins by asking after his grandfather's health, since David was recently diagnosed with renal failure, or terminal end-stage kidney disease. David responds by reporting his symptoms, listing the many medications the doctor has prescribed, and complaining about his inability to cover these costs. Beto listens and generally offers to send money himself or ask other migrant relatives for help. However, in one call, Beto ignored the financial complaint and instead responded to David's symptomatic concerns. His grandfather had lamented that pain and inflammation were keeping him from walking to the village center to watch the soccer games there, long a favorite pastime of his. Beto told his grandfather that he should have his daughter (Beto's aunt) take him there on her bike. Sharing a bicycle is indeed common practice in the village, but gendered norms dictate that men are the ones who pedal while women ride on the crossbar or a rear rack. Through the lens of this shared knowledge of village life, Beto's suggestion was obviously tongue-in-cheek. David responded in kind, "acaso puede!" (as if she could!), provoking shared laughter at this nonsensical image. At the end of their conversation, Beto bid his grandfather farewell by urging him: "cuídese mucho, haga caso, tenga dieta, no coma sal ni pan" (take good care of yourself, be obedient, follow your diet, don't eat salt or bread).

Conversations such as this one are at the heart of this book. These interactions, while poignant, may seem minute and fleeting. Nevertheless, I suggest that they are in fact crucial windows into transnational family life that can reveal both the historical forces and global inequities that these families confront as well as their creative agency and resilience in forging

Living Together Across Borders. Lynnette Arnold, Oxford University Press. © Oxford University Press 2024.
DOI: 10.1093/oso/9780197755730.003.0001

2 Living Together Across Borders

cross-border life together. Long-term transnational separation interrupts ways of maintaining family relationships that rely on shared space and physical proximity. As Beto told me in an interview six months after his arrival in the United States:

> Recién venido, como que a uno le daba desesperación por estar allá, por convivir con ellos... Más cuando alguien esté enfermo, que uno se imagina cosas, pues, al no estar con ellos, ayudándolos, apoyándolos. Pero ya cuando habla con ellos, ya se siente uno más relajado.

> (Recently arrived, it was like you were desperate to be there, to live-together with them... Specially when someone is sick, and you imagine things, you know, because you aren't there with them, helping them, supporting them. But then when you talk with them, you then feel more relaxed.)

Separation from loved ones is painful and exacerbates worry and concern. Under these conditions, communication is a salve, restoring equilibrium and relieving anxiety.

Drawing on these insights and two decades of accompanying transnational families like his, this book demonstrates that families use cross-border communication to forge *convivencia* (living-together) despite long-term separation. Such living-together is emotional and relational, as in the shared laughter through which Beto and his grandfather confront a terminal diagnosis. And although these relational moments of cross-border connection are fleeting, their impacts are lasting, laying the foundation for the ongoing material and economic provisioning necessary to family survival. Through cross-border conversations, families nurture intergenerational relations—such as Beto's ties to his grandfather—that sustain the family over the years despite ongoing separation.

However, even as transnational communication sustains cross-border *convivencia*, it simultaneously brings inequities between Global North and South into family life by continually reproducing distinctions between relatives in El Salvador and those living in the United States. Dominant discourses depict transnational family life as simply involving one-way transfers of remittances from migrants to their families back home. Everyday communicative patterns often reinforce this model of the migrant as breadwinner, positioning it within the gendered and age-graded norms that govern the inequitable distribution of care within families.[2] At the same time, however, studying cross-border communication reveals that transnational living-together consists of so much more than remittances, instead being constituted through multidirectional exchanges situated within a complex relational web. Moreover, conversations open up spaces in which family members can push back against hierarchies of gender, generation, and migration status, incrementally crafting new ways of making cross-border life. These almost imperceptible shifts gather force through their continual repetition over years of unending separation, becoming habitual ways of living life together across borders.

Through such patterned communicative practices, transnational families navigate shifting intergenerational relations as children are born and grow up, partnerships form and dissolve, and elderly relatives age and pass on, all while grappling with the precarity generated by inequitable global regimes of (im)mobility and deep-rooted legacies of violence in postwar El Salvador. The communicative perspective taken in the book therefore demonstrates how the interactional time of conversation and the everyday rhythms of family life become entangled with individual lifespans, intergenerational relations, and enduring histories of domination. Through this temporal interweaving, cross-border communication maintains migration as a collective strategy for survival by making transnational family life possible. The same communicative practices that sustain families simultaneously shore up neoliberal projects that exonerate the state of the need to provide for its citizens, instead placing this burden of responsibility onto the shoulders of individuals. But co-optation and domination are never total. This book demonstrates that language is a potent yet often implicit form of resistance through which families push back against capitalism as the foundation for social life, instead insisting—with each conversation—on the power of ongoing familial relationships for sustaining life together across borders.

Central Americans are hypervisible in contemporary discussions of migration in the United States, depicted either as criminal gang members or as traumatized victims (Gerson, Zhang, and Aguilera 2021). Yet at the same time, there is widespread ignorance about the lived realities of these communities. This book, which like all language is inescapably an act of representation, challenges the negative depictions of Central American migrants in US discourses and pushes back against dominant Salvadoran narratives that blame transnational families for causing societal disintegration. Instead, it takes seriously the importance of mundane living-together, seeking to understand how families remain connected and what this long-distance *convivencia* produces. I aim to spotlight the creative agency and steadfast resilience of these transnational families as they use language to make cross-border life together in the face of overwhelming obstacles.

Navigating Family Separation through Communication

The experiences of transnational families like Beto's may not come immediately to mind when considering the separation of Central American migrant families.[3] More salient, perhaps, are the Trump administration's practices in 2017 and 2018, under which more than 5,500 Central American children were taken from their parents, part of a policy of "zero tolerance" to punish migrants for crossing the border (Southern Poverty Law Center 2020). Images of children crowded into cages and recordings of toddlers crying for their parents led to public outcry at this horrific spectacle of family separation at the hands of the state. Media pundits, celebrities, and politicians rushed to align themselves with a protest movement that brought together longtime activists and neophytes, including many parents of small children (Yoon-Hendricks and Greenberg 2018). On June 20, 2018, Hillary Clinton tweeted "There is nothing American about tearing families apart."

Yet in reality, family separation has been a part of the United States since its founding, a means of subjugating communities of color while advancing settler-colonial projects of nation-building that concentrated wealth in the hands of a few. Slavery made the theft and sale of Black children a source of profit, while Native American boarding schools separated children from their communities, language, and culture (Mullings 2021). More recently, the state took the children of Black antisegregation and Indigenous tribal sovereignty activists, a pattern that continues still with the racialized workings of the foster system (Briggs 2020). Family separation must therefore be understood as one facet of reproductive governance (Morgan 2019; Morgan and Roberts 2012), or the way that state actors work to control reproduction and population as part of ongoing projects of racialized dispossession that consolidate the settler-colonial nation (Mullings 2021).[4]

Immigration policy has been a mechanism for bringing reproductive governance to bear on Latinx communities, in particular Mexicans and more recently Central Americans (Escobar 2018). Mass deportations of migrants beginning during the Great Depression and continuing today regularly tear families apart. Definitions of the family written into immigration policy separate multigenerational families by only admitting workers and their nuclear family members, by limiting family reunification to immediate kin, or by routinely taking children away from caregivers who aren't their parents (Enchautegui and Menjívar 2015). Trump's policy of family separation built on this history, whose deep roots are revealed by the fact that six years after the policy was ended, one thousand of the separated children had yet to be reunited with their parents (Hesson 2023). Beginning with the COVID-19 pandemic and continuing until May 2023, the use of a public health rule (Title 42) to close the US-Mexico border to most adult asylum seekers forced many Central American parents to make the painful decision to send their children alone across the border (Herrera 2021).

Although less visible in media and political discourses, the long-term cross-border separation experienced by transnational families is part of this same story of nation-building on the backs of marginalized families. For these families, lack of access to legal migration necessitates unauthorized entry, creating sustained separation. Despite living in the United States for decades, unauthorized migrants are unable to adjust their legal status and cannot initiate processes of family reunification or solicit visas so that their relatives might safely visit them. While undocumented Central American migrants once practiced circular migration to break up long periods of cross-border separation, the increased militarization of the US-Mexico border and amped-up enforcement efforts south of the border have made such visits home far more risky (Hagan, Eschbach, and Rodriguez 2008; Soltero and Saravia 2000). Migrants continue to leave Central America, pushed out by a global economy that unevenly concentrates wealth in the North, by violence inflamed by historical and contemporary US intervention in the region, and by a Salvadoran state apparatus that, fully complicit in this violence, has used migration as an escape valve and source of income (Menjívar and Gómez Cervantes 2018). Together, these forces produce a US-dominated regime of (im)mobility that naturalizes cross-border family separation, making it a way of life for hundreds of thousands of Central American families (Hallett and Arnold 2018; Menjívar and Abrego 2012).

In the face of the policies that force them to separate and then keep them apart, transnational families remain connected across time and space through everyday practices through which they collectively provide for one another's needs. Perhaps the most visible form of such cross-border provisioning is remittances, or the money migrants send home to their relatives. But there are many other ways that transnational families stay connected: shipping packages of clothing and medicine, preparing and sending nostalgic food items, taking and sharing photos of family celebrations, and participating in cross-border phone calls. This is not to say that all families sustain connections across borders. Of course, there are many kin ties that are either temporarily attenuated or permanently severed by migration. But this is a book about families that, against all odds, manage to sustain connection across space and time.

What is it that allows these families to maintain cross-border ties in the face of so many powerful forces working to separate them from their loved ones?

6 Living Together Across Borders

Answering this question by starting with transnational *convivencia* reveals that cross-border connection is sustained through care, or everyday practices of providing for others. Care sustains relationships, allowing transnational families to continually nurture intergenerational ties, thereby creating the ground upon which continued collective survival is possible. Drawing on three decades of engagement with rural Salvadoran communities, Irina Silber (2022) suggests that a shared ethic of collective care is central to the insurgent survival of those pushed to the margins in El Salvador's *longue duree* of violence. This ethic is rooted in a recognition of *debilidad* (weakness, lack of vigor or strength) in others, recognition that "can move someone to enact solidarity" (Silber 2022, 89) to provide what is needed. In the context of transnational family life, collective care emerges from recognizing the weakening of *convivencia* and prompts cross-border practices that seek to forge connection and survival despite distance. Care practices enact *convivencia*, making possible the experience of living-together despite long-term cross-border separation.

As in Beto's statements, families were far more likely to talk about *convivencia* than care, which was often backgrounded as the habitual actions that made transnational living-together possible. When they did talk about care, families themselves generally did not use the word as a noun (*cuido*); rather, they used care as a verb (*cuidar*), highlighting the action-oriented nature of providing for others. In fact, the most common use of this term was when family members urged one another to *cuidarse* (take care of yourself), as Beto urges his grandfather to do by following doctor's orders (cf. Arnold 2020). This usage underscores the active relationality of care as something that is enacted in connection with others. Indeed, exhortations to *cuidarse* might best be understood as a communicative manifestation of Silber's ethic of collective care, a means of signaling that the speaker has recognized *debilidad* and the need for care.

This book suggests that everyday conversations are a vital care practice, the most fundamental way that transnational families maintain collective intergenerational life in the face of continued, and seemingly endless, separation. To demonstrate the power of communication, I draw on my multisited ethnography of family communication, tracing fine-grained patterns of language use in everyday cross-border conversations. This close interactional analysis is supported by ethnographic insights which reveal the deep historical roots of mundane conversational strategies. The communicative practices highlighted in this book emerge from Salvadoran histories of migration, violence, and poverty, and are powerfully shaped by US economic and foreign policy, as well as by restrictive immigration laws. At the same time, these conversations respond to dominant Salvadoran discourses about migration and family that make transnational family care into a site of overwhelming significance, charging migrants with the responsibility of advancing the nation through the remittances they send home to their families; if ties between migrants and their relatives back home falter, the nation itself is at risk. These forces shape how transnational families communicate, what they talk about, and what they avoid. Indeed, cross-border communication is rife with silences about topics such as the difficulties migrants face in their everyday lives.

To develop a more precise understanding of what everyday communication across borders accomplishes, this book utilizes the tools of linguistic anthropology to understand language as a form of social action.[5] The power of language emerges in part through its inherent multifunctionality, or its ability to enact multiple forms of social action at the same time (Jakobson 1960). An utterance that seems on the surface to be doing one thing often implicitly enacts other actions, weaving a web of implicit meanings with far-reaching consequences. Crucially, attending to the multiple effects of language highlights the fact that "there is no language without politics" (Zentella 2018, 191), encouraging researchers to attend analytically to the political consequences of all forms of communication, even if these are often quite implicit. The multifunctionality of language makes transnational conversations a flexible and powerful resource for enacting care, in ways that both shape and are shaped by intersecting inequalities.

For transnational families, language acts in ways that are deeply tied to migration. Scholarship within linguistic anthropology has demonstrated that close attention to language practices sheds new light on experiences and realities of migration around the world.[6] The language used in political rhetoric, media discourse, and everyday life creates social difference, producing inclusion for some and exclusion for others (Dick 2011). Tracing linguistic practices therefore reveals how multiple intersecting borders are created, made meaningful, transformed, and at times contested. I build on this research to suggest that transnational family conversations are not simply interpersonal communication; rather, these conversations participate in the processes of differentiation and border-making in ways that have far-reaching consequences.

In particular, the significance of seemingly small linguistic practices emerges clearly in scholarship that examines how the spatial and temporal dimensions of social life are produced through language. Within linguistic anthropology, such work uses the concept of *scale* to denaturalize taken-for-granted spatial and temporal understandings of how social life is organized, for instance, in local versus national versus global dimensions (Slembrouck and Vandenbroucke 2019).[7] While it might seem that such scales are preordained

8 Living Together Across Borders

and fixed realities, linguistic anthropological analyses demonstrate how these domains are continually constituted through discursive practices of labeling and contrasting (Carr and Lempert 2016). An example of this can be seen in many protocols for human subjects' research, which allow observation of what is deemed "public behavior" without informed consent; this explicit discursive categorization of some behaviors implicitly separates social life into public and private dimension, bringing along with it assumptions about privacy, access, and values (Gal 2002).

Within migration studies in particular, scholars of language have demonstrated that hierarchies between scales are discursively constituted: what happens at "larger" scale levels is often deemed to be more consequential than "small-scale" domains that are construed as more locally confined.[8] Scalar hierarchies are often mobilized to enact and justify policies that constrain the mobility of particular migrants. Implicit in immigration policy is a scalar logic that positions the family as smaller than, and therefore subordinate to, the nation. The discursive work of scale-making thus underpins state-endorsed family separation. Linguistic anthropological insights provide tools for unpacking these suppositions and tracing how they are produced, while also making visible the ways that migrant communities enact their own scalar projects, taking up but also resisting dominant framings of how social life is organized.

In this book, I investigate the specific communicative practices that transnational families use to enact cross-border care, contending that these everyday conversations are mobilized as part of a scalar project. Through cross-border conversations, families continually enact the importance of their transnational ties, reproducing family relationships as fundamental to social life. Such conversations implicitly resist the dismissal of family life as small scale, pushing back against dominant depictions of families as subordinate to the nation-state. Instead, these conversations insistently assert and enact family relationships that span borders, thereby constituting mundane resistance through which families construct *convivencia* at a distance.

Migration and Family Care in Rural El Salvador

The rural poor in El Salvador have long turned to migration to provide for their families, as global political-economic forces have systematically stolen their resources and made their livelihoods more precarious. European colonization did away with collective land ownership, throwing Indigenous forms of family survival into crisis and concentrating resources in the hands of an elite oligarchy known as the "fourteen families" who still control most wealth and power in El Salvador (Velasquez Carillo 2010, 2011). In the nineteenth century, elite landowners established large coffee-producing *fincas* (estates), increasing the inequitable distribution of land ownership (Hamilton and Chinchilla 1991; Santana Cardoso 1975). This systemic dispossession pushed rural communities into exploitative seasonal wage labor involving regional migration to harvest coffee, cotton, sugar, and bananas (Landolt, Autler, and Baires 1999; Menjívar 2000).

Further displacement resulted from the civil war that broke out in 1979 between the government and the Frente Farabundo Martí para la Liberación Nacional (the *FMLN* or Farabundo Martí National Liberation Front), a leftist guerrilla group that many Salvadorans from rural communities joined to fight back against decades of oligarchic rule, military dictatorship, and violent repression (Mahler 1999; Miyares et al. 2003). The United States backed the Salvadoran armed forces, sending more than $4.5 billion in aid over the twelve years of the war (Quan 2005); this support prolonged the conflict and increased the suffering of rural communities whose inhabitants were forced to flee massacres and scorched-earth tactics (Carothers 1991; LeoGrande 1998). Many escaped across the border into Honduras, and a whole generation of children were raised by their grandparents or single mothers in refugee camps while their parents fought with the FMLN (Todd 2010). Others traveled to the United States, where the Salvadoran population more than quintupled from 1980 to 1990.[9] Despite the fact that they were fleeing war, most of these refugees were not granted asylum in the United States: between 1983 and 1986, only 2.6 percent of Salvadorans applying for asylum were approved, as compared to 60.4 percent of Iranians and 37.7 percent of Afghans (Smith 1996). US policy, intervention, and state terror were thus key drivers in initiating the large-scale unauthorized migration of Salvadorans to the United States that continues to this day (Coutin 1998, 2007; Menjívar and Rodriguez 2005).

At the center of this book is a rural Salvadoran village I call Cantón El Río, the location all the migrants left behind and where the nonmigrant members of these families reside. This village was founded at the end of the civil war, under a land-transfer program initiated by the 1992 Chapultepec Peace Accords which ended the civil war. This accord included a provision to redistribute 10 percent of the country's agricultural land from large landowners to ex-combatants from both sides, as well as to the civilian supporters of the FMLN (De Bremond 2007). Under the auspices of this program, legal ownership was officially transferred to the one hundred individuals—FMLN ex-combatants, supporters, and their families—who in 1991 had returned from

10 Living Together Across Borders

Honduran refugee camps to occupy the land that would become Cantón El Río (Barba, Martínez, and Morales 1996; Quintana 2007).

Cantón El Río is situated alongside the largest river in the country on low-lying floodplains with fertile land. Formerly part of large estates growing cotton and sugar cane, the area had been largely abandoned during the conflict, and so the founders carved the village from the jungle. Each adult settler received two plots of land, one for agricultural production—including the subsistence crop of corn as well as pasture for milk cows—and the other a smaller plot in the residential area of the village on which to build a house. With international support, one-room cinderblock homes and outhouses were built for each family; these projects also helped to install basic electricity and, later, to bring potable water to each home. On communally held lands, the village was able to build a child-care center, a school that offered classes up to the ninth grade, a small library, and a clinic. Community affairs are managed by an elected board made up of residents, who hold regular workdays to maintain streets and drainage, organize yearly anniversary celebrations, and advocate for governmental and international development projects, such as the construction of a dike along the river and an elevated community center to be used as a refuge in case of the flooding to which the area is vulnerable.

Despite these resources and continued organization, when I first arrived in Cantón El Río in 2001, a transition was already in process away from subsistence agriculture to dependence on migrant remittances as a primary strategy for family provisioning.[10] By the time I conducted my research (2009–2014), about half of the families in the village had at least one migrant relative living in the United States. This local experience reflects a national pattern of widespread migration: fully one-fourth of El Salvador's population lives abroad, 90 percent in the United States (Ministero de Relaciones Exteriores 2010). Emigration from rural areas is particularly pronounced: in many such communities, more than 40 percent of households have a migrant relative (Andrade-Eekhoff 2003), and 16 to 40 percent of children grow up without their migrant parents (Abrego 2014). Salvadoran women have long migrated at higher rates than women from other Latin American countries (Andrade-Eekhoff 2006; Zentgraf 2002) and women constitute 47.3 percent of all Salvadoran immigrants in the United States (Moslimani, Noe-Bustamante, and Shah 2021). However, most of the migrants from Cantón El Río were men and the few women migrants generally followed their husbands, fathers, or brothers. To make these unauthorized journeys through Guatemala, Mexico, and across the US border, migrants paid for the services of a *coyote* (guide), which cost about $3,000 in the early 2000s. The families of prospective migrants pooled resources to finance these journeys, often selling parcels of agricultural land and making the relatives who remained in the village ever more dependent on migrant remittances for family survival.

What has caused this widespread exodus of Salvadorans? In Cantón El Río, as elsewhere in El Salvador, ongoing migration emerges from the legacy of violence and social devastation left by the civil war, as well as from the unresolved inequities upon which the nation was founded. In particular, right-wing political forces used the civil war as an opportunity to implement neoliberal structural adjustment programs in El Salvador. Neoliberalism is an economic and political model that emphasizes personal responsibility in a context of free markets and free trade (Harvey 2005). Under neoliberalism, "individuals are taught not to expect state support or a social safety net but rather that they must participate in the free market to acquire funds to meet their own needs" (Osuna and Abrego 2022, 4). While El Salvador has long had an "informal-familialist" welfare system (Martínez Franzoni 2008) that relies on family care, neoliberal reforms placed increasingly heavy burdens on families through state disinvestment from healthcare, education, and other social services. The Central American Free Trade Agreement which passed in 2005 devastated rural livelihoods by swamping local markets with heavily subsidized agricultural imports (Moreno 2004). Climate change also began to affect the region, with more unpredictable rains leading to drought or flooding that destabilized agriculture even further (International Organization for Migration 2017). As rural livelihoods were made increasingly untenable, ever more families turned to migration to provide the care that they were not receiving from the state. Today, migrant remittances collectively maintain the nation: in 2022, migrants sent home $7,742 million, amounting to more than 20 percent of El Salvador's gross domestic product (GDP) (Molina 2023).

The profound economic inequality produced by neoliberal reforms has impelled continued violence, which in turn has spurred ongoing migration (Menjívar and Gómez Cervantes 2018; Osuna and Abrego 2022). Once again, US policy has contributed to the conditions that cause Salvadorans to migrate. The Illegal Immigration Reform and Immigrant Responsibility Act of 1996 authorized a zero-tolerance policy under which suspected gang members were deported from US urban centers, thereby seeding gang violence and organized crime into the volatile milieu of postwar El Salvador (Johnson 2014; Zilberg 2004, 2007, 2011). In Cantón El Río, the effects of this policy became increasingly visible beginning in 2014. A bloody territorial struggle between two gangs emerged in the environs of Cantón El Río, as a newly completed road to the coast made the area a target for drug and weapons trafficking through Central America (Lohmuller 2014). As a result, there was a sharp increase in murders in the area surrounding Cantón El Río;

12   Living Together Across Borders

most victims were young people or their adult guardians who had been killed for refusing to become foot soldiers in this gang warfare. Out of fear, people stopped attending community events and locked themselves in their houses each night at 6 p.m. when darkness fell. When a police officer who lived in the village was murdered, many other community leaders fled, fearing they would also be targeted for their efforts to increase security by installing streetlights and gates along the main streets. Families desperately gathered resources to pay the cost of the unauthorized journeys, which had more than doubled in a decade's time; to raise $7,000 in a short period of time, families often took out high-interest loans with unregulated *prestamistas* (moneylenders), who could charge up to 15 percent interest. Such loans often lock young people and their families into migration as the only viable option for paying off these large debts (Heidbrink 2019).

As a result of these ongoing drivers of migration, the transnational families I worked with comprised two generations of migrants. Adults who had left El Salvador five to ten years earlier in search of economic opportunities were joined over the course of my research by young people fleeing forced gang recruitment. Despite these different motivations for migration, both generations of migrants were denied legal status in the United States. Indeed, Salvadorans make up the fifth-largest population of Latinx immigrants but the second-largest group of undocumented migrants (Migration Policy Institute 2015). Those Salvadoran migrants who do have some kind of documentation are overwhelmingly forced to rely on vulnerable temporary statuses as the only means of accessing any sort of legal protection (Hallett 2014; Mountz et al. 2002), experiencing what Menjívar (2006) calls liminal legality. As a result of this lack of stable legal status, migrants were trapped in physically demanding jobs with no health insurance or retirement benefits. At the national level, 62 percent of undocumented immigrants hold blue-collar jobs in service, construction, and production, twice the share of US-born workers in these industries (Passel and Cohn 2015). The migrants I met moved and lifted boxes in shipping warehouses, shaped and polished marble countertops, or labored at an outdoor tire repair shop where they endured rain, sleet, freezing cold, and snow. Employers often did not pay them overtime or provide them with benefits; when they were injured on the job, they had to pay for their own medical care while taking unpaid leave until they were well enough to return to work.

Immigration policy thus licensed exploitative working conditions by keeping migrants undocumented or confining them to liminal legal positions. Migrants often described their daily lives in the United States as going "del trabajo a la casa" (from work to home), articulating economic pressure, a loss of free time to socialize, and the ever-present possibility of deportation that led them to curtail their movement as much as possible. This threat was a constant source of anxiety for migrants and nonmigrants alike. Migrant parents raising children in the United States worried about what would happen to them if they were deported.[11] Relatives in El Salvador worried about deportation too. They closely followed news of US immigration policy and often asked me to explain legal details of proposals discussed on the news. Temporary status is not well understood in El Salvador, where legality is largely conceptualized within a binary framework of "tener papeles" (to have papers or to not have papers) (Abrego 2014). Relatives of migrants with temporary status think of them as "having papers" because they have work permits and do not understand why they don't send more money or seek family reunification. Liminal legality thus not only threatened the material conditions by which families met their collective needs, but it also created affective tensions that further strained cross-border ties.

The political-economic forces and immigration policy regimes that govern Salvadoran migration to the United States thus have far-reaching consequences. Migrants themselves experienced daily the brunt of these harsh working environments and pervasive constraints on everyday life.[12] At the same time, these conditions shaped transnational care, not only impinging on how migrants provided economically but also shaping their affective and relational participation in cross-border *convivencia*.[13] The lives of nonmigrant relatives were thus also deeply shaped by US immigration policy both through family separation as well as in the ongoing care engagements that emerged under these conditions. Ultimately, the cross-border lives of transnational families are both made necessary and constrained by powerful political-economic forces that perpetuate legacies of global inequity.

This often-told narrative, while conveying important historical context for understanding Salvadoran migration, can reductively position migrants as victims of global inequalities. Recent Central American scholarship has put forward alternate ways of thinking through migration in the region that emphasize migrant hope and agency; they suggest that individual or familial projects to build a better future should be understood as collective resistance (Marroquín Parducci 2019). When Central Americans massively migrate without authorization, José Luis Rocha (2018) suggests that they are enacting a form of civil disobedience that defies and protests unjust laws limiting their mobility. These approaches resonate with decolonial perspectives that frame migration as a response to colonialism and a form of reparations for past harms (Achiume 2019; Gonzalez 2020; Patel 2021). This book builds on these theorizations of migration as a political act, turning from macrolevel conceptualizations of migrant agency to instead examine the subtle power migrants and their families wield through their communicative practices. While structural violence has painful consequences for migrants and their relatives back home, families nevertheless continue to forge ways of living-together across borders through everyday care practices, including communication. In the face of the many forces working to tear transnational families apart, sustaining *convivencia* across borders can only be understood as a form of resistance.

What Is Care?

In advancing a communicative approach to care, this book contributes to a burgeoning body of work on language and health.[14] Scholarship at this intersection of linguistic and medical anthropology demonstrates the vital role of language in organizing the interpersonal and institutional encounters through which health is navigated, while also revealing how language both shores up and potentially challenges the forms of structural violence that limit well-being for so many. Nevertheless, much remains to be done to more systematically synthesize the theoretical paradigms used within the two fields (Arnold and Black 2020; Briggs and Faudree 2016). I contribute to these efforts by developing an approach that brings linguistic anthropological conceptualizations of language into dialogue with contemporary medical anthropological theorizations of care, to elucidate how care and communication are mutually constitutive.

"Care" is a polyvalent term with a long scholarly genealogy that has been used to understand topics as diverse as health and state violence, patriarchy and climate change, kinship, and disability. To chart a path within this complex scholarship, I find it helpful to begin with definitions that are intentionally simple, what might be called *glosses,* to borrow linguistic terminology. Glosses are basic grammatical representations (for instance: first person, present tense, singular) that can be used across languages to parse the meaning of utterances and develop an understanding of particular grammatical systems. Likewise, I aim to develop a gloss that can be used as a basis for ethnographic investigations of care in a range of settings (cf. Aulino 2016). In doing so, I draw on recent ethnographic explorations of care around the world.

In her investigation of end-of-life care in Thailand, Felicity Aulino (2019) suggests that care be understood broadly as "providing for others," contending that through such an approach scholarship "can look to the patterning and embodiment of habituated actions in general to understand what values people enact and how they maintain social worlds" (Aulino 2016, 93). This definition frames care as fundamentally relational in nature, raising the question of who or what might be provided for. In her work, Aulino traces how care moves beyond the interpersonal to become care for one's group and care for the polity. Other scholars have examined the ways that care establishes relationships between humans and with nonhuman actors such as animals, plants, and the environment (Faudree 2020; Hartigan 2017; Ticktin 2019).

How does the work of relational provisioning come to matter beyond the particular relationships in which it unfolds? Elana Buch (2018), in her work on paid home care in the United States, conceptualizes care as "generative labor," referring to "the wide range of moral imaginings, practices, processes, and relations through which people work together to generate life in all its forms" (Buch 2018, 6). This understanding of care draws attention to what care produces, echoing feminist scholarship that understands care as a means of sustaining human life (Fisher and Tronto 1990; Olthuis et al. 2014; Tronto 1993) but also as fundamental to the continuation of patriarchy (Blum et al. 1980; Okin 1989). As generative labor, the care practices that maintain life simultaneously reproduce the inequities of political economic regimes (Buch 2018). Moreover, care labor is unevenly distributed in ways that create different life possibilities and shore up inequitable social relations along the lines of gender, race, class, disability, migration status, and more.[15] Indeed, care is often mobilized to shore up forms of structural violence enshrined in the policies of powerful social institutions (Mulla 2014), as when humanitarian frameworks provide legal status for sick migrants while also refusing them work permits and the right to solicit visas for their relatives (Ticktin 2011). Care is thus both necessary and violent (Arnold and Aulino 2021), with far-reaching but contradictory consequences, simultaneously sustaining people and communities, power, and inequality.

Both Aulino and Buch develop action-oriented definitions that understand care as a process rather than as a static resource. Their work is situated within the care-practices approach, which conceptualizes care not in terms of post hoc discursive accounts or in terms of the governmental policies or institutional structures that govern it, but rather through attending to the concrete ways that people enact care, giving particular priority to embodied actions (Mol, Mosser, and Pols 2010a, 2010b). That is not to say that this scholarship ignores large-scale forms of structural violence; rather, it seeks to understand how such inequities are sustained, reproduced, and potentially challenged through mundane and often habitual actions. Nevertheless, such scholarship tends to minimize the role of language in care by drawing a clear demarcation between concrete enactments of care on the one hand and reflexive accounts on the other. This relegates language to the domain of referential meaning making, eliding its pragmatic force as a form of social action and its fundamental inclusion within human experience (Ochs 2012).

The communicative care approach I develop in this book seeks to revindicate language as a vital care practice. Drawing on the definitions offered by Buch and Aulino, I understand care as *the generative and relational work of provision*, ongoing labor that produces *convivencia* and family relationships. This definition presumes that communication, as much as embodied action, can enact care. Although it may seem counterintuitive to understand communication as labor and as a means of providing for others, a long-standing body of scholarship demonstrates that language must be understood as a fundamentally material phenomenon.[16] Language is embedded within political-economic systems, as when particular ways of using language are commodified, for instance, in call centers or on phone sex lines (Cameron 2000; Hall 1995). Moreover, through the study of transnational care, this book demonstrates that language is vital in producing the relational groundwork that undergirds economic and material exchanges. For transnational families, language not only coordinates material and practical care such as remittances, but also for sustains the cross-border relationships that form the bedrock for collective provisioning.

Care and Kinship across Borders

Transnational families develop creative strategies for cross-border care that sustain both individual and collective survival. Early work described "care chains" in which migrant mothers left home to work as paid caregivers in the Global North, leaving their children behind in the care of female relatives (Hochschild 2000; Parreñas 2001, 2005). Building on this work, more recent scholarship has investigated the multidirectional extended networks that enact transnational family care and has demonstrated the active participation of relatives in both countries, including children (Baldassar and Merla 2013; Cole and Groes 2016; Kofman 2012). Increasing attention to transnational elder care and the fate of aging migrants has also productively expanded the scope of this work beyond the nuclear family.[17] This book contributes to this effort, focusing on multigenerational care in extended transnational families, care not just from parent to minor child but between elderly parents and adult children, grandchildren and grandparents, siblings and cousins, and uncles and nieces.

This focus on multigenerational families is not intended to reinforce a biological understanding of kinship. Rather, my approach to transnational family care is informed by contemporary anthropological frameworks that understand kinship as produced through everyday engagements, a social practice that is enacted rather than a biological fact that simply exists (Alber and Drotbohm 2015; Carsten 2000; Van Vleet 2008). Thus, although this book focuses primarily on kin relations based on ties of blood or marriage, I purposefully include examples of how I have been incorporated into these families through care practices. In doing so, I aim to denaturalize biology as the basis of kinship and instead demonstrate how kinship emerges from ongoing care practices.[18] Focusing on the enactment of kinship through care reveals a more complex picture, highlighting how kinship involves exclusion and hierarchy, as well as inclusion and connection (Franklin and McKinnon 2000). This processual approach demonstrates that care is fundamental not only to the production and maintenance of kinship but also at times to its dissolution.

Therefore, as care provides for others and produces *convivencia*, it is entangled within and produces relationships. Care is the ongoing labor through which such relationships are constructed and sustained over time, and language is central to this relational work (Locher and Watts 2005, 2008). Such relationality is not an either/or proposition but rather always includes both closeness and distance. Care generates both relational connection and disconnection; "concrete relations are constantly being achieved, and also failing" (Han 2012, 234). In the context of kinship, we must be careful not to simply assume that obligations to provide care emerge directly from biological kin ties, as Fayana Richards (2021) argues in her work with Black grandmothers providing intensive grandchild care in Detroit. Instead, she calls for attention to "care calculation," the affective and material process through which "caregivers actively weigh how to best deliver care amid practical constraints" (Richards 2021, 6). Care calculations are never final but rather are tied to experiences of past care and anticipation of future care (Richards 2021, 9). The communicative perspective I take in this book provides a grounded approach that demonstrates how care calculation is interwoven with the work of provision, incrementally producing relationships of obligation or, alternately, weakening such ties.

Recent linguistic anthropological work has called for attention to the role of language in producing intimacy, defined as an "emergent feeling of closeness" (Pritzker and Perrino 2021, 367). Intimacy is foundational for all relationships, not only those of a romantic or sexual nature (Perrino and Pritzker 2019). Understanding intimacy as a process allows scholars to investigate how specific ways of using language may build closeness or produce distance. For instance, while long pauses in conversation have often been studied as a strategy for creating distance between interlocutors (Gumperz 1982; Watts 1997), shared silences can also produce intimacy under the right circumstances (Basso 1970; Bauman 2009). To date, work on language and intimacy has focused on face-to-face encounters.[19] Under conditions of long-term separation such as those experienced by transnational families, communication is even more vital for producing ongoing closeness.

The work of communication as care is thus both material and affective, weaving together economic provisioning and emotional closeness (Arnold 2019a).[20] Approaching the work of kinship through the lens of care helps reveal how the relational work of sustaining family relates to neoliberal capitalism. Feminist economists have long argued that this sort of domestic labor is co-opted by capitalism to its own benefit (Folbre 2014; Fraser 2017). Capitalism relies on care work to reproduce the labor force by raising new workers, socializing them to capitalist forms of life, and then keeping them clothed, housed, and fed during their working lives. Tracing kinship through care thus draws attention to the political import of mundane actions that might otherwise be dismissed as of little significance to broader concerns about social inequality (Thelen and Coe 2017).

In particular, I am inspired by Leith Mullings's conceptualization of kin care as "transformative work" (1996, 98), a perspective that emerged from her ongoing research on Black women's "efforts to sustain continuity under transformed circumstances, and efforts to transform circumstances in order to maintain continuity" (2021, 106). Transformative work is a form of resilience that enables short- and long-term survival for individuals and communities, while also working to change the conditions that subject family ties to state violence. Nevertheless, engaging in this transformative work has a cost and can ironically impinge on women's well-being (Mullings 2005, 87). Kin care as transformative work is thus fundamentally political and deeply contradictory; it is shaped by multiple interlocking inequalities and contains the potential for both resistance and the reproduction of structural violence.

Understanding care practices as the foundation of kinship opens up insights into everyday family communication across borders. In recent years, scholars of transnational family life have increasingly attended to the centrality of communication for cross-border care.[21] Indeed, widespread access to digital communication technologies is arguably the defining feature of contemporary transnational family life, offering new possibilities for living-together at a distance. Research has demonstrated that such new communication technologies have contradictory effects for intergenerational care across borders. On the one hand, increasing access to digital technologies allows transnational families to sustain connections despite often long-term separation, greatly facilitating transnational provisioning.[22] At the same time, however, these more intensive forms of cross-border connection can create conflict in family relations. Migrants may feel harassed by constant requests for money from relatives and friends back home (Lai and Fong 2022) and making time for regular transnational communication can be challenging given their work schedules. Moreover, technologies are often used in ways that exacerbate gendered and age-graded hierarchies. For instance, left-behind children may feel they allow intense parental scrutiny (Madianou and Miller 2011a; Tazanu 2015), whereas women, both migrants and nonmigrants, may experience technologies as forms of surveillance (Cole 2014; Hannaford 2015). The impacts of technologically mediated cross-border communication for transnational family care cannot be assumed a priori but must be studied in ways that allow for complexity and contradiction. This book offers new insights into the consequences of cross-border conversations within transnational families by closely studying patterned language use through the lens of communicative care.

Communicative Care

To parse the care labor of communication, I have proposed a communicative care approach (Arnold 2020, 2021). Drawing on what I have learned from how transnational families make use of everyday communication, I suggest that language facilitates, enacts, and signifies care. The entanglement of language and care is particularly clear in transnational family life, where cross-border provisioning places a particularly heavy burden on everyday communication. Yet while this book focuses on such transnational communicative care, I suggest that this analytical framework is more broadly applicable to many other settings where language facilitates, enacts, and signifies care. Thus, in what follows, I discuss each of these three functions in turn, drawing together examples from transnational family conversations and linguistic anthropological scholarship on language and care in other contexts.

Clearly, communication is vital to many efforts to provide for others. The facilitating role of language is clear in transnational family life in which cross-border care must necessarily be communicatively coordinated. For instance, in the opening vignette, David explained to his migrant grandson the costs of his medical care as a means of implicitly requesting remittances to help cover these expenses; Chapter 4 provides an in-depth exploration of how such implicit requests facilitate remittance negotiations. Of course, language

20 Living Together Across Borders

facilitates face-to-face forms of care as well. For instance, embodied caregiving relies on communication through which participants coordinate the actions of their bodies with one another (Backhaus 2017; Sadruddin 2020; Toerien and Kitzinger 2007). Language makes care possible in medical encounters between patients and health practitioners (Drew, Chatwin, and Collins 2001; Maynard and Heritage 2005), as well as in everyday interactions between parents and children (M. Goodwin 2015; M. Goodwin and Cekaite 2018). This interrelationship also undergirds long-standing scholarship on language socialization, which demonstrates that the particular ways children learn to use language emerge from the care that they receive and engage in (Ochs 1988; Schieffelin 1990; Schieffelin and Ochs 1986). Closely tracing the ways that language is used to facilitate care can thus produce important insights into the organization of social life across multiple domains.

In addition to facilitating care, language may directly enact care. For instance, in experiences of language brokering, children of migrants interpret or translate for their parents or other relatives, thereby often caring for the family as a whole (García-Sánchez 2018; Orellana 2001, 2009; Reynolds and Orellana 2009). At times I observed the children of Salvadoran migrants engage in this kind of interpretive care work, although more often, if I was present, I was the one recruited as an informal interpreter.[23] However, the communicative enactment of care extends far beyond such situational uses. I suggest that language pervasively enacts relational care through interwoven affective and material work in ways that make it fundamental to all other modalities of care. For instance, Beto found a way to insert a joke into a difficult conversation about his grandfather's illness, producing shared laughter; this intersubjective attunement (Duranti and La Mattina 2022) brought grandfather and grandson closer despite the distance. This fleeting engagement thus consequentially fostered positive emotional connection, reassuring both grandfather and grandson that their relationship would remain a space in which challenges could be navigated despite distance.

Understanding communication as care thus requires attention to different temporal scales, both in-the-moment practices of care (Raia 2020; Svendsen et al. 2018) and longer-term engagements in care across the years (Han 2012; Thelen and Coe 2017). This book brings such approaches together, providing close analyses of communicative care practices and tracing their embedding within and consequences for long-standing care.[24] I reveal how care that extends across the individual life course and the intergenerational span of family life is produced and maintained through fleeting moments of repeated communication. For transnational families, the ability of language to forge and sustain relational ties is a vital form of care, without which all other forms of transnational provision would not be possible. Conversations provide moments of *convivencia*, such as in Beto and David's shared laughter, sustaining relationships and forging the foundation upon which ongoing collective care is enacted. Communication must thus be considered a fundamental care practice in its own right.

Finally, even as it facilitates and enacts care, communication simultaneously produces conceptualizations of care. Through language, particular actions—carried out by certain individuals, under specific circumstances—are signified as care, while the actions of other individuals in different circumstances are elided (Arnold 2020). This signification may happen explicitly, as when Beto tells his grandfather "cuídese" and then outlines specific care practices he should enact. However, the care work that makes David's self-care possible, in particular the labor of women in the family who prepare the special foods that adhere to his strict diet, is simply assumed in this directive. Language thus formulates understandings of care that draw upon and reproduce normative assumptions about how particular individuals can and should engage in care work, to what ends, and under what conditions. The gendered work of food preparation here is treated as simply part of the social world in which David must care for himself, reproducing the simultaneous reliance on and dismissal of women's social reproduction that underpins global capitalism. As this example illustrates, meanings of care are often produced directly in and through care practices (cf. Corwin 2020, 2021). Most often, these meanings emerge implicitly in the patterned ways that utterances are produced and then taken up over time (Mattingly 1998, 2010), as when financial complaints like David's are habitually treated as requests for remittances (see Chapter 4). This particular communicative pattern implicitly assigns different normative care roles to migrant and nonmigrant relatives, making migrants responsible for economic provisioning. The communicative care approach therefore insists that the enactment of care and the production of meanings of care cannot be separated but rather are fundamentally co-constitutive.

The significations produced through communicative care mobilize ethico-moral terms, evaluating people, their actions, and their relationships as "good" and normative or "bad" and deviant.[25] For instance, as I discuss in Chapter 1, Salvadoran state discourses highlight remittances as the way migrants should care for their families and by extension their nation; whether or not a migrant sends remittances thus becomes the criteria upon which migrants' moral standing is determined. These state discourses create a narrow understanding of unidirectional economic care that devalues and erases other forms of cross-border care, a discourse whose effects transnational families must continually confront.

22 Living Together Across Borders

The communicative care perspective therefore makes important contributions to long-standing debates about how ethics and morality matter for care. Euro-American theorizations have often presumed that care involves a particular moral stance of affection, concern, and interest toward others (Erikson 1995; Heidegger 2008), an assumption that formed the basis for feminist care ethics (Gilligan 1982). Simple glosses of care, such as the one mobilized in this book, instead guide analysis away from internal motivations toward concrete practice as the basis for theorizing care (cf. Aulino 2019; Buch 2018; Han 2012). This is not to say that care lacks any ethical or moral dimensions: rather, ethnographic investigations must trace to what extent particular moral motivations and ethical stances become associated with care in particular contexts. Thus, instead of assuming a priori ethical principles and moral values associated with care, this approach reveals how such orientations emerge in the complexity of everyday lived experience, often before being reflexively named after the fact (Black 2018; Zigon 2010). Therefore, rather than maintaining a strict separation between the ethical and the moral, this book takes an inclusive approach, as encapsulated in the term "ethico-moral." Studies of language use can trace how the ethico-moral dimensions of social life are invoked and produced in the course of carrying out specific forms of care work. Analytical tools such as genre and interdiscursivity, stance, and sequence organization can be mobilized to trace how such communication is patterned over time. Ultimately, language as care practice produces meanings through which the ethico-moral attributes of care are produced and negotiated in particular settings.

If language is understood as a multifaceted form of care that participates in the relational work of provision, we might ask, what then is generated by communicative care in transnational family life? On the one hand, language is clearly vital to cross-border family care. For individual relatives, communication works to sustain provisioning and well-being from day to day, week to week, and year to year. For the family as a whole, communication makes possible the maintenance of both cross-border care and the transnational family formation such care produces. From this perspective, communication is a vital form of *convivencia* that produces family despite distance; conversations are a vital resource for collective resilience under incredibly challenging conditions.

And yet, communicative care within the family is simultaneously caught up with social inequities and structural violence. Communicative care often unfolds in ways that shore up gendered and age-graded hierarchies within families, as when parents direct their young children through daily care activities, including socializing them to send certain kinds of greetings to their migrant relatives (see Chapter 3). Cross-border communication is thus also impacted by global political-economic inequities which create a divide within families between the normative communicative care practices expected of migrants and nonmigrants. At times, these familial asymmetries and political-economic hierarchies intersect, as when nonmigrant women are made responsible for the most onerous communicative tasks such as requesting remittances (see Chapter 2). Yet at the same time, language can also be used to challenge such inequalities. For instance, women may use their assumed responsibility for cross-border communication to leverage greater decision-making power in family negotiations of care (see Chapter 2).[26] Thus, even as communicative care sustains family life, it simultaneously generates interpersonal hierarchies, while also serving as a potent resource for destabilizing and renegotiating these asymmetries.

However, the consequences of communicative care go far beyond the interpersonal and relational. This book demonstrates that family communication is fundamentally implicated in the inequitable global political-economic order in which those in the Global South, living in the devastating aftermath of colonization and enslavement, and in the crosshairs of continuing intervention by dominant world powers, are forced to turn to migration for survival. Communicative care is a key resource for making migration successful in the terms of the state, which, as discussed in Chapter 1, is primarily concerned with keeping remittances flowing. In this sense, communication participates in the co-optation of family ties by neoliberalism, just as since the advent of capitalism, the family has been incorporated into heteropatriarchal capitalist projects (Fraad, Resnick, and Wolff 1994; Holmstrom 1981). However, to focus only on this co-optation would be to simplify a much more complex reality. As this book demonstrates, cross-border communication is oriented not only to economic provisioning but also to sustaining ongoing relationships and maintaining *convivencia* despite separation. Transnational conversations therefore do not simply replicate dominant political economic systems but instead forge relationships of care and collective living that rely on reciprocal obligation rather than the economic logics of capitalism. Tracing the resistance and resilience of cross-border communication requires reading the world for difference, attending to the diverse forms of social and economic organization that predate and continue to coexist alongside capitalism (Gibson-Graham 2014, 2020). Thus, even as transnational family conversations prop up inequitable political economic regimes, they can simultaneously serve to nourish and sustain more reciprocal intergenerational ties that resist capitalist logics.

Ultimately, communication as a form of care is thus both vital and violent. Although this understanding of care is not new within anthropology,

I suggest that a communicative approach provides fresh insights into how such fundamentally opposed effects of care are produced. Through the multifunctionality of language, communication as care produces communicative actions with multiple effects that do not necessarily work always in consort. Rather, a single utterance may enact explicit and implicit actions that are completely at odds with one another, or that carry out tangentially related forms of social action. For instance, in the opening vignette, Beto ignores his grandfather's economic complaints and instead provides a humorous response to his physical complaints. This action simultaneously flouts the migrant's assumed responsibility for economic care—which should normatively have been performed by treating the complaint as a request for remittances. Nevertheless, this same interaction enacts a form of relational care between grandfather and grandson even as it elides the care work of women in the family. In nurturing affective connections across borders, communication resists dominant logics that prioritize unidirectional economic provisioning by migrants, instead highlighting a more reciprocal relationship premised on relational engagement. The communicative care perspective thus provides a grounded approach for understanding how the contradictory consequences of care emerge through multifaceted practices, in this case communicative ones, that work simultaneously at multiple levels.

Methods for Studying Cross-Border Communication

In order to understand the role of communication in cross-border care, I take a multisited approach (Marcus 1995), a central method in migration studies research that traces connections across space and time to develop grounded understandings of transnationalism (Hirsch 2003). While many such studies begin with a central location in the sending country, the hub of my research was the rural Salvadoran village of Cantón El Río. I met families from this village during the four years (2001–2005) I spent living in the community and working as a volunteer with gender-development and youth-engagement programs, as I recounted in the "Prologue." My research built on these connections, deploying intimacy as a methodological stance (Barabantseva, Mhurchú, and Peterson 2021) through which I attended to my interpersonal attachments, and the sites and modes of relationality through which my complex ongoing relationship with these families emerged. From Cantón El Río, I traced family ties to migrants in three US locations: Los Angeles; Elizabeth, New Jersey; and a small town in Pennsylvania I call Marshall. Through five years of ethnographic research, I used the strategy of following language

(Dick and Arnold 2017, 398), tracing communicative practices and ideologies to understand how social spaces are constituted in ways that both create boundaries and produce interconnections (see Arnold 2022 for a more in-depth discussion of my research methods).

From 2009 to 2014, I conducted ethnographic research at these sites, making three six-week annual trips to El Salvador and one six-week trip to each of the three US sites. During these visits I lived with families or in their neighborhoods and conducted participant observation, joining in gender- and age-appropriate aspects of families' lives: preparing food, helping with housework and child care, running errands, and participating in family conversations, sometimes even being included in transnational phone calls. Families also asked me to use my research equipment to take photos or record videos to be sent to relatives in the other country, a process I discuss in more detail in Chapter 3. In addition, I conducted twenty-four recorded interviews with migrants and nonmigrants in nine different families. These open-ended conversations lasted one to two hours and discussed experiences of migration and the role of communication in cross-border lives.

During this first stage of ethnographic research, I developed particularly close ties to two multigenerational families—the Mejías and the Portillos—whose stories form the heart of this book. Both families consisted of aging parents, and several adult children, as well as their spouses and children. In both families, the original migrants came from the middle generation and tended to be men rather than women. Two of the migrant men's spouses migrated as well, but only one woman migrated independently, leading to an overall underrepresentation of women migrants among my participants, particularly in comparison to the consistently high levels of female emigration from El Salvador. Over the course of my research, some of the eldest male grandchildren in the families themselves became migrants and started families of their own, extending the transnational family by another generation.

These close and long-standing relationships with families facilitated a second phase of research that traced the complete circuit of cross-border care. In order to more closely follow the communication that linked relatives in one country to those in another, I gathered recordings of transnational phone calls—the most pervasive form of cross-border communication in these families—for four months from September 2013 to January 2014. During this period, each family received $50 per month to cover the cost of transnational conversations, a sum based on the average amount that interviewees had reported spending on long-distance communication. To gather the recordings, I collaborated with family research assistants who were young people in each family; I trained them to use the recording equipment and provided them with a monthly stipend, as well as other forms of mentoring and support. With these young people spearheading the recording process, families decided which conversations to record and which recordings to pass along to me.

Over four months, family research assistants in both families gathered a total of sixty-seven recordings of transnational phone calls. The calls ranged in length from two minutes to two hours, most averaging about twenty to thirty minutes, for a total of twenty-five hours of recordings. Family research assistants were trained to delete recorded data, so that conversations that had been recorded could be removed after the fact if anyone in the family had any concerns. I also reviewed all recordings before beginning analysis and ultimately deleted several recordings that contained sensitive legal information. All recordings—including interviews and phone calls—were indexed and inductively coded, and selected portions were transcribed using the conventions of discourse transcription (Du Bois et al. 1992).

By closely following transnational language use, this book sheds new light on the role of communication in cross-border care. Although transnational family scholarship points to the role of communication technologies for care across borders, it often pays scant attention to the specific communicative practices that these technologies facilitate. This oversight is the result of methodologies such as interviews and participant observation that limit researchers to what they are able to observe or what participants report. Participants and researchers alike may not be aware of the small but nevertheless significant communicative patterns that close analysis can reveal. Moreover, these methods do not allow researchers to track the immediate back-and-forth of conversation, or the ways that interactions in the moment are discursively tied to previous conversations, both of which are central to the ways that language acts in the world. By contrast, using linguistic anthropological methods allowed me to trace more precisely how communication participates in cross-border care by attending closely to the detailed formulation, patterning, and temporal unfolding of everyday family conversations. For this reason, the primary focus of this book is on the use of specific communicative practices including greetings, remittance requests, and joint remembering. I chose these specific practices because of their salience in the recorded conversations, but also on the basis of insights gleaned through interviews and participant observation. Through close analyses of everyday conversations, this book highlights the novel contributions of a linguistic anthropological approach to cross-border care.

Organization of the Book

The book advances a multipronged investigation in order to trace how care through communication shores up global inequities while also creating space for resistance that quietly forges *convivencia* despite separation. I begin by examining how state-endorsed migration discourse in El Salvador constitutes transnational family life as a consequential foundation for national progress. Over three decades, state discourses consistently depict transnational families primarily in economic terms, as involving the unidirectional transfer of funds from migrants—depicted as male breadwinners—to their dependent relatives back home in El Salvador. This simplistic vision of cross-border care relies on transnational imaginaries and figures of personhood rooted in heteropatriarchal models of family life. Through these discourses, the Salvadoran state seeks to incorporate migrants and their remittances into nation-building projects aligned with structural adjustment policies. Dutiful family care is thereby converted into a crucial form of relational neoliberal personhood that emerges from familial obligations, becoming the ground upon which the nation stands or falls. These dominant imaginaries of cross-border family life powerfully shape the ways that families enact transnational care and the forms of resistance they engage in, as revealed in subsequent chapters.

Shifting away from state-endorsed depictions, Chapter 2 provides an ethnographic account of the complex unfolding of transnational care and *convivencia* at a distance. I trace the moral imaginaries that undergird and are reproduced by cross-border family care. Against the simplistic models of cross-border care advanced in state-endorsed imaginaries, transnational families themselves envision and enact care as a multidirectional process in which all relatives participate. These engagements, however, are understood as fundamentally differentiated, both by gendered and generational hierarchies as well as by global political-economic inequities manifested in pervasive distinctions between migrants and nonmigrants. The chapter highlights the role of communication in transnational care, suggesting that language is a powerful resource due to its multifunctionality and its omnipresence in all aspects of transnational family care. Even as it reproduces asymmetries and hierarchies, communication opens up spaces wherein the multiple inequalities that shape family care can be negotiated. Communicative care thereby incrementally works not simply to reproduce *convivencia* but to incrementally shift the social life that care generates, implicitly pushing back against dominant imaginaries in ways that, perhaps at least partially, recover family care from neoliberal state co-optation.

The next chapter demonstrates the power of communication by investigating cross-border video greetings sent between relatives. Such greetings are never sent by migrants but only by their nonmigrant relatives. I demonstrate that transnational families understand video greetings as an important form of care that reciprocates the economic care migrants provide. Care is not simply economic but rather involves communicative and relational labor. Moreover, children in El Salvador—but not their counterparts in the United States—are socialized to send greetings. This pattern reveals how seemingly mundane asymmetries of cross-border life are deeply shaped by political economic inequities between Global North and South. These inequalities become incorporated as a pervasive feature of family care, shaping who learns to use which communicative practices. This asymmetrical socialization reveals that transnational families envision their cross-border *convivencia* as enduring across generations not through the incorporation of US-born relatives but rather through continual migration of some of those raised in El Salvador and socialized to transnational family life during their childhood. In the moment, however, greetings simultaneously work to sustain existing cross-border circuits of care, envisioning and enacting ongoing relationships of obligation. Greetings put into practice moral imaginaries in which such ongoing asymmetrical reciprocity—rather than the economic exchanges of capitalist regimes—become the foundation for social life.

The fourth chapter builds on these insights to develop a communicative investigation of the most well-known form of transnational care: remittances. Examining the regular communicative practices that families develop as they engage in remittance negotiations time and again across the years, I trace the gendered norms that govern the uneven distribution of this work. I focus on remittance requests and responses, moments in which relatives must directly confront the sustained economic asymmetry of transnational family life. The analysis demonstrates how conversational temporalities—interactional turn-taking routines and interdiscursive genre norms—structure remittance negotiations. The communicative management of time becomes a key resource through which families navigate shifting intergenerational care needs while also grappling with the effects of gendered hierarchies and global inequities. Conversational temporalities are thus central to the ways that transnational families sustain *convivencia* through cross-border care in the face of both political-economic and discursive forces that work to sever their ties.

Extending this temporal investigation, Chapter 5 explores how transnational families remember together across borders. I situate this communicative practice within the context of memory work in postwar El Salvador, where long-standing institutional silencing makes remembering a deeply political act. Inspired by local theories of communicative remembrance manifested in struggles for *memoria histórica* (historical memory) and in the rituals of *Día de los Difuntos* (Day of the Dead) celebrations, I understand remembering as a public, and often collective, form of care that stitches together social relations sundered by violence, death, and cross-border separation. For transnational families, remembering together allows them to forge new ways of living-together at a distance, creating *convivencia* by building connections from past into present. In remembering together, transnational families resist dominant discourses that depict migration as inevitably rupturing family ties, refusing the imaginaries imposed upon them and instead insisting on their continued togetherness despite long-term separation.

The conclusion synthesizes the insights into transnational care gleaned from a communicative care perspective. I begin by pointing out how language undergirds care in many contexts beyond transnational family life, arguing that the insights developed in this book have broad relevance to studies of care writ large. In particular, I draw attention to the materiality of language and its deep entanglements with global regimes of (im)mobility and political-economic structures. I also highlight multifunctionality and temporality, suggesting that these two properties of language make it a particularly forceful tool for transformative work. The book concludes by calling readers to consider how they might take action to support the struggles of transnational families for a world in which *convivencia* is a matter of self-determination rather than exploitation.

1

Making Family Care Political

State-Endorsed Migration Discourse in El Salvador

Hermano Lejano ¡Bienvenido! (Distant Brother, Welcome!)

In 1994, as El Salvador was emerging from over a decade of civil war, the mayor of the capital, San Salvador, erected the country's first postwar monument (DeLugan 2012), dedicated to Salvadoran emigrants. The tall arch of steel and concrete, supported by a smaller half-arch set at a right angle, bore a hailing cry in gold letters: "Hermano Lejano ¡Bienvenido!" (Distant Brother, Welcome!). Located at the entrance to the capital city along the highway leading from the airport, it welcomed the nation's migrants, identifying them as brothers, members of the national family. The monument's stark concrete arches broadcast modernity, as did its placement in front of a new highway overpass, the first ever to be constructed in the capital city (Baker-Cristales 2004). The monument and the overpass together constitute two material signs pointing to a vision for the new El Salvador that would rise from the ashes of war. The juxtaposition of these two signs, one indexing modernity and the other indexing Salvadoran migrants, produces an unmistakable message: the modernized and developed future of El Salvador depends on the continued involvement of its migrants. Despite their distance, these brothers are active members of the national family; through their remittances they become the economic providers who make progress possible.

Ustedes Son Embajadores Laborales (You Are Working Ambassadors)

On December 19, 2019, the first contingent of fifty migrants with temporary H2A visas left El Salvador to complete three months of agricultural work in Mississippi. Their departure followed a months-long selection process in which applicants—all men—had to demonstrate their agricultural vocation, a

Living Together Across Borders. Lynnette Arnold, Oxford University Press. © Oxford University Press 2024.
DOI: 10.1093/oso/9780197755730.003.0002

spotless police and immigration record, and, most importantly, strong ties to family that depended on them for economic support (Guzmán 2019a). On the day of their departure, the fifty temporary migrants and their families were driven to the airport in a caravan of white microbuses, each bearing a large sign with the slogan "El Salvador: Listo para Trabajar" (El Salvador: Ready to Work) (Ministerio de Trabajo de El Salvador 2019b). Press coverage lingered over footage of the travelers having their passports and tickets scanned at airline counters (Gómez and Pastrán 2019), a spectacle of legally sanctioned migration. Cameras zoomed in as the men said goodbye to their tearful wives and children, to their mothers and extended families, promising with an almost supernatural certainty to see them again in three months (Guzmán 2019c). At a farewell event, Rolando Castro, the Salvadoran Minister of Labor who had coordinated the program, hailed these temporary migrants as *embajadores laborales* (working ambassadors) and sent them off with this charge: "a trabajar duro, a trabajar fuerte, y a dejar en alto a nuestro querido El Salvador" (work hard, work with determination, and elevate our beloved El Salvador) (Guzmán 2019b). Twenty-five years after the Hermano Lejano monument was built, migrants continue to be envisioned as central to nation-building projects in El Salvador, now being called not only to support the nation but to improve the country's transnational image in the face of xenophobic US rhetoric targeting Central Americans.

State-Endorsed Migration Discourse

For the past thirty years, public discourse about migration in El Salvador has actively woven together understandings of family, gender, care, and nation. Such discourses put immense pressure on transnational family relationships and fundamentally shape cross-border communicative care. This chapter therefore examines Salvadoran migration discourse, or language focused on migration, its causes, and its consequences (Dick 2010), seeking to understand how conceptualizations of family and care are mobilized and to what ends.[1] In particular, I focus on state-endorsed discourses, those that are articulated or authorized by state actors or their proxies (Dick 2018, 14). As shown in the opening vignettes, these discourses are sometimes directly generated by government officials. However, state-endorsed discourses also emerge in popular culture as well as in the media, which, according to Salvadoran communications scholar Roxana Martel (2006, 965), functions "como caja de resonancia del discurso oficial" (as a sounding board of official discourse).

32   Living Together across Borders

Of course, state actors are not the only authors of migration discourse; indeed, the rest of the book focuses on migration discourses produced by migrants and their families, examining how they contest and resist the terms laid out in dominant discourses. State-endorsed migration discourse is particularly powerful because of its direct connection to migration policy; dominant discourses such as these thus have profound consequences for the ways that migration is regulated, experienced, and made meaningful. This is clear in immigrant-receiving nations, as for instance when the Trump administration constructed the figure of the "MS-13 animal" to depict all Central American migrants as threatening criminals belonging to the Mara Salvatrucha gang; this imagery was used to justify border militarization, increased enforcement efforts within the United States, and inhumane policies like the "zero-tolerance" approach that tore children away from their parents (Arnold and Dick 2018). The migration discourses that circulate within sending contexts like El Salvador are no less consequential, although they receive far less scholarly attention. Focusing on state-endorsed discourses in El Salvador is not a parochial project, however. As we will see, Salvadoran migration discourses are shaped by US foreign and immigration policy and the inequalities of global neoliberalism, while also playing a crucial role transnational moral panics.

This chapter therefore traces how dominant Salvadoran migration discourses mobilize depictions of migrants, contrasting heroic figures such as the *hermano lejano* or *embajador laboral* with visions of failed migrants who threaten the nation. I demonstrate that these state-endorsed visions function as an ideological companion to neoliberal projects of economic structural adjustment, advancing certain visions of migrant subjectivity that induce migrants, and nonmigrants as well, to think and act in particular ways. But whereas the neoliberal subject is often assumed to emphasize an atomized and self-sufficient form of existence (Brown 2003), state-endorsed Salvadoran discourses depict fundamentally relational selves that call migrants to take responsibility for the nation by enacting their moral obligation to provide for their family. Thus, the heroic *hermano lejano* becomes a brother in the national family by consistently sending remittances to his relatives back home. The *embajadores laborales* sent out in 2019 serve as ambassadors for the nation precisely by enacting their dedication as providers for dependent wives and children. In both cases, the migrant is envisioned as an ethico-moral individual who provides economically for both his family and his nation, thereby taking responsibility for the well-being of the nation through relational care work. Cross-border family care is thus deeply political in El Salvador, mobilized as a strategy that urges individuals to take on a neoliberal risk-taking subjectivity and absolves the state of abandoning its responsibility to care for its citizens. Acts of transnational provisioning are thereby imbued with immense significance, made to sustain not only families but also the material and ideological foundations of the nation itself.

These dominant discourses make the *convivencia* (living-together) of transnational families into a fraught site of struggle and signification. Such rhetoric consistently mobilizes heteronormative and patriarchal understandings of family care, depicting it in restricted and fixed terms. Care is understood as a unidirectional phenomenon, sent by migrants to their dependent relatives back home. Thus, economic care in the form of remittances is elevated, while other family care practices are erased. Migrant remittances become contributions to the development of the nation, co-opting relationships of obligation between cross-border relatives and placing responsibility for the well-being of the nation firmly on the shoulders of migrants. While such dominant discourses ignore communicative forms of care altogether, they nevertheless powerfully shape the unfolding of cross-border family communication, influencing what communicative practices are used, by whom, to what ends, and with what meaning.

This chapter therefore sets the stage for the rest of the book through an analysis of state-endorsed discourses that contrast depictions of successful and failed migrants. I examine the emergence of these figures in government rhetoric, media discourse, and popular culture, while also drawing on interviews with migrants and their families to demonstrate the impact of these depictions. I suggest that these seemingly contradictory representations are connected by understandings of care. Migrants are envisioned alternately as those who provide care, as victims who need care, and as those undeserving individuals who represent threats to care and thus to the nation. State-endorsed discourses cast individual actions as the main determinant of familial experiences of migration, eliding the global political-economic inequities and ongoing legacies of US imperialism that drive and fundamentally shape the contours of Salvadoran migration. Ultimately, depictions of migrants that mobilize family care create a powerful interpretive framework that make cross-border communication, in particular, into a charged locus of political and personal signification.

Contrastive Migrant Personhood: Heroes or Dangerous Failures?

Over four decades of widespread emigration, Salvadoran migration discourse has focused on figures of migrant personhood, or representations of the types of people involved in migration (Arispe-Bazán 2021; Dick 2018). These typified figures of personhood set up ethico-moral guidelines for evaluating individuals and their actions as moral and praiseworthy or as deviant and censurable (Ingold 2011; Povinelli 2002; Taylor 1985). In contexts of migration, these ethico-moral figurations of personhood are fundamentally spatial and temporal in nature (Dick 2018; Karimzad and Catedral 2021). For instance, both the *hermano lejano* and the *embajador laboral* embody notions of national progress that are fundamental to understandings of modernity (Dick 2010). Through their efforts from abroad, these heroic migrants will help their national family, thereby enacting themselves as ethico-moral individuals who fulfill their obligations.

Migrant figures of personhood are discursively embedded and interconnected within broader imaginaries of migration. I define imaginaries as ways of understanding the social world that are continually invoked and thereby come to shape many forms of collective life (Gaonkar 2002, 4). Imaginaries envision and create connections between individuals and larger collectivities such as the nation (Hansen and Stepputat 2001; Warner 2002).[2] Although state actors often actively work to maintain such national imaginaries, anthropological work reveals how individual actors take up and respond to dominant imaginaries in ways that both constitute and incrementally transform large-scale social collectivities.[3] Linguistic anthropology, in particular offers crucial analytical tools for a grounded investigation of imaginaries, since, as Hilary Parsons Dick (2018, 13) points out, "most of the imagining in what we call imaginaries happens discursively." In other words, visions of social collectivities are produced through language use, both in specific moments of talk and writing as well as in the processes of circulation through which imaginaries move across time and space. A linguistic approach anchors investigations in the complex discursive practices through which national imaginaries are produced, allowing explorations of how national belonging is envisioned, by whom, and to what ends.[4]

The importance of imaginaries is particularly clear in instances where mobility disrupts taken-for-granted assumptions about the geographic basis of national belonging (Salazar 2011; Schmidt Camacho 2008). In El Salvador, which has been obliged by neoliberal globalization to position itself as an explicitly transnational state (Hallett 2019), imaginaries of connection across distance are fundamental to how the Salvadoran nation is understood (Baker-Cristales 2004; Dyrness and Sepúlveda 2015; Rivas 2014). For instance, the Salvadoran diaspora is often labeled *Departamento 15* (the fifteenth department), discursively expanding the fourteen departments (or states) that make up the territory of El Salvador to include a fifteenth diasporic department (Rodríguez 2005). Since April 2000, one of El Salvador's two largest newspapers (*La Prensa Gráfica*), has dedicated an entire section—named Departamento 15—to news about the diaspora (Rivas 2014).

However, even as imaginaries work to produce transnational belonging, these processes are fraught with contestation over who is included in the nation, who is excluded, and what the terms of such inclusion might be. In Salvadoran migration discourse, depictions of successful and failed migrants lay out the terms that migrants must follow if they wish to remain part of the national family. This anchoring contrast depicts migrants either as national heroes or as having failed to meet this ideal (DeLugan 2012; Marroquín Parducci 2019; Rivas 2014). The figures of failed migrants serve as a disciplining tactic, presenting migrants and potential migrants with cautionary tales of the pitfalls that must be avoided to achieve the heroic ideal.

The salience of this contrast emerges clearly in table 1.1, which lists figures of migrant personhood that have been dominant in Salvadoran imaginaries for the past thirty years. Figures are listed in chronological order, with a brief description and example for each. Some figures are named, as indicated by the use of Spanish names, while others remain unnamed but are nevertheless typified depictions of migrant personhood. This list was compiled first through a synthetic review of the literature on Salvadoran migration, which focused mostly on the first four figures. The two more recent figures emerged from original research I conducted on media coverage of migration in two major Salvadoran newspapers between June 2018 and July 2020 (Arnold 2023). Table 1.1 briefly characterizes each figure of migrant personhood and provides an example from media discourse, state rhetoric, or popular culture.

State-endorsed figures of migrant personhood emerge at particular moments in ways that respond to shifting national imperatives. Even as figures change and multiply, the contrast between successful and failed migrants remains. Kin care is continually mobilized in attempts to discursively harness migration to state projects. This chapter examines heroic figures of migrant personhood before turning to depictions of failed migrants. It focuses on the foundational figures of the heroic *hermano lejano* and the deplorable selfish migrant, which have the most profound consequences for transnational family life.

The Heroic Migrant as Economic Provider

The migrant as a national hero is the most constant figure of migration in El Salvador. The heroic migrant emerged as the twelve-year civil war drew to

36 Living Together across Borders

Table 1.1 State-Endorsed Figures of Migrant Personhood

Figure	When Emerged	Characteristics	Example
Hermano lejano (distant brother)	Early 1990s	Heroic male figure who sacrifices to send money home to maintain both his family and his nation	'Hermano lejano, las gracias le damos, por darnos la mano' (Hermano lejano, we thank you for giving us a hand) (song entitled 'Hermano Lejano' by Tony Acosta, lyrics transcribed from Acosta 2013)
Selfish migrant	Mid-1990s	Deadbeat dad and faithless husband who abandons his family back home	'Los que se van se olviden un poco de sus seres queridos. Ya no vuelven a llamar' (Those who leave forget their loved ones a little. They no longer call) (from TV show 'Reencuentros Hermano Lejano' UNIVISION 2016)
Criminalized deportee	Late 1990s	Dangerous young male figure whose only loyalty is to his gang	'Los antisociales deportados de los Estados Unidos representan una bomba de tiempo' (The antisocials deported from the United States represent a time bomb) (statement by René Figueroa, ARENA senator, cited in Marroquín Parducci 2008, 30)
Victimized migrant	2010s	Migrant who suffered violence during their unauthorized journey north and needs care	'Migrante que perdió un pie al caer de tren solicita ayuda. El joven es el único sostén económico de su familia y por ahora no puede trabajar' (Migrant who lost his foot after falling from the train asks for help. The young man is the only economic support of his family and he is unable to work right now) (news headline, Díaz 2019)
Entrepreneurial returnee	2018	Migrant who is deported to El Salvador and is redeemed through entrepreneurship	'La historia de tres migrantes salvadoreños que fueron deportados y ahora emprenden en su país' (The story of three Salvadoran migrants who were deported and now are entrepreneurs in their country) (news headline, Arévalo 2019)
Embajador laboral (working ambassador)	2019	Heroic male figure whose work and compliance with immigration law recuperates the nation's global reputation	'A trabajar duro, a trabajar fuerte, y a dejar en alto a nuestro querido El Salvador. Son nuestros embajadores laborales' (Work hard, work with determination, and elevate our beloved El Salvador. You are our working ambassadors) (Minister of Labor Rolando Castro at farewell event for H2-A visa recipients, reported in Guzmán 2019)

a close in the early 1990s. At this crucial moment, there was a veritable explosion of media discourse about migration (Marroquín Parducci 2008, 27), which envisioned how migrants would participate in postwar projects of nation-building. These discourses quickly cohered around the figure of the *hermano lejano*, the migrant celebrated in the eponymous monument erected in 1994. In this figuration, the migrant is a national hero whose remittances—sent to family back home—will provide the resources to build a new and modernized El Salvador.

The emphasis on remittances in these depictions emerged in the context of neoliberal structural adjustment programs in El Salvador that increasingly made social provisioning dependent on remittances. Beginning in 1985, the United States started demanding structural adjustment in exchange for the military aid they sent to the Salvadoran government. Neoliberalism functioned as a counter-revolutionary response by global capital against the *campesino* (peasant) and working-class rebellion that had sparked the Salvadoran civil war, then in its fifth year (Osuna and Abrego 2022). Elites in El Salvador collaborated with neoliberalism, paving the foundation for a far-reaching economic liberalization campaign which in 1989 began reducing government spending, privatizing banks, and eliminating state regulation of price controls and interest rates (Moodie 2010, 44). The end of the war accelerated these processes, and El Salvador has since led neoliberal restructuring in the region, privatizing and cutting more public services, and opening up the movement of goods and investments through dollarization in 2001 and participation in the 2005 Central American Free Trade Agreement (Hallett 2019).

In this economic context, migrant remittances were made to bear increasing social weight. International agencies such as the World Bank touted remittances as means of poverty reduction (Pedersen 2013), although attempts by the Salvadoran government to convert remittances into a development economy have largely failed (Wiltberger 2014). Nevertheless, the state co-opted migrant remittances a "a substitute for social security" (*Estudios Centroamericanos* cited and translated in Dyrness and Sepúlveda 2015, 108). Migrant remittances—which are overwhelmingly used by families to meet basic needs of food, shelter, education, and healthcare—have relieved the state of its responsibility to provide for the well-being of its citizens, allowing for the continued adoption of neoliberal reforms.

Cultivating a continuing stream of migrant remittances thus became a crucial state endeavor, a project of fomenting national belonging in which imaginaries played a central role. To keep remittances coming in, government officials theorized, "faraway citizens need an affective bond of loyalty, or sense of belonging to the nation" (DeLugan 2012, 104). However, in order to

38 Living Together across Borders

cultivate such relational bonds, the state needed to gain the trust of its migrant citizens, trust that had been severely eroded after years of abandonment and outright violence (Hallett and Baker-Cristales 2010). Susan Coutin (2011) argues that the Salvadoran state strategically used representations of migrants to foment this trust, giving rise to prevalent depictions of migrants' national pride and nostalgia for the homeland. Government rhetoric, media discourse, and forms of popular culture have worked together to mythologize the heroic migrant, who has become "a valuable commodity in the symbolic economy of El Salvador" (Rodríguez 2005, 25). Imaginaries that figure migrants as heroes are thus a crucial component of ongoing state efforts to co-opt migration to nation-building projects.

This section provides a close analysis of the specific discourses through which heroic figurations such as the *hermano lejano* and *ambajador laboral* were produced. This approach can reveal the specific constellation of characteristics for each figure, revealing how particular understandings of family care undergird Salvadoran national imaginaries. In particular, popular music is an important means of constructing the figure of the heroic migrant (Martel and Marroquín Parducci 2007). A plethora of songs, in a range of musical genres, are dedicated to the *hermano lejano*. Examining such musical renditions of state-endorsed imaginaries can shed light on the precise figuration of the heroic migrant, as these cultural forms allow for greater specification of imaginaries.

Perhaps the most well-known musical representation of the *hermano lejano* is an eponymous 1998 song by *Orquesta Los Hermanos Flores*, the world-famous Salvadoran musical group. The lyrics of the song purport to give voice to an imagined distant brother who sings of his longing for homeland and family (see Excerpt 1.1, English translation by author).

These lyrics illustrate the specific characteristics of the *hermano lejano*, features that are fundamentally linked to family care. The lyrics of this song not only identify the *hermano lejano* as male—a distant brother, not a distant sister—but this gendering is also performed through the voice of the male singer. This masculine depiction elides the fact that women have long made up a substantial proportion of Salvadoran migrants.[5] Moreover, the migrant is envisioned here in generational terms, as an adult son whose aging parents remain back home in El Salvador. The deeply affective depiction in the song reinforces these familial ties; the migrant experiences profound sadness and loneliness as he misses the warmth and love of his parents. Throughout the song, the migrant alternately dreams of returning to El Salvador and of being once again at his dear mother's side. Longing for family closeness is thereby conflated with a longing for the homeland. Just as the migrant in the song

Excerpt 1.1 Lyrics from El Hermano Lejano by Los Hermanos Flores

Estoy tan lejos de mi tierra bella	I am so far from my beautiful land
Muriendo de tristeza y soledad.	Dying of sadness and loneliness.
Extraño tanto el calor de mis padres	I miss the warmth of my parents so much
Y los consejos que solían darme	And the advice they used to give me
Con mucho amor y sinceridad.	With so much love and sincerity.
A Dios le pido que me dé un consuelo	I ask God to give me some comfort
Para olvidar la distancia y poder luchar	To forget the distance and be able to fight
Por mi familia que tanto quiero	For my family, which I love so much
A los que siempre soñé brindarles	To whom I always dreamed of giving
Un mundo lleno de felicidad.	A world full of happiness.

cares for his parents, so too the *hermano lejano* takes on his filial role as brother in the national family by caring for his *madre patria* (motherland). Thus, it is through these intergenerational ties that the loyalty of the *hermano lejano* is made to extend from the family to the nation. Dedication to the family becomes dedication to the nation.

Depictions of the *hermano lejano* in Salvadoran migration discourse thus constitute national imaginaries founded on particular understandings of family and of care. Visions of the nation do not emerge in a vacuum (Alonso 1994; Bauman and Briggs 2003; Herzfeld 1997); rather they are inevitably produced in conjunction with other ways of envisioning collective social life. In particular, national imaginaries often draw on particular understandings of kinship by envisioning the nation as a family (Eley and Suny 1996). Feminist scholars have demonstrated that patriarchal and heteronormative visions of the family are often foundational to national imaginaries (Boehmer 2005; Yuval-Davis, Anthias, and Campling 1989), particularly in Latin America (Skurski 1996; Sommer 1993). Contra to Andersonian accounts of an egalitarian national community, such work suggests that national imaginaries draw on tropes of patriarchal kinship that license the subordination of women and children in order to naturalize social difference as hierarchy (McClintock 1996, 262). National imaginaries extend kin hierarchies to reproduce and justify social inequality along the lines of class, race, and ethnicity (Alonso 1994, 387).

I suggest that care is central to the ways that national imaginaries mobilize visions of kinship; it functions to grant moral meaning to social difference and thus serves to sustain inequality. In Latin America, nation formation was often imagined as a process of male civilization and domination of a wild and

40 Living Together across Borders

feminized national territory (Skurski 1996). In these visions, marriage is seen as a force that stabilizes the nation by anchoring heteronormative care relations (Sommer 1993). Gendered understandings of public space as male continue to have immense cultural force (Radcliffe and Westwood 1996), with the domestic sphere viewed as the domain of the good woman (Dick 2017). Visions of kin care thus convert national imaginaries into gendered ethico-moral projects that lay out fundamentally different ways of participating in the national community for men and for women. Moreover, the moral meanings of kin care also become vehicles for creating distinctions of race and class within the nation. Wealthier, lighter-skinned women are envisioned as the maintainers of tradition and producers of citizens, granted respect due to their reproductive capacities (Pratt 1994). However, the care labor of poor women and those from racialized groups is ignored or vilified, even as it is actively appropriated to generate national wealth (Alvarez 1990; Stepan 1991).

The discursive mobilization of kin care to create national belonging is clear in depictions of the *hermano lejano*. As shown in the song lyrics, the figure of the *hermano lejano* relies on a normative imaginary of kin care in which relationships of familial obligation extend across the life course, and adults are expected to care for their parents to repay the care they received from them when they were children. The multigenerational extended family—rather than the nuclear family—serves as the basis for care, as Chapter 2 discusses in greater detail. The migrant here is understood as occupying the care slot (Leinaweaver 2010), the middle generation that has care responsibilities both for elders (their parents) and children. In Salvadoran understandings of kinship, this care slot is gendered as well as generational; particularly in rural families, the youngest daughter has traditionally been expected to remain unmarried, staying with her parents and taking care of them with the economic support of her brothers. It is precisely this understanding of kinship that is mobilized in discursive depictions of the migrant as a distant brother who provides for his national family.

While caring for his family back home is central to this figuration of the heroic migrant, the specific care he provides for his family is left implicit. This pattern is widespread in Salvadoran migration discourse, which celebrates the heroic migrant but glosses over the details of what and how he provides. I suggest that it is the mobilization of particular understandings of kin care that makes such inferences possible. Migrants' role as economic providers for their families is indirectly indexed by the gendered and generational characteristics associated with the *hermano lejano*. As an adult male member of the family, he must be an economic provider. Crucially, this assumption is licensed by a patriarchal and heteronormative model of the male breadwinner. But this is a particularly relational form of heteronormative masculinity: the migrant is not a macho man—fiercely independent and devoid of feelings—but rather a family-oriented and emotionally involved provider.

In the three decades since the figure of the *hermano lejano* emerged, the repeated mobilization of imaginaries of kin care have created a default depiction of the heroic migrant. Indeed, the connection between migration and remittances has been so naturalized through this imaginary that, for many Salvadorans, a migrant is by definition one who sends money to his family (PNUD El Salvador 2005, 383). The gendered and generational attributes of the *hermano lejano* have created a foundation of preexisting meanings upon which new significations can be built. In other words, new depictions of the heroic migrant can take up the assumptions embedded in the figuration of the *hermano lejano* to extend what it means to be a heroic migrant. As these new meanings are built, the models of kin care upon which they are based become ever more implicit and gain increasing normative force. This process of signification can be seen in the emergence of the figure of the *embajador laboral*, first invoked in the 2019 temporary visa program.[6]

In order to be considered for a temporary work visa, male applicants had to show that they had "arraigo familiar sólido en El Salvador" (strong family roots in El Salvador) (Ministerio de Trabajo de El Salvador 2019a), ties that were substantiated by listing the dependent wives, children, and elderly parents for whom applicants provided. Media coverage of the temporary visa program regularly included interviews not only with prospective migrants themselves but also with their wives, mothers, and children, all of whom emphasized their reliance on this masculine provider. In this program, the understandings of kin care embedded in the figure of the *hermano lejano* become the terms through which individuals demonstrate that they deserve a chance at legally sanctioned and safe migration. Moreover, by substantiating such relationships of familial obligation, applicants establish their ethico-moral personhood and readiness to take on the additional labor of representing the nation to the world as *embajadores laborales*. In the face of heightened anti-immigrant rhetoric that increasingly targets Central Americans, it is no longer sufficient for migrants to provide for their nation and their family by sending remittances. Rather, the Salvadoran migrant must also care for the reputation of his nation on the global stage.

Crucially, these figurations of the heroic migrant as *hermano lejano* or *embajador laboral* both draw the relatives of migrants in El Salvador into national imaginaries of migration. The migrant who provides economically must have dependent family members who rely on his support, and celebrations of the heroic migrant implicitly cast nonmigrants in this role.

Care here is a unidirectional economic transfer from the provider to his dependent relatives. Just as the providing migrant is envisioned as a man who occupies the care slot, so too the nonmigrant is imagined as possessing gendered and generational characteristics. Nonmigrants are generally depicted as women, children, or elderly individuals, all of whom are assumed to be in need of care. For instance, the *hermano lejano* in the song imagines his aging parents back home as those to whom he wants to provide "a world full of happiness." Similarly, prospective migrants applying for temporary visas had to list their dependent wives and children on their applications.

Imaginaries that mobilize kin care are thus a key mechanism for producing differentiated forms of national belonging.[7] Migrants must participate through economic care, though of course this is a form of inclusion based on exclusion: the *hermano lejano* can only belong to the nation by remaining forever distant, while the *embajador laboral* takes on his representational role by leaving the country in search of economic opportunities not available there.[8] Relatives of migrants, on the other hand, have an even narrower and more marginal mode of participation by which they may belong to the nation. Indeed, nonmigrants are imagined as participating in the nation through care engagements that are largely defined in terms of passive dependence on migrant kin. In this imaginary, to be a nonmigrant member of the national family is to depend on migrant remittances. No doubt it is in part this extremely limited figuration that provides the mythologized *hermano lejano* with such allure: far better to be an active hero—even one who must suffer and sacrifice—than one who must forever passively depend on others.

The discursive constitution of figures of personhood within imaginaries of migration is thus part of the coercive ideological apparatus that underpins the deeply inequitable distribution of care labor in our world today (Nakano Glenn 2010). In these depictions of the heroic migrant, care is understood as not as a reciprocal practice but rather as involving a care recipient and a care provider, who each remain in a fixed role with regard to the other. Patriarchal norms are deeply woven into this imaginary, such that while the economic provisioning provided by male migrants is widely celebrated, the care contributions of nonmigrants are made invisible and devalued. At the same time, noneconomic forms of care provided by migrants are also completely elided. Thus, these imaginaries mobilize an extremely limited understanding of care as involving unidirectional economic provisioning, thereby positioning migrant and nonmigrant relatives in a fixed relationship of provider and recipient of care.

Moreover, this depiction of nonmigrants grants significance to migrants' economic support by highlighting affective and ethico-moral qualities. For instance, the song portrays the *hermano lejano* as a sacrificial figure; being away from his beloved family and homeland is deeply painful for this familial and patriotic migrant. The *hermano lejano* misses his parents because he loves them, and this longing thus signifies his deep moral attunement to his familial ties and obligations.[9] Similarly, media coverage of the temporary visa holders depicted men saying heartfelt farewells to wives and children and aging mothers, while also highlighting their sorrow at having to miss the end-of-year festivities in El Salvador. The money sent home by the heroic migrant is thus earned through sacrifice; it becomes the visible manifestation of the migrant's ethico-moral personhood.

Indeed, tropes of sacrifice are widespread in Central American migration discourse, a conceptualization that is deeply gendered. Ideas of sacrifice woven into understandings of motherhood lead migrant women to work longer hours and endure suffering in order to support their children back home; as a result, women migrants consistently send more remittances than their male counterparts, despite earning less (Abrego 2009). Left-behind grandmothers who care for the children of their migrant daughters frame this intergenerational care as a shared sacrifice (Yarris 2017). The heroic migrant, on the other hand, is envisioned as overcoming loneliness and longing to struggle and provide for his loved ones. He embodies a masculine approach to sacrifice as hardships confronted and obstacles overcome. However, in both cases, gendered conceptualizations of sacrifice woven into kin care work to compel migrants to care for their families, providing the life-sustaining resources that the neoliberal state will not offer to its citizens.

Thus, as patriarchal and heteronormative understandings of kin care are incorporated into national imaginaries, the remittances the migrant sends to his family become economic provision for the nation as a whole. Discourses of kin care thus place responsibility for national wellbeing squarely on the shoulders of individual citizens, advancing a neoliberal agenda. Neoliberalism is not only an economic program, but also an ideological project that is advanced through "technologies of subjectification"; these technologies work to make individuals into subjects who govern themselves in accordance with neoliberal ideals of self-sufficiency (Ong 2006, 14). The discursive constitution of imaginaries is central to this ideological project, a powerful means of shaping understandings of self and society. This is clearly seen in the case of the *hermano lejano* and the *embajador laboral*, both of whom are made responsible for the wellbeing of their nation. Although migrants are presented as entrepreneurial individuals who generate revenues through their hard work, these actions are understood to be motivated not by a desire for individual advancement but rather by a duty to provide for dependent others.

44   Living Together across Borders

State-endorsed depictions of the heroic migrant mobilize the heft of kin relationships of obligation to more powerfully induce individuals to take on the social responsibility that used to belong to the state. Thus, through these imaginaries, kin care is harnessed to neoliberal projects of self-governance.

Failed Migrants as Scapegoats in Transnational Moral Panics

The ethico-moral status of the heroic migrant is consolidated in part through consistent contrast to representations of failed migrants, those who do not contribute resources but rather take from their families and their nation. While these figures were not explicitly named like the *hermano lejano* and the *embajador laboral*, they are typified through moral panics, which take amorphous social fears and project them onto a particular social group. While moral panics purport to generate solutions, in reality they work to obfuscate root causes by directing attention to a particular scapegoat (Hall 2017; Hall et al. 1978). Depictions of failed migrants do this work, making individuals responsible for the structural violence of neoliberalism. As with the heroic migrants, care is used as the hook that makes individuals responsible. In the case of depictions of failed migrants, however, state-endorsed discourses emphasize how migrants' failures to provide expected care have dire consequences for the nation.

Importantly, figures of failed migrants become scapegoats in transnational moral panics (Osuna 2020). While these narratives of failure emerge from material conditions in El Salvador, their consolidation and mobilization in state-endorsed discourses is part of transnational processes "interconnected through flows of social knowledge, people, capital and policies that cross nation-state borders" (Osuna 2020, 8). To demonstrate how care becomes central to such transnational moral panics, I briefly outline state-endorsed discourses about the criminalized deportee before turning to a more in-depth discussion of a figure who was particularly impactful for transnational families: the selfish migrant.[10]

The figure of the criminalized deportee emerged in El Salvador in the late 1990s, largely in response to US immigration policy that dramatically increased the number of immigrants deported from the United States, as well as the percentage of deportees who had been criminally convicted (Zilberg 2011).[11] Beginning in 1995, Salvadoran media discourse began to include depictions of deportees as criminals, representations that continued to increase every year for the next decade, creating a sense of a continuous flood of dangerous returned migrants (Marroquín Parducci 2008). Political discourse contributed to this moral panic, as when René Figueroa, a senator for the ARENA party, stated, "Los antisociales deportados de los Estados Unidos representan una bomba de tiempo que debe ser desactivada con una ley que proteja a la ciudadanía honrada" (The anti-socials deported from the United States represent a time bomb that should be deactivated with a law that protects honorable citizens) (cited in Marroquín Parducci 2008, 30). Deportees here are depicted as a dehumanized threat, drawn in sharp contrast to decent citizens who need state protection from this scourge. The criminal deportee is part of a dangerous mechanism that must be neutralized, a euphemistic description that seems to license even murder as an antidote to this danger. Such extreme responses emerged due to the conflation of the deportee with the figure of the gang member whose only loyalty is to the criminal organizations that destabilize Salvadoran society.[12] The deportee is thus the polar opposite of the heroic migrant, with the criminally disordered social relations of the deportee highlighting the morally valorized relationships of the heroic migrant as a good family man and a contributing member of society. In this depiction, the criminalized deportee has no ethico-moral compass and lacks dedication to family provisioning; he is therefore a threat to the well-being of the nation and must be removed from society by any means necessary.

These depictions of criminalized deportees have not remained in El Salvador, but have been taken up in transnational moral panics about immigration in the United States. Visual imagery in Salvadoran news media often involves such depictions of deportees as animals, taking up a common metaphor that circulates in print media as well (Martel 2006, 969). For instance, this cartoon from *La Prensa Gráfica* (cited in Marroquín Parducci 2008, 31), entitled *Maras* (Gangs), shows a police officer catching and locking up a shirtless and heavily tattooed gang member, only to turn around and find that the hand of Uncle Sam (labeled "deportation") has dropped an identical gang member onto Salvadoran soil. Such visual media draws on a particular set of codified material signs (tattoos, loose pants) that signify gang membership (see fig. 1.2), literally projecting these onto the bodies of deportees.

Crucially, the deportees—but not the police officer—are depicted with pig-like snouts. Such dehumanized depictions are precursors to the rhetoric of the Trump administration that portrayed all Central American migrants as "MS-13 animals" who threatened US national security. For the Salvadoran state, depictions of a threatening horde of criminal deportees served to justify increasingly authoritarian policies, many of which violated the terms of the 1992 Peace Accords (Martel 2006, 961). Fifteen years later, the Trump administration took a page out of the Salvadoran playbook, consistently drumming up fear of invading hordes of MS-13 gang members in order to justify increasingly harsh immigration policies and inhumane treatment of Central American migrants (Arnold and Dick 2018).

Depictions of failed migrants as lacking an ethico-moral compass are thus powerful resources in the arsenal of state-endorsed migration discourses. Consolidating these figures in transnational moral panics provides discursive justification for the mistreatment of migrants. Moral panics produce failed migrants as scapegoats who threaten the nation; they thereby draw attention to the actions and decisions of migrants, while eliding the global inequalities and histories of imperialism that form the root causes of gang violence. Through figures of failed migrants, individuals are made responsible for resolving large-scale structural inequities.

The Selfish Migrant: Family Disintegration as a National Threat

The centrality of family care to such transnational moral panics becomes particularly clear in the case of the selfish migrant. Like the criminalized deportee, the selfish migrant is positioned in opposition to the figure of the heroic migrant. While the heroic migrant faithfully remembers his duty to provide care, the selfish migrant rejects his role as male provider. He no longer sends remittances, nor does he stay in regular contact with his relatives in El Salvador. Hilary Parson Dick's work in Mexico traces a similar discourse in which migrants who abandon familial responsibilities are described as *desobligados* (disobliged). These migrants are imagined as having been corrupted by the individualism of the United States, such that they no longer embody the purportedly Mexican values of relational personhood (Dick 2018, 133). In El Salvador, the figure of the selfish migrant similarly symbolizes a threat to the nation through the abandonment of family care duties; for this reason, I refer to this figure of the selfish migrant with the more precise name of the *migrante desobligado*.

It is precisely because the mythological migrant is imagined as a national provider that imagining his dereliction of duty becomes such a threat. What will become of the nation if migrants fail to send remittances? Perhaps due to the existential threat that the *migrante desobligado* represents, this figure was omnipresent in everyday conversations about migration during my fieldwork in El Salvador. For instance, when I was first beginning my research and would tell people in El Salvador that I was interested in studying transnational

Making Family Care Political **47**

family communication, I was often told that I would be lucky to find anyone to study, since most migrants quickly forgot about their family back home and stopped calling and sending money. The widespread presence of this figure demonstrates the normative force that accrued to the models of care underpinning depictions of migrants as celebrated male breadwinners.

The *migrante desobligado* was evoked regularly in the interviews I conducted with relatives of migrants in El Salvador. For instance, in one conversation with a mother and her adult son who had several migrant relatives in the United States, the son stated:

> Mucha gente que se ha ido para allá, yo me he dado cuenta, no solamente en esta comunidad sino en muchas comunidades de acá, en muchas partes del país, que se van, y ya no le vuelven a hablar a la familia. Y después de que la familia los ha apoyado tal vez para que se vayan. Ya no les hablan, porque ya tienen dinero, por todo eso. Ya no les interesa la familia.

> (Many people that have gone there, I have realized, not just in this community but in many communities here, in many parts of the country, they leave, and then they don't call their family anymore. Even when the family has maybe helped them to go. They don't call them anymore, because now they have money, because of all this. They are no longer interested in their family.)

His mother agreed: "Ya lo toman como que no es nada la gente" (It's like people don't mean anything to them anymore). Here, the family is envisioned as supporting the migrant's journey to the United States, likely using land or houses as collateral for the informal loan used to pay the several thousand dollars that the *coyotes* (guides) charge for their services. But the family's help is ultimately not reciprocated: once they have money themselves, *migrantes desobligados* lose concern for their family and treat them as if they no longer meant anything to them. Interestingly, mother and son avoid depicting their own family in these terms, although earlier in the interview they reported seldom receiving remittances from their migrant kin. Instead, the figure of the *migrante desobligado* is used to characterize a generalized familial experience of migration not only in this particular village, but in neighboring communities, and indeed throughout the country.

Close attention to the language of this representation provides a deeper understanding of the significance of this depiction. In this account, there is recurrent use of the adverb "ya" (four times by the son and once by his mother). This term is not directly translatable; as an adverb, it is used to temporally mark when transitions from previous states occur, but it can also be used as

Figure 1.2 Cartoon Entitled "Maras" (Gangs). Published in *La Prensa Gráfica,* August 25, 2005.

a discourse marker to convey emotional intensity (Koike 1996). Because of its productive multifunctionality, this term is very high frequency in general and appears in many of the examples in this book. In this particular instance, the multiple uses of "ya" suggest that the figure of the *migrante desobligado* emerges at a specific temporal juncture. In three of these five cases, "ya" is combined with a marker of negation to produce "ya no," a collocation that marks a dramatic and total change in migrants' behavior. A similar usage of "ya no" appears in the next example as well. Migrants are thereby represented as having changed as a result of their migration and their improved financial prospects.

This linguistic analysis reveals the importance of temporality in this depiction, which highlights the moment in which migrants become corrupted. Although they leave El Salvador as responsible family members, their moral compass is quickly destroyed by the allure of wealth and individual enrichment in the United States. The figure of the *migrante desobligado* thus envisions the heroic migrant as primarily threatened by moral pressure that begins as soon as he steps foot in the United States, and that may at any moment convert him into a *migrante desobligado*. The transnational dimension of this moral panic is thus revealed through this temporal framing. Crucially, in this depiction, cross-border communication becomes a vital diagnostic for determining whether migrants have lost their sense of obligation to family back home. Because migrants tend to call home more frequently than they send remittances, a lapse in communication can be the first sign of a migrant relative's corruption.

The ever-present threat of this ethico-moral corruption is presented as the motivation behind the popular television show "*Reencuentros Hermano Lejano*" (Hermano Lejano Reunions), which has aired since 2009 and boasts a viewership of 85.5 million worldwide in Central and South America, Mexico, and the United States. The show profiles stories of families that have experienced decades of cross-border separation due to migration, featuring tearful interviews with migrants and relatives back home, as well as highly emotional family reunions. The producer and host of the show, Salvadoran media personality Berta Luz Campos, plays a prominent role in each episode, using the family stories to advance an explicit message about migration that consistently mobilizes the figure of the *migrante desobligado*. In each episode, she emphasizes that separation due to migration often breaks up homes, causing familial disintegration. Migrants say they are only going for a few years, to achieve a specific goal, pero cuando sienten, Estados Unidos los ha atrapado, el tiempo va pasando (but when they realize it, the United States has trapped them, time keeps passing by) (UNIVISION 2018). Here the United States is a seductive sorceress who entices migrants in and then captures them, reorienting their moral compass away from family and toward selfish ambition. And over the years of separation, migrants se olviden un poco de sus seres queridos y eso no es bueno. Ya no vuelven a llamar (forget their loved ones a little and this is not good. They don't call anymore) (UNIVISION 2016b). Just as in the quote from the interview with the mother and son, here the lack of communication is understood as a sign that migrants have been corrupted by the United States, which has not only trapped them physically but also morally, converting them into *migrantes desobligados*.

The show depicts these experiences of abandonment as widespread realities of migration for many families. But at the same time, such familial disintegration is not inevitable, as Berta Luz Campos emphasizes over and over again. She exhorts migrants: "Mantengan esos lazos de unión" (Preserve those ties of unity) (UNIVISION 2016a). Migrants should choose to remember relatives back home, should engage in the communicative work necessary to sustain relationships across borders. The tearful narratives of abandonment that are presented in each episode are cautionary tales that warn migrants of the deeply painful consequences of letting themselves be lured into selfish pursuits. And it is not only nonmigrants who suffer, but migrants themselves who miss out on valuable experiences with loved ones. The show offers them a chance for redemption by sharing their stories and working toward reunification with family back home.

The circulation of the figure of the *migrante desobligado* in everyday conversations and media stokes a simmering moral panic that focuses on

50 Living Together across Borders

individual migrants' corruptibility as the root cause of negative familial experiences of migration. In other words, the migrant must ward against ethico-moral corruption so that he may remain a heroic provider and not inflict suffering on his loved ones, or threaten his nation through his lack of responsibility.

In reality, of course, the challenges that migrants face in fulfilling this idealized role are primarily political-economic rather than ethico-moral. A long legacy of US immigration policy targeting Central Americans in particular has produced tenuous legal status for most Salvadoran migrants in the United States, leaving them vulnerable to exploitation by employers, as well as to the constant possibility of arrest, detention, and deportation (Menjívar and Abrego 2012). The figure of the *migrante desobligado*, through its emphasis on moral threats, works to discursively elide the global inequities that make the heroic migrant an unobtainable ideal for so many.

Moreover, the moral panic that consolidates the figure of the *migrante desobligado* converts cross-border kin care into a potent meaning-making sign. Examining migrants' contributions to family care—particularly the regularity of their communication—becomes a diagnostic that indicates whether they are starting to be seduced by the lure of material wealth into selfish pursuits that will lead them to abandon their familial responsibilities, and ultimately to become a threat to the nation. This oversignification of cross-border kin care has important impacts for transnational families, providing a far-reaching interpretive framework through which to understand their experiences.

The meaning-making power of this framework emerged in an interview I conducted with Bárbara, the wife of a migrant who had remained in El Salvador with their daughter. Remembering back to when her husband was first talking about migrating, she recalled:

> Mi mamá sí me decía, fíjese, mi mamá me decía, "No lo dejes ir. Porque si se va, se va a olvidar de ustedes," me decía. "Se casa por allá," me dice. "Se casa por allá, ya no va a volver." . . . Me decía mi mamá, "Muchos hombres se van y se acompañan por allá, y después pero ni cinco le mandan. Olvidan de la familia," me decía. Y eso a uno le da miedo usted.

> (My mom would tell me, listen, my mom would tell me, "Don't let him go. Because if he goes, he is going to forget you all," she would tell me. "He will get married there," she tells me. "He will get married there and then he won't come back.". . . My mom would tell me, "Many men go and they get a new partner there, and then they don't send a penny. They forget their family," she would tell me. And this is frightening, you know.)

The figure of the *migrante desobligado* emerges in part from normative understandings of gendered care roles: in this case, the migrant is depicted as forgetting his wife when he finds a new partner. Bárbara's account resonates with a common Salvadoran discourse on migration that Leisy Abrego documents, which "maintains that migrant fathers 'say they're leaving for their kids, but as soon as they step on U.S. soil, they forget that they ever had a family'" (2014, 134). Thus, in Salvadoran imaginaries of migration, the *migrante desobligado* is specifically envisioned in gendered terms as a faithless husband and deadbeat dad, the opposite of the dedicated male provider mythologized by the figures of the *hermano lejano* and *embajador laboral*.

Moreover, family abandonment is described as a cognitive and affective process of forgetting kin ties, a framing that resonates with the emphasis Berta Luz Campos places on remembering in her exhortations to migrants in her TV show. Indeed, remembering and forgetting are extremely charged in transnational family life, as I explore in greater detail in Chapter 5. In accounts of the *migrante desobligado*, forgetting family ties is not simply an internal process but rather one with significant material consequences: selfish migrants who do not remember their family back home do not send them even five dollars. The forgetting suggested by a lapse in communication thus may signal impending financial disaster for the family back home.

Just as with the first interview example, the corrupting process that turns dutiful remittance-sending family members into *migrantes desobligados* is depicted here as a generalized experience, a seemingly inevitable part of transnational family life. The *migrante desobligado* is thus ever present, shadowing the footsteps of the heroic migrant. This figure casts a pale of constant worry over transnational family life as nonmigrants wait to be abandoned by their migrant kin. This anxiety emerges clearly in Bárbara's statements. Although she deploys reported speech in a distancing strategy that articulates the fear of abandonment in her mother's voice, her own voice surfaces as she summarizes this narrative, saying, "Eso a uno le da miedo usted" (This is frightening, you know). Bárbara uses the generic third-person pronoun that avoids explicitly claiming this as a personal fear, yet the prosody of her statement—characterized by rapid speech, higher pitch, and increasing volume—along with her use of the vocative "usted," highlights the immediacy of what is ultimately a very personal emotional experience. Such is the power of this imaginary that even three years after her husband's migration, years in which he has regularly sent remittances that have allowed them to expand the family house and pursue continued education for their daughter, Bárbara nevertheless still fears that at any moment his moral fortitude may be worn down, and he may be corrupted.

52 Living Together across Borders

The constant state of worry prompted by this imaginary impacts migrants as well. A year after speaking with Bárbara, I interviewed her husband Gerardo in the United States. We talked for almost two hours, and Gerardo used this time to express his sadness and frustration with his current situation. Although he was proud of how hard he worked and the home construction projects he had been able to fund with his remittances, he was lonely. He missed his wife and daughter desperately, but felt they did not understand the sacrifices he was making: working extremely long hours at a physically exhausting warehouse job, and then coming home to a room the size of a closet, for which he paid $100 per month. As Gerardo talked about his relationship with his family back home, the potent impacts of depictions of the *migrante desobligado* became clear. He said his wife would get upset with him for not calling her as frequently as he had previously, and would suggest that he had changed:

> A veces me dice que yo he cambiado. "No," le digo yo, "a veces uno, no es que cambia," le dije, "sino que a veces, es el trabajo. . . . Pues, o a veces, la misma gente lo hace cambiar a uno. Porque a veces se, pues por, a veces la gente habla cosas que no son."

> (Sometimes she tells me that I have changed. "No," I tell her, "sometimes, it isn't that you change," I told her, "but rather that sometimes, it is because of work . . . Or, sometimes, it is people who make you change. Because sometimes, because, sometimes people say things that aren't true.")

Here, Gerardo expresses his frustration with his wife's constant expectation that he has changed in some fundamental way. Her fear that migration will cause him to eventually forget his family back in El Salvador leads her to interpret all of his actions as possible indications of moral corruption. Gerardo uses the generic *uno* to present these experiences as generalized and shared. This helps to keep some distance between himself and the painful experiences he describes, just as reported speech displaces the conversation in space and time. In reporting these conversations with Bárbara, he positions himself as resisting expectations of inevitable change, insisting that his intensive work schedule interferes with more frequent calls. Moreover, he alludes to the effect of constant comments about how migrants change, suggesting that such talk may ultimately push the migrant away, ironically causing the feared change.

Thus, this specter of the *migrante desobligado* served as a pervasive frame of reference for transnational family life that caused significant pain. The depiction of care as a unidirectional transfer of economic provision from migrants to those left behind erased the agentive engagement of nonmigrants in cross-border care, as well as the noneconomic forms of care migrants regularly provided. As a result, nonmigrant kin, afraid that they would lose connection with their migrant relatives, along with the concomitant material support, often put significant pressure on their migrant kin. The singular focus on moral corruption as the cause of diminished remittances obscured the political-economic inequities that fundamentally shaped migrants' ability to provide for their relatives back home. And because this narrative emphasized individual actions and moral personhood, it simultaneously produced potent silences about the ways that structural violence impacted family life. For instance, many nonmigrants told me that they did not know much about the jobs that their migrant kin held or the conditions in which they lived. The anxieties and silences provoked by this imaginary could lead to frustration and growing distance within transnational families.

However, the powerful workings of this imaginary were consistently masked by a widespread discourse in which migration itself was presented as the cause of familial disintegration. For example, a mother whose son had migrated several years earlier described transnational families as follows: "Es una familia desintegrada. Cuando la familia, alguien piensa en irse, es una desintegración. Y aquí vamos a la realidad" (It's a disintegrated family. When the family, when someone thinks of leaving, it is disintegration. And this is the reality). Such depictions of migration as inevitably causing families to fall apart also circulate widely in Salvadoran media;[13] indeed, this premise is the basis of "Reencuentros Hermano Lejano," which depicts transnational families as fundamentally disintegrated and needing the assistance of a TV show to reunite them.

Of course, descriptions of transnational families as inherently disintegrated rely on a strong contrastive assumption about co-present families. The presumed dissolution of kin ties after migration is only possible if premigration families are assumed to be fundamentally cohesive units made up of individuals who consistently fulfill their gendered and generational care obligations. Thus, Berta Luz Campos's exhortation to migrants to maintain family ties implicitly suggests that such ties necessarily adhere in co-present families, which are assumed to be characterized by intrinsically united and loving forms of *convivencia*. This idealized understanding of family life of course glosses over the serious challenges many co-present families face in El Salvador, from domestic violence and child abuse to alcoholism and grinding poverty to the high percentage of households with absentee fathers that are headed by single mothers (Abrego 2014). But this idealized vision of family life is ultimately what gives the image of disintegration such ideological force.

Crucially, the depiction of disintegrated transnational families is the first step in a logical chain that puts forward a single, simple explanation for the many challenges afflicting Salvadoran society. According to this framing, migration causes familial disintegration that is directly responsible for increasing gang violence in the country (Moodie 2010; PNUD El Salvador 2005). It was the children of Salvadoran migrants—raised in the United States and abandoned by migrant parents who were too busy working to raise them properly—who became criminal deportees, bringing the gangs with them when they were deported to El Salvador. And today's transnational families are unable to care adequately for children in El Salvador; migrant fathers and mothers make left-behind children into easy targets for gang recruitment and abuse. Discourses that emphasize the negative impacts of migration on families thus turn cross-border kin care into the scapegoat for all of El Salvador's problems.

Depictions that position migration as causing family disruption obscure a deeper reality, hiding the conditions that necessitate migration, which are the true roots of the disruption of social reproduction (Gamburd 2000). Transnational families are an easy scapegoat, and targeting them conveniently conceals how global political-economic inequities and the abdication of the state from the care of its citizens make cross-border life a necessary strategy for family survival. State-endorsed imaginaries mobilize the language of kinship to blame transnational families for widespread social problems, obscuring how the inequitable distribution of resources produces the conditions that push families to the brink (Mullings 1996; Rapp 1978). Thus, dominant imaginaries of migration in El Salvador carry out vital ideological work that shores up the global political-economic inequities that have placed an overwhelming burden of responsibility onto migrants and their families, even as they make ever more challenging the conditions under which they must struggle to survive.

Conclusion

Dominant migration discourses in El Salvador rely on deeply contradictory depictions of migrants as they attempt to harness migration for state projects. I have demonstrated that kin care is consistently mobilized in each of these migrant figures as an observable sign of ethico-moral personhood or of its absence. Salvadoran transnational imaginaries are thus interwoven with imaginaries of kinship and care that mobilize gendered and generational hierarchies to determine the distribution of responsibilities for care. Such imaginaries also envision a fixed divide between economic providers and dependent care recipients, providing a static and overly simplistic vision of care in transnational family life. Through these figures of migrant personhood, heteronormative and patriarchal understandings of kin care become the foundation for deeply inequitable forms of national belonging for migrants and nonmigrants alike.

Moreover, in these imaginaries, kin care is strategically mobilized to support neoliberal projects. The emphasis on kin care as a sign of ethico-moral personhood places the onus on individual actions as the determining factor in experiences of migration. Transnational moral panics highlight the corruptibility of migrants, blaming them for negative outcomes such as familial disintegration and social disorder. Thus, in these figurations, kin care becomes the modality of a particular local form of neoliberal personhood. Salvadorans—both migrants and nonmigrants—are responsible for social ills, not as independent individuals but rather as relational and familial beings. Familial relationships of obligation thus become the grounds upon which Salvadorans are induced to take on risk-taking neoliberal subjectivity. This emphasis on individual actions obscures the ways that neoliberal economic restructuring—in conjunction with long-standing US hegemony—make transnational separation a necessity for so many Salvadoran families.

Thus, in dominant Salvadoran imaginaries of migration, kin care is profoundly political, constituting national belonging and advancing neoliberal projects. While this oversignification of care is deeply local, it is at the same time fundamentally global, shaped by US immigration policy and by transnationally circulating discourses of migrant criminality and victimization. Care within transnational families is weighted in signification that extends far beyond the immediate experiences of family. Cross-border kin care becomes the ground upon which the nation itself stands or falls: it is understood either as what sustains the nation or as the point of rupture that becomes its undoing.

However, while the state deploys tropes of kin care as the foundation for national belonging, such frameworks also open themselves up to co-optation. For instance, Salvadoran migrants have taken up the state's singular focus on remitting to advance their own projects for national belonging. In order to lobby for voting rights from abroad, migrant activists highlighted their long-standing and substantive economic support for the nation, an argument that ultimately led to new legislation that made overseas voting possible (Hallett and Baker-Cristales 2010). Continued participation in the nation by sending remittances ultimately became the ground upon which migrants were able to claim the right to transnational political participation.

56 Living Together across Borders

But resistance may also take less overt forms. As Herzfeld suggests, "because national ideologies are grounded in images of intimacy, they can be subtly but radically restructured by the changes occurring in the intimate reaches of everyday life—by shifts of meaning that may not be registered at all in external cultural form" (Herzfeld 1997, 31). In other words, mundane experiences and the meanings they create have crucial and often unseen consequences that can impinge upon and incrementally destabilize state imaginaries. The subsequent chapters of the book examine these subtle shifts of meaning that occur in the intimate reaches of family life, focusing on everyday communication within transnational families.

Cross-border communication constitutes a form of response to state-endorsed discourses, a means by which transnational families engage with the dominant imaginaries that put such pressure on kin care. Tracing a range of communicative practices, the book documents the pervasive influence of state-endorsed imaginaries on transnational family life, which constitute an ever-present interpretive frame whereby cross-border care can be evaluated and its meaning understood. At the same time, however, cross-border care is far more complex and nuanced than the simplistic portrayal these imaginaries invoke. It does not simply involve unidirectional economic transfers to passive dependents. Rather it is constituted by shifting reciprocal engagements in many different kinds of care, all of which are shaped by and simultaneously reproduce multiple overlapping relationships of obligation. In particular, attending to communication reveals subtle forms of contestation in the ways that cross-border care is simultaneously enacted and made meaningful. Everyday conversations weave relationships together across space and time in minute but nevertheless consequential ways. Such cross-border communication is the means through which families forge *convivencia*, finding ways to live-together despite long-term separation. The next chapter describes the complex entanglements of cross-border care and highlights the role of language in these exchanges.

2

Transnational Care in Multigenerational Households

Asymmetrical Practices and Moral Meanings

Quinceañera

My goddaughter Verónica, who lives in Cantón El Río, was about to turn fifteen. It seemed like only yesterday that I held her in my arms as holy water was poured over her head, an act that officially brought me into Verónica's family—the Mejías—making me a *comadre* (co-mother) to her mother Sara, responsible for helping her raise this child. And now, suddenly, it was time to plan her *quinceañera* (fifteenth birthday party, an elaborate celebration throughout much of Latin America that marks the transition between girlhood and womanhood). To choose a date, Sara called those of us who would be traveling to El Salvador for the celebration: myself and her migrant brother Patricio. In response, we both agreed to send money to help cover the costs of the party as planning began in earnest: how many people would be invited and where would the event be held? What food would be offered and what would Verónica wear? I excused myself from this detailed planning, but Patricio suggested to Sara that instead of buying the traditional extravagant gown, which Verónica would only wear once, Sara should buy her daughter a nice dress that she could wear again. Pleased by the practicality of this suggestion, Sara followed his advice.

In the week before the event, more relatives became involved in the preparations. Sara's mother and sisters came to her house in the evenings to make decorations, recruiting older children (and me) to help out or to watch the younger children. On the day of the party, we rose with the dawn to get everything ready. Men set up tables and chairs; Sara's brother Fermín arrived from another part of the country and organized a sound system for the playlist he had curated on his laptop. Women worked even harder: cleaning, putting up decorations in trees and on the tables, getting children scrubbed and dressed in their party attire, shoes polished, and hair combed. Sara and her sisters had asked their brothers to provide enough money so that they could

Living Together Across Borders. Lynnette Arnold, Oxford University Press. © Oxford University Press 2024.
DOI: 10.1093/oso/9780197755730.003.0003

hire other village women to prepare the food for the party, thereby relieving themselves of a significant form of gendered care labor. Sara asked me to take photos and videos throughout the day to share with those migrant relatives— another brother and his two teenage sons—who had been unable to attend due to lack of legal status. They had pooled their resources to send Verónica the gift she most coveted: a smartphone. Upon returning to the United States, I shared the photos online and made a photo book that I sent to Sara and Verónica as a memento of the occasion. In return, Sara gifted me with a *manta* (cloth) she had made for my daughter, embroidered with her name, a heart, and a rabbit, her favorite animal.

Thanks to everyone's efforts, the celebration was a wonderful success. Even the weather cooperated, and the rain held off until the last guests had left. But our collective work had produced more than just a party. It had fostered and strengthened transnational *convivencia*, producing a way of living-together across borders. Putting together this celebration involved multidirectional care of many kinds: not only economic transfers, but material gifts, contributions of time, and many different forms of labor. These reciprocal— although asymmetrical—care engagements drew on existing relationships of obligation between members of the Mejía family (and me) in both countries, ties that were simultaneously reinforced through this collective endeavor. The *quinceañera* was a multigenerational undertaking to which everyone in the family had contributed, although in uneven ways shaped by gendered and age-graded kinship norms as well as by global political-economic inequities that produced inequitable access to resources within this transnational family.

Cross-border communication was crucial to this collective project. Through communication, whether in-person or across borders, the family made collective decisions and coordinated multiple forms of care; such conversations were vital to the successful celebration of this milestone. At the same time, such long-distance conversations opened up spaces in which individuals could negotiate their engagements in this joint project. Once again, such negotiations were uneven, and those with greater access to economic resources (Patricio and I) had an outsized say in decision-making. Communicative engagements in care were therefore vital to the ways that we enacted asymmetrical relationships of obligation across borders.

* * *

While the previous chapter examined dominant state-endorsed discourses about migration and family, this chapter shifts focus to investigate how transnational families enact living-together across borders through care practices.

Transnational Care in Multigenerational Households **59**

I suggest that simplistic state-endorsed visions of transnational care involving unidirectional remittance transfers are grossly inadequate for understanding the complex realities of cross-border care. Rather, I trace multidirectional exchanges of care that span both space and time, demonstrating that language plays a crucial role in these exchanges.

This chapter examines how cross-border communication participates in cross-border care, arguing that language bears a heavy weight for maintaining transnational *convivencia*. In contexts of sustained separation across borders, relationships of obligation can no longer be maintained through the constant small contacts of daily life entailed in the exchange of plates of food, in working together in the kitchen, or in conversations over meals. Moreover, families can no longer rely solely on information about care needs or available resources gleaned from such living-together; separated relatives cannot see growing children bursting out of their clothes and shoes, cannot witness the ripening of vegetables and fruit or the emptying of sacks of corn with each days' tortillas, cannot track the number of eggs laid by the hens, cannot see the maturing of calves ready to sell. Rather, under conditions of transnational separation, multigenerational care needs and the family resources available to meet them have to be negotiated through cross-border communication, just as the relationships that undergird such care must be communicatively sustained. Such transnational conversations mobilize grammatical and linguistic resources, making use of different communicative technologies. Technologically mediated communication across borders becomes a lifeline without which transnational care would fail.

Language is a powerful resource for care labor because of its inherent multifunctionality (see the "Introduction" chapter). As with Verónica's *quinceañera*, communication facilitates practical and material care, such as scheduling the event and negotiating the amount of money Patricio and I were to send. At the same time, this communication itself enacts care, as in Patricio's suggestion about his niece's dress, or in the videos and photos I shared with relatives in both countries. Moreover, language simultaneously creates meaning from particular actions enacted by specific individuals in the context of certain relationships. Sara's care-ful gift for my daughter—including not only thread and cloth, time and creativity, but also communicative labor to find out my daughter's favorite animal and colors—simultaneously enacted and signaled a close relationship between us.

Crucially, the organization of family conversations across space and time through different communication technologies powerfully shapes how language may simultaneously facilitate, enact, and signify care. This chapter therefore attends to the kinds of communicative actions that different

60 Living Together across Borders

technologies afford, while also examining the ways that specific cross-border conversations are embedded within ongoing negotiations of family care that play out in face-to-face conversations among relatives in both countries.

Analyzing these complex care practices reveals that for transnational families, cross-border life is undergirded by a more nuanced imaginary of care. Whereas state-endorsed visions imagine transnational care as a one-sided and fixed relationship of economic provision and dependency, transnational families envision and enact care as a participatory project in which everyone in the family engages. Rather than the sole emphasis on economic care in state-endorsed imaginaries, transnational families enact care through multiple shifting forms of care work. As shown by the family's efforts around Verónica's *quinceañera*, such reciprocal understandings of care do not do away with asymmetry. Rather, different family members provide varied forms of care, with expectations tied deeply to gendered and generational norms, as well as to migration status.

Thus, even as it sustains family life, communicative care reproduces hierarchical kin relations and asymmetrical care engagements. Moreover, the chapter demonstrates that political-economic inequities are embedded in and extended through communicative care in transnational families. At the same time, however, communication also opens up spaces wherein these intersecting inequalities may be challenged in ways that incrementally work to shift the social life that care generates. To better elucidate the contradictory consequences of communicative care, this chapter provides an ethnographic account of how such language practices are situated within transnational family life. Although this discussion is informed by long-standing engagements with several transnational families, in this chapter I draw primarily on the experiences of the Mejía family (the family of Sara and Verónica and of Beto and David from the vignette in the "Introduction" chapter) to develop a more cohesive picture of cross-border kin care. This focus is not accidental but rather reflects the greater depth of my connection with this specific family, built over two decades of ongoing care engagements.

Signifying and Enacting Obligations with Relational Grammars

I first became attuned to the communicative dimensions of care by developing ongoing relationships of obligation with transnational families. My connection with the Mejía family began with Sara, who—like me—was a single young woman in her early twenties when I first arrived in Cantón El Río.

Our shared positionality in gendered and age-graded social hierarchies provided common ground on which we could begin to build connection, despite our significantly different life experiences and our inequitable access to resources. Along with other young women, Sara and I participated in the small all-female choir that sang at community masses and played on the village's women's soccer team. Over the months, our friendship deepened and to reflect this growing closeness, I began to address Sara using the linguistic forms that I had heard the young women of the choir and soccer team using among themselves: the informal second-person pronoun *vos* (you) and its associated verbal forms (e.g., *¿Lo conocés?* [Do you know him?]).

Forms of address like these are part of what I call relational grammars, highlighting the ways that habitual language practices not only reflect and but also enact shifting interpersonal relationships over time.[1] Second-person pronouns and verb forms used when speaking directly to another individual are a particularly potent component of such relational grammars, given their pervasiveness in everyday conversations (R. Brown and Gilman 2003). The grammar of Spanish requires individuals to choose between formal and informal second-person (you) options every time they address someone. In Salvadoran Spanish, the default used in most relationships is the formal pronoun *usted* and its associated verbal forms (e.g., *¿Lo conoce?* [Do you know him?]) whereas the informal *vos* used among the young women is more restricted to particularly intimate relationships.[2] Relational grammars are fundamentally interactive; when one person addresses another using a particular form of address, the other decides whether to respond with the same form or a different one.

The importance of address forms in constituting relationships is illustrated by the fact that metalinguistic conversations about these grammatical patterns are quite common. For instance, during my fieldwork in the United States, one of the young migrant women I had gotten to know suggested that we should "hablarnos de tú" (use *tú* forms with one another), as she felt that using *usted* was too formal, a request I was happy to honor. In Cantón El Río, discussions about whether people *se hablan de vos* (use *vos* forms with one another), particularly across gender lines, are a frequent aspect of village gossip.

When I began to use *vos* with Sara, however, she continued to address me using the more formal *usted*, resulting in a situation in which I used informal forms with her and she used formal forms with me. Such asymmetrical patterns of address tend to characterize relationships with significant power differentials, such as those between parents and children or teachers and students. Every time Sara and I conversed, this asymmetrical pattern was repeated over and over again, signifying a hierarchical relationship that did not reflect the intimate friendship I thought Sara and I had developed. When I asked her why she did not use *vos* with me, she told me that for her, using *usted* emphasized the respect she felt for me as her close friend.[3] Rather than reverting back to *usted* myself and accepting Sara's understanding of how address forms reflected our relationship, I asked Sara to address me using *vos* forms, and she acquiesced. Ironically, even as I pursued a symmetrical form of address to signify a close egalitarian relationship, my status as a community outsider—a US citizen with access to greater resources—allowed me to unilaterally impose my own understandings on the grammar that would be used within our relationship, insisting on a symmetrical use of *vos* forms.

Despite this disagreement over forms of address, Sara and I have remained close in the two decades since then. When Verónica was born, I became Sara's *comadre* and our relational grammar shifted: although we continued to use *vos* verb forms, we began to address each other primarily as *comadre*, rather than using the generic *vos*, communicatively reiterating in every conversation the specific relational ties and obligations between us. When I moved back to the United States just a few months after Verónica's birth, we stayed in close contact through phone calls that became more regular once Sara got her own cellphone. I often sent money to cover medical and educational expenses for Verónica, and on my yearly visits, brought ever more complicated puzzles for my goddaughter, as well as vitamins, clothes, and school supplies. Sara opened her home to me each time, rearranging beds to make space for me, and preparing my favorite foods: *pupusas* and *tamales pisques,* freshly baked Salvadoran quesadillas, *refrescos de jamaica*, and *maracuya*. Now that I am a mother too, we refer to my daughter as Sara's *sobrina* (niece) and Sara as her *tía* (aunt). Thanks to the accessible multimodal communication afforded by smartphones, we exchange friendship memes, photos of our gardens and children, and audio messages on an almost daily basis.

Becoming Sara's *comadre* also brought me into relationship with her family: her aging parents, her migrant brothers, her sisters and nieces and nephews in El Salvador. This formalized relationship has especially facilitated cross-gender interactions with her brothers and nephews. These men often remark "te sentimos como familia" (we feel you are like family), a deft framing that draws me close to the family affectively even as it maintains some distance (you are like family, *not* you are family). Yet I am often treated as family when it comes to resolving care challenges, particularly when crises occur in either country. When funds are required to resolve a crisis, we strategize in phone calls or text messages about how much money each of us can contribute. Over the years, the Mejías have also called on my social capital as a well-educated, white, English-speaking citizen, mobilizing these privileges as resources to help migrant relatives navigate the complex educational and legal landscape of life in the United States through translating documents or interpreting conversations with lawyers and teachers. My contributions to the family are reciprocated through large and small acts of care. Most significantly, every member of the family agreed without hesitation to participate in the research that formed the foundation for this book, repeating time and again that they did this to help me achieve my goals as part of our mutual care obligations to one another.

By getting to know Sara and becoming incorporated in her family, I experienced the power of the relational grammars that form the basis for relationships of obligation, ties that shift over the years and are inescapably shaped by global political-economic inequities and kin hierarchies. By participating in the ongoing exchanges of communication and affection, money and food, I experienced the ways that language is vital to the care that keeps family relationships alive over the years, supporting *convivencia* despite separation across space and time. From the Mejía family I learned how communicative care enacts transformative work that sustains continuity even as it subtly operates on the conditions under which social reproduction occurs. For these potent teachings, I remain forever in the debt of Sara and her family.

This experience of becoming incorporated into a family over time while still not quite being a part of it reveals the consequentiality of small-scale language practices. Seemingly mundane and unimportant grammatical features have the power to signify and thereby enact the social world, a force gained in part through their continued repetition in everyday usage. I am Sara's *comadre* because we articulate this connection explicitly every time we speak, even as we enact this relationship through shared care practices. In addition, people may overtly attend to particular linguistic forms, actively ascribing meaning to them. As seen in the differing interpretations Sara and I drew from the use of *usted*, such significations can vary radically in ways that sometimes create conflict. Of course, not all forms of communicative signification are this explicit and consciously articulated; the subsequent chapters analyze communicative practices with powerful significations that emerge much more implicitly. Whether implicit or explicit, relational grammars create meaning about individuals, their actions, and their interrelationship with others. As language signifies repeatedly who people are in relationship to one another, these ties are communicatively enacted. It is on this relational ground that ongoing care engagements are forged.

Care in Multigenerational Extended Households

Just like relational grammars, communicative care practices are inextricably interwoven with the many forms of nonlinguistic care—embodied, material, affective, and economic—through which transnational families collectively sustain themselves. In this section, I therefore outline how multigenerational extended families organize and enact care through asymmetrical relationships sustained across borders. I do so by tracing how the Mejía family has navigated shifting relationships of obligation through multidirectional care engagements over the years.

When Sara was pregnant with Verónica, her first child, it quickly became clear that her boyfriend had no intention of assuming any paternal responsibilities. Her family built her a small room of her own: it was attached to her parents' cinderblock house, made from tin sheeting and just big enough for her bed and a few belongings. When I went to visit her, Sara proudly showed me her new *casita* (small house). Living in her own home freed her—and her family—from the social stigma of being a pregnant woman still living under her parents' roof. By the time Verónica was two years old, Sara had been able to build a cinderblock house of her own through funding from an international development project. The funders required that she own the land where the house would be built, so her parents signed over a corner of the family plot to her and other small pieces to her sisters.

Despite this more formal separation, the family continued to share resources across residences. For instance, each morning and evening, Sara's mother sent a thick stack of tortillas to each of her daughters' homes. Sara's sisters, and eventually Verónica and other female grandchildren, took turns taking the corn to the communal mill to be ground and then helping their grandmother turn the *masa* (dough) into tortillas. The corn for the tortillas was grown by Sara's father and nephews in the family *milpa* (cornfield). At mealtimes, children went from house to house, carrying plates of *con que* (literally "with what," the part of the meal that accompanies the tortillas) prepared in their home and coming back with food from relatives' houses. The *con que* was often made with eggs from chickens raised by the women of the family, vegetables from their gardens, and cheese made from the milk of the family's cows. Until she was able to save enough money to install electricity, Sara ran a long extension cord from her parents' house to light her home and stored perishable food in the refrigerator at their house. In 2015, when a violent power struggle between gangs and organized crime exploded in their area, the family was concerned for the safety of Sara and her children at night. So her teenaged nephew Adán, who was being raised by her parents, was tasked with coming to sleep at her house at night to provide a masculine presence that might help to protect this single mother. In turn, Sara made him dinner, often cooking his *con que* precisely to his specifications, an indulgence his grandmother would never have countenanced. After the children were in bed, they would stay up watching TV and talking about topics both light and more serious.

Across the years, the Mejías consistently organized care through the extended family rather than in nuclear families. In rural El Salvador, such multigenerational families—spanning at least three and sometimes four generations—are the hub of kin care. Within these multigenerational extended families, nuclear families may have their own dwellings, particularly in rural areas. However, just as in the Mejía family, everyday kin care in the form of electricity and money, labor and food, continually circulates across residential boundaries.[4] I suggest that this widespread Salvadoran family form should be understood to function as a multigenerational extended household.[5] Extended households allow relatives to pool resources for care in the face of a national and global economy that pushes their families to the margins. Just as the Mejía family cared for Sara when she was pregnant, the multigenerational extended household provides individual members of the family with greater protection, serving as the social safety network that the state fails to provide for its citizens.

The organization of everyday care within the multigenerational extended household involves labor by multiple members of the family, all contributing to provisioning in ways that are fundamentally shaped by gendered and generational norms as well as by local political-economic dynamics. In the Mejía family, for instance, while men worked the *milpa* and raised cattle, women took on a daunting set of care responsibilities ranging from child care and food preparation to gardening and caring for small animals to paid wage labor. In kinship studies, these sorts of care engagements are often described as operating according to a principle of asymmetrical reciprocity, in which the differing care obligations that hold between individuals are shaped by social hierarchies such as age and gender (Shohet 2013, 204).[6] These hierarchies determine what care an individual is expected to provide to whom, and how they will reciprocate the care that is provided for them.

Crucially, asymmetrical reciprocity not only organizes daily provision, but also structures longer-term exchanges of care that extend across the individual life course through shifting intergenerational relationships. For instance, Sara's mother, Rosario, had worked as a cook at the local child-care center, and her small salary had helped to supplement the family diet and provide other necessities. As she aged, the accumulation of years of heavy work began to take a toll on her body, and at the urging of her grown children, Rosario left formal employment. When Verónica was only six weeks old, Sara took a job at the same child-care center, leaving her daughter in the care of her mother and younger sisters so that she could earn a salary to contribute to the family economy.

As these experiences show, individuals' positions in webs of social hierarchy are not static but shift over time. Obligations to others may not be reciprocated immediately when they are accrued, but rather are understood to determine future responsibilities later in the life course. Asymmetrically reciprocal care is thus organized through an intergenerational contract (Göransson 2013); as children move into adulthood, they become responsible for supporting those who raised them, thereby reciprocating the care they received when they were younger (Benavides et al. 2004; Merla 2015). This intergenerational contract was cited as the motivation justifying Sara in leaving her six-week-old infant with her mother in order to take a paying job.

The intergenerational contract was also the explanation given when I asked both migrants and nonmigrants about why people migrated. In this discourse, responsibility to care for aging parents as well as one's own children was a driving motivation for migration. And this discourse was reflected in practice: Sara's migrant brothers, and later her nephews after they migrated, regularly sent money home, despite having formed their own nuclear families in the United States.

Such consistent remittances were the result of continued struggle and sacrifice on the part of migrants, who juggled transnational family obligations while raising their US citizen children in mixed-status families. The uneven protection of family members under US immigration law had concrete consequences; families constantly had to navigate differentiated access to healthcare, education, bank loans for small businesses, and other resources, negotiating how best to obtain and distribute these resources to meet family care obligations (Castañeda 2019; A. Flores 2018; Mangual Figueroa 2012). Migrants worked long hours and often lived in overcrowded conditions, so that rental costs could be shared and meager earnings stretched. For instance, one migrant family of four I knew shared their one-bedroom apartment with another adult relative, having converted the living room and a hallway closet into additional sleeping spaces.

Remittance amounts and recipients fluctuated over time according to migrants' employment and expenses, as well as in conjunction with the needs of those in El Salvador. All of this had to be negotiated through cross-border communication. During the time of my research, families relied primarily on transnational phone calls, which occurred at least once a week and became more frequent in times of crisis or celebration. Cellphones in both countries were passed around from person to person, with a series of short dyadic conversations resulting in phone calls that generally lasted at least thirty minutes. Like other transnational care practices, this cross-border communication was characterized by asymmetry. Conversations included much more detail about life in El Salvador than in the United States; relatives would not only discuss family news but also share updates about broader village life. This conversational asymmetry is based on differentiated knowledge. While migrants know the social and physical environs of their relatives' lives in El Salvador, the same is not true for nonmigrants; for them, the United States is unknown (Dick and Arnold 2018). While conversations could have been used to remediate this lack of knowledge, migrants shared very little about their everyday lives, and their relatives in El Salvador remained surprisingly incurious, such that they often knew next to nothing about where their migrant kin lived and what their work entailed. The United States—and migrants' lives there—remained unknown in part because they were treated in conversation as unknowable. This dynamic doubtless shaped the fact that migrants often complained about transnational phone calls and said relatives back home only called to request money; of course, this narrative was overly simplistic, as subsequent chapters will demonstrate, and migrants themselves often made transnational calls of their own accord.

With migration, the multigenerational extended household of the Mejías became a global household (Safri and Graham 2010), or a single entity for care provision that includes the homes of individuals living in different countries. For Safri and Graham, global households are consequential because of their collective role as a macro-economic actor that moves significant financial resources around the globe through remittances. Crucially, the global household must be understood as a noncapitalist economic actor organized on the basis of collective care provision rather than capitalist logics of production. For Safri and Graham, investigating the lived realities of different kinds of global households can thus help to develop a "household-based politics of economic transformation" (Safri and Graham 2010, 101).

I suggest that in order to more deeply understand the transformative politics of the global household, it is important to understand how such households emerge from the organization of care practices prior to migration. The families in my study had all managed care across multigenerational extended households before migration, and this experience proved to be an important resource as the distance between homes within the extended household was stretched across borders. In particular, the organization of care through an intergenerational contract often created obligations of reciprocity that extended beyond the parent-child relationship, potentially solidifying a more expansive web of care. For instance, Sara and Adán's previous exchanges of care in El Salvador created relational obligations between aunt and nephew that continued to hold even once Adán migrated to the United States. As a result, Adán sent remittances to Sara on a fairly regular basis, but not to his other aunts. In another case, Francisco Portillo rarely sent remittances to his mother, instead sending funds regularly to his elderly grandparents. Although his mother complained, other members of the family and community saw this distribution of remittances as justified. After all, during the country's civil war, he had been raised by his grandparents in a refugee camp in Honduras while his mother fought with the guerrillas. Here, the intergenerational contract narrowed the web of care obligations due to particular visions of what kinds of actions must be reciprocated as care. Childrearing was widely accepted as the quintessential form of care labor that needed to be reciprocated by elder care, but participation in a collective struggle to improve rural livelihoods in El Salvador was excluded from incurring intergenerational debts of care.

Thus, transnational family care is not always enacted harmoniously. Indeed, migration often introduces greater economic disparities between nuclear families within the multigenerational household, producing tensions over how to prioritize the needs of migrants' children versus those of relatives in the extended family back home. Thus, there are often conflicts within the multigenerational family around different understandings of who owes which debts of care to whom. In navigating these tensions, particular ways of articulating and envisioning relationships of obligation become deeply consequential for how transnational kin care is enacted.

Envisioning Asymmetry and Reciprocity

Negotiations about multigenerational kin care are grounded in moral imaginaries, defined as "shared but diverse ideas about how life should be lived" (Buch 2018, 15). Moral imaginaries lay out a vision of the "good life": the types of actions and goals, the kinds of individuals and relationships, in short, the ways of being that are valorized as "good." They are thus powerful normative frameworks that specify the way things should be, how people should act in order to be considered ethico-moral individuals.

Moral imaginaries are both mobilized and reproduced as multigenerational families enact asymmetrically reciprocal care within global households. For example, the everyday act of sharing food within the Mejía family is undergirded by an imaginary in which men, women, and children all enact particular roles: growing corn, making tortillas and *con que*, and carrying food to other dwellings. Moral imaginaries are not static but rather processual and dynamic, emerging and shifting as families continually work and rework their visions of a good life through their everyday engagements in care. When Sara became pregnant, her family made changes to their care arrangements. By building her a house—which Sara agreed to live in—the family reproduced an ethico-moral vision of family life in which adult daughters form their own distinct household when they have start to have children; this moral imaginary valorizes the nuclear family in a way that is at odds with the foundational role of the multigenerational family in collective survival, a tension made manifest in Sara's small tin sheeting room attached to the family's cinderblock house.

Moral imaginaries thus manifest in the world in consequential ways. Imaginaries live in our embodied and linguistic habitus, carried and enacted through habituated forms of bodily action such as the making and distribution of food.[7] Language is perhaps particularly crucial to the ways that moral imaginaries emerge through care. For instance, the relational grammar that has developed over time in my relationship to Sara—moving from *usted* to *vos* to *comadre*—has emerged alongside changing care obligations undergirded by shifting moral imaginaries of our relationship to one another. Communication powerfully creates ethico-moral meaning, not only in explicitly articulated value judgments, but perhaps even more powerfully through implicitly signifying individuals and their actions in grammatical choices made in the encoding of events (Duranti 1994a). The subsequent chapters demonstrate how language practices such as greetings, remittance negotiations, and collaborative reminiscing implicitly assume and simultaneously reproduce particular imaginaries of family care.

Understanding such moral imaginaries provides vital insights into the ongoing consequences and maintenance of social hierarchies. Just as these imaginaries underpin judgments of worthy "good" ways of being, at the same time, they serve to devalue or denigrate ways of being considered "bad." Such ethico-moral judgments can be mobilized to shore up social inequities. I maginaries "provide the social and moral basis upon which systems of resource distribution are justified" (Buch 2018, 15). Moral imaginaries thus undergird large-scale assemblages such as neoliberal late capitalism as well as more localized family economies. This book attends closely to the ways that cross-border care within transnational families mobilizes moral imaginaries in ways that weave asymmetrical social relations and political-economic inequalities deeply into the fabric of social life.

This dynamic emerges clearly in the ways that ethico-moral meanings are used to justify the inequitable division of care labor along gendered lines. In

El Salvador, particularly in rural areas, families are based on heteronormative understandings of kinship (Abrego 2014).[8] Heterosexual partnerships are unquestioningly viewed as the basis of family life.[9] This normative heterosexuality is tied to patriarchal ideals of asymmetrical kin care: men should be the heads of households, responsible for providing for their families. In rural areas, men normatively provide for their families through subsistence agriculture such as cultivating corn and raising cows, through seasonal labor cutting sugar cane, or other forms of paid agricultural work. It is this vision of the male provider that underpins the imaginaries discussed in Chapter 1, where the migrant is figured as a heroic distant brother who provides for his family and by extension his nation. Women, conversely, are expected to be responsible for the domestic domain: cooking, cleaning, and washing clothes, while also bearing primary responsibility for childrearing.

These gendered expectations are linked to a person's age as well. Starting at a young age, children are asked to make contributions to kin care, responsibilities that increase as they grow. The smallest children are often sent to deliver messages or fetch and carry between the separate dwellings of an extended family household, and as they get older, are sent to buy things at the village store. Girls like Verónica are often charged with responsibility for watching younger siblings or cousins. By the age of seven, girls start taking corn to the communal mill and helping to make tortillas. Boys accompany men to work in the *milpa*, and by the age of ten are often responsible for taking family livestock to and from the pasture. Children's participation in care advances concrete projects of family provisioning while also continually socializing them into the gendered moral imaginaries that undergird kin care (Arnold 2019a).

These imaginaries treat the inequitable distribution of care labor as an ethico-moral concern by drawing on depictions of gracious personhood, which "locates what it means to be human in the successful occupation of social roles that exist outside and endure beyond any one individual" (Dick 2018, 86). That is, people are understood not in terms of intrinsic personal characteristics but rather through the ways in which they occupy relational roles.[10] Individuals constitute themselves as moral persons through actions that are carefully fitted to normative social roles that are often gendered and generational; by doing so, they make their actions visible and meaningful under shared interpretive frameworks.

Kin care is a vital site for mobilizing moral imaginaries that enact gendered and generational forms of gracious personhood. From the moment of birth—and often even before—people enter into social roles defined by care given and received, a form of role-constituted personhood that remains pervasive across the life course. Children are socialized into gracious personhood through the care practices they are expected to enact, roles they then begin to impose on the younger children in their care. Similarly, Sara and her siblings encouraged their mother to retire, and once she did, they provided for her and the rest of the family through their earnings, even as she took responsibility for raising her grandchildren so their parents could work. In these examples, gracious personhood is enacted by fulfilling age-graded care responsibilities, obligations that crucially intersect with other forms of social difference such as gender. Gracious personhood is thus the ethico-moral infrastructure that shapes asymmetrically reciprocal care.

Nevertheless, the ethico-moral force of gracious personhood does not apply equally to all members of the family, as is clear with the inequitable gendered distribution of kin care. Within the Mejía family, women's engagements in care were the glue that held this multigenerational extended household together. In El Salvador, men often abdicate their contributions to kin care, a pattern most obvious in the widespread phenomenon of absentee fathers who, like Sara's boyfriend, take no responsibility for their children. Nationwide, female-headed families currently constitute almost 36 percent of Salvadoran households (ISDEMU 2014). The unreliability of male partners means that normatively patrilineal models of kinship—in which descent is traced through the father's line—exist in uneasy tension with matrilocal practices of kin care centered on the mother's family (Yarris 2017, 39). As in the Mejía family, young women often remain part of their natal household once they become mothers, with children incorporated in the mother's extended household rather than that of their father. Thus, Sara built a house near her parents, as did her sisters, who brought their male partners to live with them. In a context of widespread absentee fathers, these multigenerational extended households provide a safety net for women, who can turn to their own male relatives for traditionally masculine care: Sara's father grew corn for tortillas, her nephew provided nighttime protection, and her migrant brothers sent economic resources.[11] This preference for kinship based on shared ancestry rather than on marriage emerges from ongoing asymmetrical exchanges of care that begin in childhood and forge relationships of obligation that make male relatives, in general, a more reliable form of support than male spouses.

However, the frequent abandonment of paternal care is simply the most visible sign of a broader pattern in which women bear a disproportionate burden of responsibility for care. Of course, this dynamic is not unique to El Salvador and has been a common theme in feminist literature and ethnographic research around the world.[12] In addition to child care, food preparation, and housework, rural Salvadoran women often engage in provisioning labor. Many cultivate vegetable gardens and fruit trees, as well as raising small

72 Living Together across Borders

animals like chickens and pigs. These efforts produce eggs, meat, vegetables, and fruit that enrich their family's diet, and they often use these ingredients to make tamales or other food that they sell locally to supplement family income. Other women earn money by working as seamstresses or opening small stores that they run from their homes. Some even participate fully in the traditional male domain of agricultural labor; a local development agency near Cantón El Río provides funds to help women purchase and maintain herds of cattle. Availability of paid employment outside the home is limited in rural areas, but those women who do take on such work such as Sara's mother, Rosario, nevertheless remain responsible for managing the care of the home, outsourcing specific tasks to other female relatives. Women's care engagements thus regularly extend far beyond the domain of responsibility suggested by dominant moral imaginaries.

Abrego (2014) suggests that this gendered inequity in the distribution of care labor is rooted in radically different ideologies about masculinity and femininity in El Salvador. For women, motherhood and other care-based roles are understood as the defining feature of feminine personhood, whereas men enact their masculinity not only through fatherhood and provision but also through their independence and through having multiple sexual partners. These gendered norms compel women to provide care in order to enact valorized forms of femininity; on the other hand, although men are also expected to enact gracious personhood through kin care, the moral pressures they face are far less intense. These gendered norms result in migrant mothers sending more remittances more consistently than their male counterparts, even though this means working longer hours at lower-paying jobs, often in gendered and devalued fields of care work such as housecleaning and child care (Abrego 2009). These gendered visions of gracious personhood also impact nonmigrant women, as in the case of the grandmothers and other female relatives who step into the caregiving roles that women migrants leave behind (Yarris 2017).

Thus, for transnational families, gendered and age-graded inequities in the enactment of gracious personhood are interwoven with distinctions related to migration status. Migrant and nonmigrant relatives are expected to participate in care in fundamentally different ways. As discussed in Chapter 1, these expectations are deeply shaped by state-endorsed migration discourses that depict migrants as providing economically for their families, while simultaneously eliding the care contributions of nonmigrants by depicting them as dependent on migrant remittances. Of course, as the experiences of the Mejía family demonstrate, these dominant discourses elide the complexity of transnational care. In addition to remittances, migrants often send thoughtful personalized gifts to El Salvador. They also call home regularly, and these conversations involve not only discussion of collaborative plans for care provision, but also simultaneous ongoing emotional and relational labor. Moreover, far from being passive care recipients, nonmigrant relatives of all ages participate in collective projects of provisioning, as well as caring for their migrant relatives by, for instance, sending packages of nostalgic food, clothing, and small gifts. Transnational communication is central to nonmigrant care as well, both in everyday phone conversations and in times of family celebrations when they arrange to have family events in El Salvador photographed and these images shared with those not present. Unlike simplistic dominant depictions, transnational kin care thus involves many forms of care, moving in multiple directions between many individuals.

However, despite the complexity of transnational care in practice, the moral imaginaries undergirding transnational kin care emphasize the persistent economic asymmetry between migrants and nonmigrants by linking it to differentiated forms of gracious personhood. For migrants, remittances are envisioned as the basic requirement of valorized personhood, whereas for nonmigrants, this involves dependency and gratitude for the economic support of migrants. The analyses in subsequent chapters will demonstrate that moral imaginaries link kinship norms and global political-economic inequities, making them work together in ways that compound the inequitable effects of care. Thus, in addition to managing the gendered and generational asymmetries of kinship, care in transnational families must navigate global inequities in a very immediate way. It is precisely through care engagements that such inequalities are reproduced and their compounding effects navigated from day to day.

The impact of global inequities on kin care is clearly visible in the ethico-moral meanings attributed to cross-border communication. Of course, communication is vital to the care engagements of both migrants and nonmigrants, as shown in the experience of Verónica's *quinceañera*. However, the normative value granted to such communication was radically different for migrants and nonmigrants. While migrants are expected to stay in touch with relatives back home, this communicative care is envisioned as ancillary to economic provisioning. That is, migrants who remain in touch with their families but do not send remittances are likely to face increased pressure from relatives back home; over time, this insistence on remittances can lead migrants to stop calling altogether. For nonmigrants, however, cross-border communication is imagined as the single most important means of enacting gracious personhood in transnational care. But not just any communication will do. Rather, communicative engagements in care—for both migrants

74 Living Together across Borders

and nonmigrants—are organized through regular practices of participation that shape who says what to whom, and when and how such communication occurs. The following section therefore develops a focused exploration of how transnational families utilized communication to enact cross-border care, and argues that particular communication technologies were mobilized to navigate normative forms of gracious personhood and their concomitant imaginaries of family care.

Communication Technologies and Affordances

Transnational families have long found ways to communicate across space and time through letters, recordings on cassette tapes, international phone calls, and of course, most recently, social media and video calls. For transnational Salvadoran families, the first generation of migrants in the 1980s and 1990s had very constrained possibilities for communication with relatives back home, particularly in rural areas where there is no mail delivery and where phone lines never reached. Relatives in El Salvador had to walk or take long bus rides to the public telephone office in the nearest sizable town to receive phone calls that had been planned months in advance via letters (Mahler 2001). So when cellphone technology arrived in the country, it quickly took off: from 2000 to 2005, El Salvador remarkably numbered among the ten fastest-growing cellphone markets in the world (Ros et al. 2007). By 2012, 88 percent of all Salvadoran households had at least one cellphone, while only 25 percent had a landline. During the time of my research, internet access was available to only 11 percent of Salvadoran households (International Telecommunication Union 2014), primarily those in urban areas. This reliance on cellphones and lack of internet access has also characterized the Salvadoran diaspora in the United States (Benítez 2006). When I first began preliminary research for this book in the summer of 2009, none of my participants in either country had internet access at home. The arrival of the smartphone dramatically changed this picture over the subsequent five years. Migrants were the first to adopt this technology, starting in 2010. By 2013, smartphones were increasingly common in the village in El Salvador as well. These smartphones provided relatives in both countries with regular access to the internet for the first time, although they continued to lack access to sufficient bandwidth for video calling. For the most part, smartphones were used to access applications such as Facebook or WhatsApp, providing relatives with low-cost ways of exchanging photographs, voice memos, and texts.

Despite these changes, the phone call remained the primary form of cross-border communication for these families during the time of my research. Why did these families rely so heavily on phone calls, given the availability of lower-cost alternatives for cross-border communication? I suggest that this reliance had to do with the ways that phone calls facilitated asymmetrically reciprocal forms of communicative care. In particular, phone calls allowed for accessible, multidirectional, and accountable communication within transnational families, allowing individuals to enact gracious personhood "on the record" as it were, thereby allowing collective monitoring of moral imaginaries of care.

Understanding language as care in transnational families thus requires close attention to "communicative affordances," or the different opportunities and constraints that technologies provide for action through language (Hutchby 2001b, 2001a). For instance, the social media platform formerly known as Twitter allows users to make posts but limits the number of characters posters may use. Affordances are often understood as determined by properties of the technology itself. For instance, synchronous technologies like phone calls and video chats allow for real-time dialogic interactions between participants, while asynchronous technologies such as letters and emails introduce a lag time between responses. Technologies also differ in terms of the extent to which they give access to nonverbal aspects of communication. Text-based modalities are the most constrained in this regard, while phone calls give access to the affective information encoded in voice qualities, and video-based technologies include the widest range of embodied communication.

However, this deterministic view of affordances ignores the ways that people take up technologies to accomplish particular interactional goals (Bloomfield, Latham, and Vurdubakis 2010; Faraj and Azad 2012). For instance, Twitter users developed conventions for creating threads to get around character limits for posts on the platform. Thus, communicative affordances must be understood as providing opportunities for action by particular people in specific circumstances and can therefore only be ascertained through close ethnographic exploration of how particular technologies are taken up. This book provides just such an investigation, focusing on how people use different technologies to enact gracious personhood as they negotiate care. The following unusual sequence of events within the Mejía family provides a clear example of the connection between communicative affordances and gracious personhood.

Luis Mejía saw computers as the way of the future and wanted his teen-aged sons in El Salvador to learn how to use this technology. So he sent them a laptop and paid for computer classes. His sons—seventeen-year-old

Adán and fifteen-year-old Beto—used this new technological access to set up Facebook profiles. They then sent online messages to their father in which they complained about their grandparents, who had been caring for them since Luis migrated eight years earlier. They told their father that their grandparents made them work too hard in the family *milpa*, didn't let them spend time with their friends, and didn't buy the food and clothing that they wanted. In this family context, Facebook messaging allowed Adán and Beto to communicate privately with their father, since their grandparents could not read and did not have the computer literacy to understand what the boys were using the laptop to do. The boys could thus send Facebook messages without their grandparents realizing the content of their messages or even that they had contacted their father. Through this private channel of communication, the teenagers pushed back against the care their grandparents provided and the obligations they expected the boys to fulfill as a means of enacting gracious personhood. Communicative affordances allowed them to create a one-sided account that characterized these asymmetrically reciprocal forms of care as exploitative and authoritarian in a way that ultimately produced a great deal of conflict.

Within multigenerational extended households, young people like Adán and Beto tend to be more technologically savvy than their elders and are the ones most likely to have cellphones or social media accounts. This technological expertise often means that young people take on a more significant role in cross-border care than in comparable co-present care. In particular, they are often responsible for helping elders navigate transnational communication by setting up technology and troubleshooting problems that arise. As the experience of Adán and Beto shows, young people can use this expanded participation to attempt to make changes in family care arrangements.

Luis was angered by the picture of multigenerational care painted for him by his sons' accounts. After all, he worked hard to send sufficient remittances home so that his sons would be well cared for. He called his mother, Rosario, and reprimanded her sharply, saying that if she no longer wanted the boys with her, he would pay for someone to take care of them. Like his sons' account, Luis's critique implicitly challenged the moral imaginaries that undergirded the organization of care within this extended household. Drawing on his position as the boys' father, he asserted the primacy of these nuclear ties in determining what counted as "good" care and equated paid care with the care his mother had long provided for his sons. His comments threatened the ongoing reciprocal exchanges of asymmetrical care that formed the basis of gracious personhood and familial relationships, while also eroding the respect that adult children owed their parents.

Rosario was unable to respond directly to her son's threat. Instead, she became physically ill. When Sara asked her what had happened and found out about her brother's words, she was outraged. After all, she said, Luis hadn't raised the two boys, but had left this childrearing labor to Rosario and to her, as the eldest daughter of the family. The fact that Sara took on her brother's critique as targeting her as well as her mother reveals how this conflict over intergenerational care across borders implicitly mobilized gendered care norms. To begin with, Luis called his mother rather than his father to express his dissatisfaction, treating childrearing as a feminine domain of responsibility. This gendered assumption resonated with Sara's statements. Although Luis had sent remittances for his sons, she and her mother were the ones to do the everyday work of actually raising the boys. Luis's position as a man and a remittance-sending migrant allowed him to devalue this feminine care labor, an injustice Sara sought to rectify through additional cross-border communication.

Interestingly, when Sara interceded, she did not call Luis directly. Instead, she called her other migrant brother Patricio, with whom she had a much closer relationship, mobilizing this sibling relationship of obligation to extend responsibility for the conflict to him. She told Patricio what had happened and urged him to call Luis and hold him to account for his disrespectful words. Patricio protested that it wasn't his place to correct his older brother's actions, but eventually he agreed to make the call; both he and Sara recognized that his position in the web of familial relationships—as a man and a fellow migrant—gave him a more influential location from which to issue normative statements about care arrangements in their extended household. And indeed, their strategy was effective: after Patricio talked to him, Luis called his mother to apologize for his words, and the conflict was smoothed over for the time being. Adán and Beto remained in their grandparents' care until they unexpectedly migrated to join their father in the United States a few years later.

In direct contrast with private Facebook messages, phone calls functioned as a much more collective form of communication, one that facilitated multidirectional negotiation within complex webs of familial relationships. Phone calls provided this sort of collective function in part because they constituted public events within the family. In El Salvador, several cellphones were shared between all the members of the household, so that Luis spoke to his mother on Sara's cellphone, or that of another sister, making it quite straightforward for people to keep track of who had spoken to whom and when. In both countries, small living spaces made it possible—and normal—to listen in to calls others were making. After calls, relatives would regularly ask those who had been on the phone call what they had discussed. Perhaps in recognition of this public function, transnational calls generally involved a series of dyadic conversations in which the phone would be passed from hand to hand among relatives in both countries, with each of these subsequent pairings often discussing similar topics. Thus, while cellphone calls are often assumed to afford more private conversations through direct access to individuals (Deumert 2014), for these families, they functioned in quite a different way, serving as a multidirectional and publicly accountable form of communication. They thus allowed relatives to enact gracious personhood in ways that were visible within the family, and to collectively correct those lapses that occurred, as in the example described above, working to repair asymmetrically reciprocal relationships of obligation.

Moreover, other technological properties of phone calls contributed to this function. Phone calls were accessible: members of the family in both countries had the necessary technology. There was also no need for literacy or complex technological skills, meaning that everyone from young children up through elderly adults was able to participate in this form of cross-border communication. Phone calls thus created space for the inclusive but differentiated participation that characterized care in these families. In addition, because phone calls are synchronous—unfolding in real time—they facilitated immediate response that could fluidly shift as conversations progressed. On the phone, relatives could hear the inflections of one another's voice and gain important clues to unspoken—often affective—meanings that were being conveyed. Phone calls thus allowed for a more direct form of communicative care in which relatives could respond to these implicit meanings. Even as they were more intimate than written communication, phone calls also provided more communicative distance than video calls. For members of transnational families, video calling can be emotionally difficult, providing painful reminders of long-term separation when actually seeing distant loved ones (Madianou and Miller 2012b). Video calls also involve a more intensive preparation of oneself and one's physical environment, labor that is particularly onerous for migrants who share very curated visions of their life in the United States with family back home. Video calls may inadvertently break carefully maintained silences about the real struggles and sacrifices of migrants' lives. Phone call technology was thus a perfect fit that provided some intimacy, but not too much.

The confluence of these technological properties—and the way families took them up to facilitate communicative actions—made phone calls a powerful technology for managing cross-border care. For these families, phone calls were publicly accountable and accessible, offering just the right balance of communicative intimacy for the often quite charged conversations through which cross-border care was negotiated. The subsequent chapters provide a closer look at the specific communicative practices that families employed to enact care and living-together through cross-border phone calls. However, phone conversations did not exist in a vacuum. The content of calls was often discussed both before and after the fact in face-to-face conversations in both countries. Transnational phone calls were thus embedded in ongoing communication about kin care, and as discussed in the next section, this conversational interweaving can have consequences for the gendered and generational norms that structure familial relationships of obligation.

Contesting Asymmetries through Interwoven Conversations

Patricio Mejía had sent money to his father David back in El Salvador for seed so that he could plant the *milpa* that would provide the family with corn for tortillas for the rest of the year. But the rains had been unusually heavy, causing flooding that had rotted the seed in the ground. Someone needed to tell Patricio of this unfortunate outcome and ask him to send more money for a second planting. Time was of the essence since the rainy season was already well advanced, and if the corn was planted too late, it would not mature before the rains stopped. Agricultural matters such as this were generally left to the men of the family, but David went to see his eldest daughter, Sara. It was common knowledge in the family that she and Patricio were close and that he called her more often than anyone else. So David asked Sara to tell her brother about the situation with the *milpa* when he called next.

As in this case, relatives in El Salvador often planned which family member should be the one to communicate particular information to migrants. These decisions were sometimes based on relational dynamics between migrants and specific family members, as when David asked Sara to speak to her brother because of their close relationship. However, this allocation of communicative labor—as with the distribution of all care work—was also shaped by gendered and generational understandings of gracious personhood. In particular, as with care work more broadly, women were often tasked with taking on the most unpleasant communicative labor (what Fishman 1978 calls "interactional shitwork"). In this instance, Sara's father, David, attempted to avoid a difficult phone call reporting bad news and additional expenses to his migrant son by passing the responsibility to his daughter. Age-graded understandings of intergenerational care could also factor into decisions about who should initiate cross-border conversations. In interviews, several mothers told me

80 Living Together across Borders

that they did not call their migrant children because the communicative responsibility of initiating phone calls was part of the care that children owed to those who had raised them. Similarly, Adán complained that his migrant father tended to speak more often to his younger brother Beto. He felt that this communicative pattern disregarded his primary position as eldest brother and understood it as a signal that his father preferred his brother over him. The transnational distribution of communicative labor, like all forms of cross-border care, thus emerged from and reproduced moral imaginaries, although not always in straightforward ways, as we will see.

A few days after David asked Sara to talk to her brother about the *milpa*, Patricio put prepaid minutes onto her cellphone. This strategy was often used to facilitate transnational communication because calling rates were cheaper from El Salvador to the United States than vice versa. It was also Saturday, which Sara knew was Patricio's day off from work, so she treated the arrival of the prepaid minutes as a request to call him. Attuning her communication to his more demanding work schedule, as well as their familial obligations, she waited to call until that evening, when all of their children would be in bed. They spoke for forty-five minutes, sharing family news and commiserating about their mother's poor health. But against her father's request, Sara did not mention the *milpa* at all. Instead, she complained that their father had sold one of the family's calves without consulting her. When Patricio asked for details about which calf had been sold and for how much, she said she didn't know anything, articulating frustration at her exclusion from this significant familial decision. At the end of the call, Sara suggested that Patricio call their parents the next day when he got home from work to ask their mother about her health and to ask David about the sale of the cow. Rather than telling her brother about the *milpa*, she used the call to set up a communicative scenario that returned responsibility for this conversational task to her father. On the surface, this was a fairly unsurprising communicative action; relatives regularly suggested that their immediate interlocutor speak to another family member about an issue that had arisen.

However, in this case, Sara used this communicative move as another form of leverage against existing gendered distributions of decision-making within the family. Early the next morning, David came to Sara's house, likely having heard the news of her phone call with Patricio from one of his grandchildren who ran freely from house to house and often transmitted news in the course of their peripatetic play. After giving her father the usual morning coffee and sweet bread, she commented in a joking tone "Patricio dice si ya va a haber elotes para que venga a comer" (Patricio wants to know if there will be fresh corn soon for him to come and eat). "¿Te llamó?" (Did he call you?) asked

David, to which she responded, "Estuvimos hablando anoche" (We were talking last night). A long pause followed, but when his daughter did not provide any further details about the call, David asked if she had told Patricio about the *milpa*. In a pointed response, she commented, "Como no me dicen nada a mí, ¿cómo le voy a decir a él?" (If no one tells me anything, how am I going to tell him?), before abruptly ending the conversation by walking away to attend to another task. Sara had of course known all about the *milpa*, so here she must be referring to another situation from which she had been excluded. While this may seem to be a vague statement, in fact the meaning is quite clear in context: Sara's statement indirectly asserts a complaint that she was not consulted in the sale of the calf.[13]

This vignette reveals the complex temporal dynamics of care communication that flowed from face-to-face to phone call and back. This temporal organization opened up spaces in which family members could maneuver within normative gendered and generational visions of gracious personhood. Even as such conversations focused on concrete considerations—the sale of calves and the cultivation of the *milpa*—they also served as opportunities to subtly renegotiate the moral imaginaries that shaped asymmetrical familial relationships of obligation. Such moments reveal the transformative potential of communication as a resource for shifting the distribution of care work and thus reworking the ground upon which collective continuity is enacted.

Ironically, the gendered assignation of communicative care work created opportunities for women to maneuver within a system of inequitably divided care. For instance, Sara did not simply go along with her father's request to speak to her brother about the failed *milpa*. Rather, she used the conversation with her brother to assert her own role in collective care by complaining to him about how she was excluded from her father's decision to sell the calf. In the transnational phone call, this exclusion was presented as making it impossible for Sara to share important details of family care with her migrant brother. In doing so, she made clear to the family's primary economic provider—Patricio—why it was important for her to be included in such decisions in the future. She thereby used her gendered responsibility for communicative care to advocate for a more expansive role for herself in agricultural matters, a domain from which she was routinely excluded as a woman.

The negotiating power that communicative spaces opened up was not limited to phone calls. In El Salvador, information gleaned through cross-border communication was a valuable resource that could be shared strategically. Thus, when David asked his daughter Sara about her conversation with Patricio, she turned this request for information into an opportunity to voice an indirect complaint to her father about how he had excluded her from his

82 Living Together across Borders

decision to sell the calf. She pointed out that in order to carry out the communicative care work he had asked of her, she needed to be involved even in conversations about agricultural matters. Ultimately, the gendered expectations of gracious personhood that often made women responsible for particular kinds of transnational conversations turned communication into a transformative resource for renegotiating the gendered division of care work in the family.

Such negotiations over transnational phone calls were far less pronounced among migrants. During my research, I spent several months at a time with members of the Mejía and Portillo families in the United States. In both cases, migrants resided in multigenerational homes with two generations of migrants as well as the children of the first generation of migrants. Despite navigating similar intergenerational care relations, migrants engaged in far less preplanning of cross-border calls. Moreover, instead of asking for information about what had been discussed in these calls, those who had spoken to family in El Salvador readily shared news with their fellow migrant relatives, in particular juicy bits of gossip or funny anecdotes. Discussions among migrants often focused on requests for remittances that had been made in phone calls, as they worked to prioritize family care needs in light of available resources.

This imbalance in communicative negotiations between El Salvador and the United States reflects and reproduces the ways that asymmetrically reciprocal care in these families was structured not only by gendered and generational aspects of gracious personhood but also by political-economic inequities between Global North and South. Non-migrants relied on cross-border communication as a vital resource for family survival, a means of maintaining contact with relatives who had greater access to economic resources. For migrants, on the other hand, transnational communication was less a matter of survival than a source of increased obligations; indeed, migrants often told me that they sometimes avoided transnational conversations to reduce these pressures.

Moreover, these imbalances in communicative negotiations were likely shaped by state-endorsed imaginaries of cross-border kin care. Within these dominant discourses, migrant obligations for kin care are clearly delineated as economic in nature, whereas the care engagements of nonmigrant kin remain quite amorphous and undefined, as shown in Chapter 1. Because nonmigrant care practices are not explicitly addressed in state-endorsed discourses, these practices were discursively left more undetermined; arguably, they were thus more subject to moral imaginaries of family care that highlighted gendered and generational forms of gracious personhood. In El Salvador, cross-border communication therefore constituted a powerful site for negotiations about the distribution of care labor, as seen in Sara's struggle to expand her participation in family decision-making as well as in Adán and Beto's attempt to shape the care they received from their grandparents and their own participation in asymmetrical care. These communicative dynamics reveal the ways that distinctions between migrants and nonmigrants in transnational families interacted with gendered and generational care norms in sometimes unpredictable ways.

These stories illustrate that cross-border communication mattered for transnational care in several different ways. It is through such conversations that families collectively negotiate material provisioning, finding ways to meet the needs of relatives in both countries. Communication thus functioned as a vital form of labor, with its distribution within the family deeply shaped by the gendered and generational asymmetries of kin relationships. Yet even as communicative labor enacted care, it opened spaces for renegotiating the moral imaginaries that undergirded asymmetrical care in these families. The signifying power of language emerged from the complex temporal organization of cross-border communication, which created opportunities for women and young people in particular to challenge the gendered and generational asymmetries that formed the basis of moral imaginaries of care. Particularly for relatives in El Salvador, for whom cross-border conversations were more heavily weighted with signification, communicative care thus functioned as transformative work (Mullings 1996) that incrementally shifted the kin hierarchies undergirding distributions of care. However, it is important to note that the differential care obligations of migrants and nonmigrants were not subject to the same communicative renegotiation as gendered and generational norms. Subsequent chapters trace this dynamic in greater detail, seeking to more fully understand the possibilities—as well as the limitations—of communicative care as transformative work.

Conclusion

The generative power of care is clear in the shifting practices the Mejía family used to sustain collective provisioning over the years of transnational separation. Care iteratively draws upon and reproduces many facets of social life, and in particular, this chapter highlights the ways that kin care enacts moral imaginaries. Through kin care, families continually mobilize and reproduce visions of the forms of personhood and types of relationships that are fundamental to the "good life." I have suggested that transnational families enact a moral imaginary of care as a multidirectional and inclusive practice, made up of shifting asymmetrically reciprocal relationships of obligation in which many different forms of care circulate. The imaginaries produced by transnational families thus implicitly challenge state-endorsed capitalist visions of care as involving a fixed relationship of unidirectional provision between a male provider and his dependents. For families, care is about collaborative *convivencia*.

Family imaginaries of multidirectional and participatory care do not mean that such exchanges are entirely free of tension. Indeed, the chapter has examined several conflicts over multigenerational kin care, disagreements that mobilize different moral imaginaries of care and understandings of how gendered and age-graded forms of gracious personhood should be enacted. Care thus does not have unmitigatedly positive effects, but rather produces social relations shot through with multiple forms of inequality. I have particularly highlighted how hierarchies of gender, age, and generation are reproduced through kin care. Moreover, even as it counters state-endorsed imaginaries, transnational family care is shaped by depictions that celebrate heroic migrant provision through remittances, while eliding the care engagements of nonmigrants. Such discourses shape how transnational families envision and enact care obligations in ways that are often characterized by profound distinctions between migrants and nonmigrants. These distinctions in turn intersect with gendered and generational kin hierarchies, producing compounding negative effects. Everyday engagements in care thus bring global political-economic inequities into the intimate domain of family life. Kin care is a vehicle for inequality and violence, even as it sustains individual lives, collective *convivencia*, and the multigenerational transnational family form.

Communication in particular is vital to the contradictory consequences of care, and it is an important resource for generative care labor because of its ability to simultaneously facilitate, enact, and signify care, with these different functions sometimes working at counter-purposes. Communication often contributes to the violent effects of care, reproducing gendered and generational hierarchies as well as political-economic inequities within ongoing family relationships. However, communication also opens up spaces for negotiation, providing opportunities to maneuver within care hierarchies. In particular, newer technologies and gendered distributions of communicative care labor can ironically create opportunities for young people and women to renegotiate constraining moral imaginaries, using communication as a resource for transformation. Communicative care thus provides possibilities for incremental changes that may, over time, imperceptibly shift social relations.

The next three chapters build on this understanding of care and communication. Each examines in depth a specific practice of communicative care: greetings, remittance negotiations, and collective reminiscing. Each practice is understood as a form of communicative care labor whose complex organization and enactment produces powerful and far-reaching consequences. While these communicative practices are shaped by state-endorsed visions of kin care, close analysis reveals the ways that these everyday instances of language use constituted transformative work, enacting much more inclusive visions of kin care that counter dominant discourses about transnational care and that at times may subtly shift the social relations that form the basis of collective life.

3

"Les Mando Saludos"

Sending Greetings, Envisioning Family, and Grappling with Inequality

Communicative Emissaries

The corn stood a handspan high in the *milpa* (cornfield), the rows of bright green interspersed with the rich brown of soil recently turned by Olivia Portillo's weeding. Now, freshly bathed, with her hair combed into a tidy knot and wearing her best clothes, she stood in front of the *milpa*, preparing to speak to her three adult sons and teenage daughter, undocumented migrants living in Southern California. To facilitate this cross-border communication, she had asked me to record a video for her so that she could *mandar saludos* (send greetings) to her migrant children. Along with the labor-intensive preparation of herself and her surroundings, Olivia incorporated my research equipment and access to transnational mobility into a communicative project that aimed to span the distances of long-term cross-border family separation. Her work set the stage for carefully chosen words: after greeting her children, she complimented her sons on being responsible fathers and hoped "que sepan educar a sus hijos porque ya en otro país, pienso que no es igual que aquí en El Salvador" (you know how to raise your children, because in another country, I think it is different than here in El Salvador). She urged her nineteen-year-old daughter Serena to "cuidarse" (take care of herself), highly gendered advice to remain chaste and avoid pregnancy. She roughly brushed tears from her eyes, concluding: "yo siempre tengo la fe que les voy a ver de vuelta" (I always have faith that I am going to see you all again).

Migrants and their families have long relied on communicative emissaries such as this video *saludo*. Mobile forms of communication—whether letters (Blegen 1955; Vargas 2006), or more recently, audiocassettes (Madianou and Miller 2011b; Richman 2005)—carry out relational work when migrants and their kin are unable to travel themselves. In the digital era, the families I worked with sent digital cameras back and forth across borders with *viajeros* (couriers). When I was asked to carry cameras and viewed the recordings with the permission of the families, I noted that different messages were moving

Living Together Across Borders. Lynnette Arnold, Oxford University Press. © Oxford University Press 2024.
DOI: 10.1093/oso/9780197755730.003.0004

Sending Greetings, Envisioning Family, and Grappling with Inequality   **87**

in each direction. Migrants sent photos documenting family celebrations and footage of the urban environments in which they lived. Relatives in El Salvador sent photos of the home village and family members, but they also frequently included video *saludos* like the one Olivia sent, a communicative practice that, strikingly, migrants never used in these recordings.

Why were video *saludos* sent from El Salvador to the United States but not vice versa? Why were they only sent by nonmigrants and why were they not reciprocated in kind by migrant relatives? This chapter seeks to answer these questions by investigating the role of *mandar saludos* as a communicative genre in transnational family life. I trace the discursive patterns of the *saludos* families send across borders, suggesting that *mandar saludos* is a specific genre of greeting which includes ritualized salutations, well-wishing, advice-giving, and other affectively oriented communicative actions. By attending closely to the content and form of this genre, as well as to the contexts and consequences of its production, the chapter demonstrates that families treat *saludos* as a form of care and *convivencia* (living-together) which plays a crucial role in sustaining family over the years of separation.

Viewing *saludos* as care opens up the significance of Olivia's recording. The *saludo* carries a potent message of relational ties and obligation embedded in her words, her embodied actions, and her choice of the *milpa*—symbol of Mesoamerican sustenance and survival—as a backdrop. Alongside her words, the recording mobilizes material signs of care, juxtaposing the *milpa* with Olivia's aging female body to implicitly represent her migrant children's obligations to her. These images subtly remind them that in their absence, she has had to take on the traditionally masculine care work of cultivating corn; it implicitly invokes their obligation to send money to Olivia so that she can hire help and not have to do this heavy work herself. In addition to this economic component, the *saludo* involves emotional labor, seen most clearly in the tears that begin to gather in Olivia's eyes as she articulates her desire to see her migrant children again one day. The *saludo* also involves explicit articulations of concern and affection, which are entangled with normative gendered models of care: Olivia's sons are expected to be responsible fathers who raise their children properly, while her daughter should care for her own body in a particularly gendered way by maintaining chastity. *Mandar saludos* is thus a communicative practice that projects relational connection across space and time, cultivating the relationships of obligation that sustain cross-border circuits of economic, material, and affective care.

Moreover, even as they nurture cross-border relationships, *saludos* like these lay out a vision of transnational family life. Olivia's *saludo*, for instance, articulates kinship as involving long-term separation and the unknowns

88   Living Together across Borders

of life in the United States. At the same time, this distance can be bridged through active care practices, with different family members responsible for enacting varied forms of care, including communicative care. Cross-border *saludos* like Olivia's, which are sent in pre-recorded videos, are a particularly potent site for the envisioning and enacting of such imaginaries. Although as discussed later in the chapter, families do *mandar saludos* in synchronous phone calls, video *saludos* like Olivia's utilize an asynchronous communicative technology. Video *saludos* preclude immediate response by the addressee, and as such, they afford interlocutors space for uninterrupted talk. Video *saludos* thus constitute a communicative practice in which greeters can produce extensive imaginaries of migration and family care.

Attending to these video *saludos* therefore provides a useful counterpoint to the dominant Salvadoran imaginaries—outlined in Chapter 1—through which the state works to co-opt transnational kin care to its own ends. *Saludos* articulate and enact visions of cross-border kin care from the perspective of those who live these experiences. Through *saludos,* individuals produce the moral imaginaries that are foundational to cross-border relationships of obligation. They situate the sender and the receiver within a transnational relational web wherein particular individuals are responsible for carrying out specific kinds of care work, explicitly and implicitly laying out the terms of differentiated care obligations.

Of course, such imaginaries of family care are not without tensions and hierarchies (see Chapter 2). Imaginaries of belonging necessarily involve exclusion, as when Olivia greets her migrant children but not their offspring; her omission of the US-citizen grandchildren she has never met discursively excludes them from the transnational care circuit. These moral imaginaries also reproduce hierarchy through gendered and generational asymmetries in the distribution of care, as seen in Olivia's differentiated advice to her sons and daughters. The unidirectional nature of the genre itself reveals pervasive distinctions between the responsibilities of migrants and nonmigrants. An analysis of *mandar saludos* thus reveals how communicative care brings together inequalities between North and South with the gendered and generational hierarchies of family life.

However, the genre of *mandar saludos* is not simply a vehicle for extending inequality and structural violence. Rather, it represents a quiet, everyday mode of resistance that refuses the ways that dominant discourses seek to mobilize kin care to state projects and neoliberal regimes (see Chapter 1). By sending *saludos*, transnational families enact more expansive understandings of care that go beyond a capitalist emphasis on economic provision to valorize the affective and reproductive labor that communication carries out. Tracing the communicative specificities of *saludos* reveals how they insist on multi-directional relationships of obligation as the basis for collective survivance. That is, *convivencia* is sustained and continually reenacted through the asymmetrically reciprocal forms of care through which families provide for one another. Through this communicative envisioning and enacting of family life, *saludos* have effects that go far beyond the moments in which they are spoken or viewed, profoundly shaping long-term experiences of cross-border care.

How Greetings Matter

Greetings as a communicative genre have been the focus of substantial anthropological scholarship (e.g., Caton 1986; Milton 1982; Salmond 1974), though largely focused on face-to-face communication. Greetings are often understood as everyday "little rituals" (Haviland 2009) that occur at the beginning of interactions and thereby manage the consequences of spatio-temporal mobility for social relations (Enfield 2009; Frake 1975). As people encounter one another and utter greetings, they essentially invoke social connections that endure despite times of physical separation. It is thus not surprising that transnational families mobilize greetings through the genre of *mandar saludos* to enact important relational work.

Because of their clear relational function, greetings are often understood as a genre of communication that primarily involves establishing contact and connection between interlocutors, what Malinowski called "phatic communion" (1923, 314–15). But, as ethnographic scholarship shows, even as greetings articulate social connection, they often produce exclusion by invoking hierarchical social relations. Most fundamentally, greetings treat the greeted person as worthy of social recognition (Firth 1972), and low-status individuals such as children or servants are often excluded from greetings (Duranti 1992; Irvine 1975). For instance, in Olivia's *saludo*, while she greets her migrant children individually, she does not address their children directly, instead only mentioning her grandchildren in passing.

Moreover, focusing on greetings as primarily phatic elides the ways in which this genre can convey and even elicit information, thereby serving as a means of social control (Duranti 1997, 89). Indeed, work on phatic communication often emphasizes that it is characterized precisely by its lack of content. Malinowski suggests that in such communication "there need not or perhaps even there must not be anything to communicate" (1923, 316). Jakobson (1960) builds on Malinowski and considers the "phatic function" as one of the six primary functions of speech. To exemplify such communication, he

90   Living Together across Borders

derisively describes the sort of small-talk pleasantries exchanged at cocktail parties as "entire dialogues with the mere purport of prolonging communication" (1960, 75). Such depictions of phatic communication suggest that what matters most is simply the act of talking, rather than any particular meaning being conveyed.[1]

I argue against such reductive understandings of phatic communication, demonstrating that transnational *saludos* are in fact highly consequential communicative acts that simultaneously construct important meanings even as they constitute relationships. Greetings situate the encounter between greeter and greeted in a much broader context, suggesting that it "is taking place under particular sociohistorical conditions and the parties are relating to one another as particular types of social personae" (Duranti 1997, 89). In other words, greetings are powerful communicative tools used to articulate imaginaries of particular relationships and the social order in which they are embedded and which they continually reproduce. Tracing the imaginaries envisioned and enacted through cross-border *saludos* can reveal how transnational families themselves understand cross-border kin care.

Sending Greetings in Latin America

When transnational families *mandar saludos* across borders, they take up a well-established Latin American communicative practice of sending greetings indirectly through an intermediary. As Brody (2000) documents, such greetings were traditionally sent in indigenous communities when someone traveled from one relatively isolated settlement to another. In this communicative practice, known as *spatilab'il sk'ujol* in Tojolab'al Mayan, the traveler brings verbal greetings that specific individuals send with them to others they plan to meet on their journeys. These indirect greetings (Brody 2000, 3) articulate a connection between the sender and the recipient, and the nature of their relationship is often specified in the greeting itself. Because the greetings are mediated through the individual charged with carrying the greeting, the relationship between sender and receiver is also publicly enacted as it is passed along.

The public nature of the relational work accomplished by indirect greetings has expanded as this practice has been adapted to technologically mediated communication. Radio stations have replaced travelers as the primary means of sending greetings, with DJs commonly reading out greeting messages that people deliver to the station (Brody 2000). Radio shout-outs are also broadcast on Spanish-language radio stations within the Latin American diaspora

Sending Greetings, Envisioning Family, and Grappling with Inequality 91

in the United States (De Fina 2013), where individuals call in, sometimes even transnationally, to deliver their greetings on air. In other cases, the delivery of indirect greetings has become incorporated into transnational musical performances. Cathy Ragland (2003) documents how DJs who circulate between Mexico and US diasporic communities read out audience greetings during dances. Alex Chávez (2017a) traces how *huapango arribeño* musicians from Northern Mexico respond to audience requests for *saludados* by improvising poetic greetings that they speak out as part of their musical performances. Many of these performed greetings are transnational, directed to individuals who are not physically present at the celebration. In all of these technologically mediated cases, the person to whom the greeting is sent may not hear it in the moment, though someone who has will almost certainly tell them about it later. In these instances, the public articulation of relationships becomes the central function of technologically mediated greetings.

Such indirect greetings were prevalent in Cantón El Río, where I observed greetings being sent both in person and through technological means. On my visits to the village, those individuals with whom I had a close relationship would regularly ask me to carry greetings to my parents, or to my spouse and child in the United States. These were relatives of mine whom they had never met, but to whom they nevertheless claimed connection by way of our relationship. Radio greetings were also widespread in the rural area where Cantón El Río was located, particularly those sent through the local community radio station. People of all ages listened to and participated in such radio shout-outs, and indeed, discussions about who had greeted whom provided continual grist for the gossip mill.

The cross-border practice of *mandar saludos* must be understood within this local landscape of communicative practices. When transnational families used my video camera and cross-border mobility as resources to *mandar saludos*, they used technology to send indirect greetings. They thereby took up a powerful communicative tool for articulating and enacting relationships across distance, a communicative practice whose impact was even more amplified given the long-term cross-border separation that these families experienced.

Although I observed video *saludos* being produced without my involvement, for ethical reasons I focus here on cross-border *saludos* that I recorded with my camera at the request of members of transnational families; my analysis is also shaped by viewing other *saludos* that the families recorded themselves. Of course, my presence as cameraperson often shaped the recorded *saludo*. Family members sometimes explicitly referred to me when sending greetings, for example, prefacing their *saludo* by extending thanks to me. For instance, before greeting her migrant children, Olivia thanked me for coming to visit her, saying "me alegra mucho que se vea allá con mis hijos, que eso me ayuda bastante" (it makes me very happy that you see my children there, it helps me a lot). The transnational mobility that allowed me to be present in the lives of both Olivia and her migrant children is signified here as a form of care. In particular, Olivia highlights her gratitude for what I carry with me when I travel: news of her migrant children and US-citizen grandchildren, as well as physical items such as digital cameras, food, clothing, medicine, and other goods. Beyond these explicit references to me, however, the *saludos* I recorded and those produced by families themselves show a striking consistency in both content and style. Regardless of how they were recorded, these video *saludos* began with an opening salutation that identified who was being greeted, followed by well-wishing often framed in religious terms, and then, optionally, explicit articulations of affection or words of advice.

Mandar Saludos as a Genre of Communicative Care

It was evening in Cantón El Río and the oppressive heat of the day was finally lifting. In our usual end-of-day routine, my *comadre*, Sara Mejía, and I were chatting while resting in a hammock on her patio. She asked if I would use my video camera to make a recording of the two new rooms her parents had recently added to their home, with the help of funds that her migrant brothers Patricio and Luis had sent. The family wanted their migrant relatives to see for themselves these new additions to the house. I readily agreed, and when I went to her parents' home a few days later, her father, David, took charge, narrating the building process as I recorded, including details about the cost of specific materials and labor for each part of the project. Upon completing the tour and accounting, he spontaneously turned to speak directly into the camera as follows:

> Nosotros estamos muy agradecidos con Patricio y con Luis, porque Luis nos ha ayudado también con una parte y Patricio puso lo demás. Y también le mando muchos saludos a Patricio y a Luis. Y la esposa de Patricio, y la esposa de Luis también. Porque siempre se acuerdan de nosotros. Espero que siempre se encuentren alentados, trabajando. Sí.

> (We are very thankful to Patricio and to Luis, because Luis also helped us with part of it and Patricio sent the rest. I also send many greetings to Patricio and to Luis. And to Patricio's wife and to Luis's wife as well. Because they always remember us. I hope that they are always in good health, working. Yes.)

David's *saludo*—like the other instances I observed—differs in significant ways from the face-to-face greetings that have been the basis of much anthropological discussion. Duranti (1997, 67) has distilled this scholarship into six criteria by which to identify greetings cross-culturally. Greetings generally (1) occur near the beginning of an interaction, (2) establish a shared perceptual field, (3) elicit a matched greeting response, (4) have relatively predictable form and content, (5) establish a spatiotemporal unit of interaction, and (6) identify the person greeted as a distinct being worthy of recognition.

Because they are recorded and sent across borders, video *saludos* clearly do not meet three of these six criteria. Whereas face-to-face greetings reliably occur as people encounter one another in paired utterances exchanged by both individuals, thereby creating a shared field of in-the-moment engagement (criteria 1, 2, and 3), this is not the case for video *saludos*. Instead, they are delivered asynchronously, as is characteristic of indirect greeting practices throughout Latin America. Nevertheless, video *saludos* do meet the other three criteria. As the analysis below will demonstrate, these *saludos* are quite consistent in linguistic design (criterion 4) and serve to recognize specific individuals as worthy of recognition as members of the family (criterion 6). Moreover, while it may seem counterintuitive, I contend that video *saludos* also produce a spatiotemporal unit of interaction (criterion 5). Whereas face-to-face greetings primarily function to establish interactional units, video *saludos* recreate a larger unit: the transnational family as an entity that spans space and time. Video *saludos* thus arguably carry out the most fundamental work of greetings: the use of formulaic language to adapt to and create new forms of social organization (Duranti 1997, 88). For this reason, I understand the practice of *mandar saludos* as a specific genre of greetings, one that is mobilized to particularly powerful ends in the context of cross-border communication.

In making this claim, I understand communicative genres like greetings not as fixed forms but rather as processes through which a given stretch of discourse becomes identified as instantiating a particular genre (Bauman 1999). Speakers may design their utterances to more clearly fit the model of a particular genre. Similarly, decisions about what kind of genre a text is shape how its recipients hear it (Briggs and Bauman 1992). For instance, a speaker may frame their talk as a story by using particular kinds of openings (Labov 1972), and whether the audience takes up this narrative frame will in turn influence how they respond (Lerner 1992). This processual understanding of genre-making thus fundamentally involves comparison and relationship between different communicative practices. Indeed, the term *mandar saludos* suggests such an understanding, one in which seemingly related forms of talk

94 Living Together across Borders

are differentiated from one another. While immediate greeting exchanges are referred to with the verbal form *saludar* (to greet), the noun form *saludo* (greeting) is used to name the process of sending indirect greetings.[2] This nominalization implies that the greetings involved in *mandar saludos* are more substantial and elaborate texts, as indeed is the case with video *saludos* such as David's.

The placement of David's *saludo* illustrates how these genre conventions became linked to transnational family care. As with Olivia's recording, David's *saludo* emerged on the heels of an acknowledgement of debt. Olivia thanked me for carrying news and packages, while David thanked his sons for sending the funds that allowed for the renovations to the family home. This placement is significant, revealing how families understand *saludos* to participate in the cross-border care circuits through which these families are maintained. It suggests that families conceptualize *mandar saludos* as a modality of communicative care that asymmetrically reciprocates the economic care provided by migrants.

David explicitly articulates this understanding, saying that he sends the greeting to his sons and their wives "porque siempre se acuerdan de nosotros" (because they always remember us). Remembering here is understood not only as an internal cognitive process but rather as an externally visible enactment of obligations to relatives; this framing highlights both the affective and the material aspects of remembering (Arnold 2019a).[3] David knows that his sons and their wives remember their family in El Salvador because they continue to fulfill their care responsibilities by sending remittances. His sons have sent money, and so he sends his *saludo*, which simultaneously reciprocates economic support and reminds migrants of their continuing obligations to those back home. Here, a particular communicative practice—in this case the genre of *mandar saludos*—becomes incorporated into the family economy. Language is thus shown to be part of the political economy (Irvine 1989), entangled with profound inequities between Global North and South. These inequalities shape the articulation of a seemingly straightforward asymmetrical division of care work in which migrants are understood as responsible for economic care while nonmigrants reciprocate through affectively laden communicative labor. The imaginaries voiced by transnational families here seem to align to some extent with dominant state-endorsed imaginaries that emphasize migrant breadwinning. But as the subsequent sections demonstrate, this communicative genre is complex; families use *saludos* to forge cross-border *convivencia* that subtly resists widespread assumptions about transnational care.

Envisioning Kin Care through Reference Patterns

Analyzing the content of video *saludos* provides insight into less explicit forms of social action enacted by this genre. Kin care obligations were implicitly envisioned and enacted in these recordings through relational grammars (see Chapter 2), in particular through the reference terms used to identify different relatives. Those sending *saludos* alternated between using personal names, kin terms, or more general gendered and age-graded terms to pick out the specific relatives to whom they sent their regards. *Saludos* also varied in terms of the order in which migrant individuals were identified and then greeted. Attending closely to these linguistic details reveals a consistent pattern that articulates a particular imaginary of family relationships of obligation.

To demonstrate this relational grammar, I examine David's *saludo* alongside two others produced by other members of the Mejía family later the same day: one by David's wife, Rosario, and one by their youngest daughter, Camila. Although all these *saludos* were recorded on the same day, neither Rosario nor Camila was present when David recorded his *saludo*. After David completed his recording, Rosario came into the house from the outdoor kitchen where she had been making tortillas. At David's urging, she recorded the following *saludo*, which was strikingly similar to the one her husband had recorded.

> Yo les mando saludes para Patricio, y para la muchacha Marlene, y las nietas, las dos niñas que tienen allí. Les mando muchos saludes. Les quiero mucho a ellos. Y también, le mando saludes a Luis, la otra nieta, la Inés, y la, y la, la . . . ¿Cómo se llama esta muchacha?[4]

> (I send greetings to Patricio, and to Marlene, and the granddaughters, the two girls they have there. I send them many greetings. I love them a lot. And also, I send greetings to Luis; to the other granddaughter, Inés; and to, to, to. . . What is that young woman's name?)

When she could not remember the name of Luis's wife, she turned to David and asked him "¿Cómo se llama, vos?" (Hey, what is her name?) to which David responded, "Yo solo (dije) la esposa de Luis" (I just said Luis's wife). This exchange shows explicit concern with finding the right reference terms for particular individuals, confirming the importance of relational grammar to the practice of *mandar saludos*. Rosario then took up this form of reference, continuing:

96 Living Together across Borders

> Sí pues la esposa de Luis. Es que se me olvida el nombre. Haydee parece que se
> llama. Entonces, les mando muchos saludes.
>
> (Yes, Luis's wife. I forget her name. I think she's called Haydee. So then, I send them
> many greetings.)

Rosario laughed in embarrassment as she explained having forgotten her daughter-in-law's name. But she did not request that we re-record or edit the video. After explaining that Luis's teenage sons had not wanted to send a *saludo*, she reiterated her greetings and concluded:

> Los quiero mucho a ellos y a las nueras y las nietas también. Que se cuiden mucho.
> Allí a saber para cuándo nos vamos a ver otra vez. Solamente esto.
>
> (I love them a lot and the daughters-in-law and the granddaughters too. I hope
> they take good care of themselves. And who knows when we will see each other
> again. Just that.)

In comparison with her husband's *saludo*, Rosario uses much more explicitly affective language, twice mentioning her love for distant relatives, while also referencing the pain of separation, with tears welling in her eyes as she wonders when she will see them again.

The third *saludo* was sent by their daughter Camila. She had gone to pick up her daughter from the village child care center, and as she did most days, she stopped by her parents' house on the way home. Her parents urged both Camila and her three-year-old daughter Ora to send a *saludo*. When the child refused to speak, Camila sat Ora on her lap and sent her own message:

> Hola Patricio. Espero te encuentres bien. Y deseándote que estés alentado, esté
> alentada la niña. Marlene también. Y que seas feliz en tu boda. Que te salga todo
> bien, así como lo esperas.
>
> (Hello Patricio. I hope you are well. I hope that you are in good health, that your
> little girl is in good health. Marlene as well. And that you are happy in your wedding.
> That everything turns out well, just the way you hope.)

She then explained why her daughter hadn't sent her own greeting, before continuing: "Tambien a Luis, deseándole que esté bien, y la niña también." (Also to Luis, I hope he is well, and the girl too). Rosario interjected "La Haydee" from the background, using the name she herself had forgotten earlier to remind her of the third family member, Luis's wife. Without acknowledging this contribution, Camila continued, "Y Haydee. Que estén alentados. Saludos a todos y que siempre sigan adelante. Y, solamente." (And Haydee. That they all are in good health. Greetings to all and may they all always forge ahead. And, that is all.)

These three greetings are very similar in form: beginning with a salutation followed by well-wishing, which may be generic ("take good care") or more targeted, as in Camila's mention of her brother's upcoming wedding. The content of the *saludo* does seem to vary somewhat in connection to the gendered and generational characteristics of relationships between sender and recipient. While her parents use the phrase "les mando saludos," Camila instead uses a more informal direct salutation ("hola"), a pattern that held in other *saludos* I recorded. Similarly, the explicit articulation of affect seems to be particular to mothers' greetings, as seen in the striking similarity with which both Olivia Portillo and Rosario Mejía articulated love interwoven with the pain of separation in their *saludos*. At least for these mothers, and perhaps less visibly for other relatives as well, *mandar saludos* was a form of affective labor that brought up difficult emotions tied to the very real losses of transnational separation.

A less immediately noticeable but nevertheless significant point of comparison between these *saludos* is the reference terms used and the order in which individual relatives are identified. Through these variations, each greeting produces a slightly different imaginary of transnational kin ties, as shown in table 3.1, which lists the reference terms used in the order they appeared in each of the greetings. David's *saludo* prioritizes consanguineal over affinal kin, greeting first his sons and then their wives and making no mention of their children. Rosario and Camila, on the other hand, group the relatives into two nuclear families, within which children are mentioned before their mothers. While Luis and Patricio are consistently named, children are generally referred to with kinship terms (granddaughter) or other general terms (girl). This relational grammar locates the children with regard to gender and generation, and their identities are inferred through reference to their fathers. This pattern of reference creates a vision of kinship in which the individuality of the male migrants is foregrounded, while children are represented solely in terms of their kin relationships. The daughters-in-law are placed even further in the background. When they are mentioned, they are represented at times by kin terms (wife) or by gendered and generational terms (young woman). When Rosario attempts to remember one of their names, she actually gets it wrong, with the result that both she and Camila send greetings to a misnamed individual (Haydee), highlighting the marginal position she had in the family

98 Living Together across Borders

Table 3.1 Reference terms in Mejía family video saludos

	David's Saludo	Rosario's Saludo	Camila's Saludo
Individuals in order mentioned	Patricio	Patricio	Patricio
	Luis	la muchacha Marlene (Marlene)	la niña (the girl)
	la esposa de Patricio (Patricio's wife)	las nietas (the granddaughters), las dos niñas (the two girls)	Marlene
	la esposa de Luis (Luis's wife)	Luis	Luis
		la otra nieta, la Inés (the other granddaughter)	la niña (the girl)
		cómo se llama esta muchacha (what is this young woman called), Haydee	Haydee

from their perspective. Taken together, the linguistic design of these *saludos* reproduces an imaginary of kinship shot through with differentiation along the lines of gender, generation, and blood relation.

However, kin structures are not always reproduced straightforwardly. In all three *saludos*, the younger brother, Patricio, is always greeted before his older brother Luis, thereby disregarding birth-order status. Moreover, Camila's greetings for her two brothers are quite distinct. While her salutation of Luis is almost perfunctory, her *saludo* for Patricio is much longer and warmer; Patricio is also the only person she addresses using the informal second-person forms, and she greets him directly, saying "Hola Patricio." This move aligns her greeting with the action of *saludar*, the reciprocal greeting exchange of face-to-face encounters, suggesting a vision in which she and Patricio are not only affectively but also physically close. Across these *saludos*, Patricio was granted a central status in imaginaries of transnational kinship.

Why was Patricio so prioritized in the Mejía *saludos*? One answer may lie in the fact that he was the migrant who was currently sending the most money home. I traced this pattern across the video *saludos* I gathered. In families with more than one migrant relative, the first individual greeted was always the current primary remitter. Moreover, the lack of participation in remittances could result in a migrant being excluded from *saludos*. On another occasion, for instance, the Portillo family recorded *saludos* to several migrant siblings. The son who had stopped sending remittances was not included in the list of those being greeted.

By prioritizing consanguineal male migrants over children and affinal kin, the relational grammar of *saludos* articulates and reproduces a vision of family life in which migrants who have the strongest normative kin obligation to provide care are figured as more central to the family. This ranking is interwoven with remitting power, tied to the male gendering of the breadwinning role, as suggested by the consistent prioritization of the primary remitter and the exclusion of nonremitters.[5] The hierarchies and exclusions of the imaginaries produced by video *saludos* reaffirm migrants' participation in care through remittances, rewarding migrants who remit and pushing those who do not to the periphery. As such, the communicative care enacted by *saludos* nurtures cross-border relationships in ways that simultaneously sustain hierarchy within the family. Like other forms of care, communicative care in the form of *saludos* is therefore fundamentally contradictory (see "Introduction" chapter). Through this genre, gendered and generational distributions of care within the family become inflected by uneven access to the material and economic resources concentrated in the Global North.

Moreover, as they envision cross-border kin ties, *saludos* lay out an imaginary of transnational family life that is based on obligations to care in certain ways. In particular, they underscore asymmetrical cross-border care, emphasizing a distinction between migrants, who normatively care through remittances, and nonmigrants, who use *saludos* to enact communicative care that sustains transnational family connections. Nevertheless, this asymmetrical normativity is not totalizing. Migrants' engagements in family care extend beyond remittances to include consequential forms of communicative care (see Chapters 4 and 5). And indeed, nonmigrants at times articulate clear expectations of migrant communicative care. For instance, in Camila's *saludo* to Patricio, she requested that her brother send them more recent photos of her newest niece: "Ojalá nos mandas pronto unas fotos de la niña. Ahorita cómo está ella, no tenemos fotos para conocerla." (Hopefully you can send us some photos of your girl soon. We don't have photos to know how she looks right now.) Thus, even as *saludos* envision and enact care in ways that continually shore up boundaries between migrant and nonmigrant relatives, the multifunctionality of communication nevertheless offers possibilities for subtly subverting this process and instead pursuing more symmetrical engagements in relational care across borders.

Learning to Send Greetings and Family Futures

Like all genres, *mandar saludos* was a communicative practice that had to be learned. In El Salvador, socialization to *mandar saludos* began early on, as

100   Living Together across Borders

soon as preverbal children were able to hold a cellphone up to their ear. In play—that is, without an actual call in progress—relatives would prompt the infant to send greetings to migrant kin, individuals who had often migrated before the child's birth. This prompting practice extended to video *saludos*, though generally with more verbal older children. For instance, before Camila recorded her *saludo*, she unsuccessfully tried to get her three-year-old daughter to greet her uncle, telling her to face the camera and then prompting her over and over again to say "hola tío" (*hi uncle*). Although socialization to *saludos* was very common in El Salvador, I never observed the children of migrants being socialized to send greetings to relatives back home. As with the sending of *saludos*, socialization into the genre was also limited to those living in El Salvador.

Prompting children to *mandar saludos* is an example of language socialization, the process whereby children (and other novices) simultaneously learn to communicate as they learn the social norms of their community. As Bambi Schieffelin and Elinor Ochs (1986, 168) write in their groundbreaking article, "The process of acquiring language is deeply affected by the process of becoming a competent member of a society. The process of becoming a competent member of society is realized to a large extent through language." Thus, gaining communicative competency in a given context is about acquiring both specific language skills as well as knowledge about how to use those skills. While learning to *mandar saludos*, children in El Salvador learned about the transnational family and their place within it. Children were taught about their kin ties to different migrant relatives and learned how to enact the communicative care labor that was expected of them as nonmigrants.

The communicative practice of prompting—or telling a child to say something—is a common routine by which adults socialize children into valued communicative competencies.[6] Examining prompts can reveal ideologies about what kind of speech is important and must be taught, as opposed to that which children are assumed to learn spontaneously (Moore 2012). Prompting necessarily occurs in multiparty interactions that involve the prompter, the child prompted, and a third party whom the child is encouraged to address as their recipient (Field 2001; Pfeiler 2007). Because it is used in multiparty interaction, prompting teaches children about who can say what to whom, in what setting, and to what ends (De León 2011). Prompting can therefore be considered a form of metacultural positioning (B. Smith 2012); in other words, prompting articulates imaginaries in which particular ways of acting, being, thinking, talking, and feeling are depicted as normative. Elsewhere, I demonstrate that prompting is a crucial means by which transnational families frame particular kinds of material and communicative

Sending Greetings, Envisioning Family, and Grappling with Inequality   101

exchanges as normatively enacting care (Arnold 2019a). In cross-border conversations, different relatives are prompted to take on the forms of care expected of them.

Prompting children to *mandar saludos* is no exception. A particularly compelling—but also troubling—instance of this socialization to care occurred one day when I had gone to Rosa Portillo's home to video record her house and surrounding lands at the request of her migrant siblings in the United States. From the porch, her young son Zacarías, age five, watched avidly, and asked his mother if he might go visit these distant aunts and uncles. Even at this young age, he had learned that he belonged to a cross-border family made up of distant relatives, most of whom he had never met. Rosa denied her son's request without explanation, but then urged the child to send a *saludo* to his aunt Serena, the most recent migrant and the only one whom her son remembered. She prompted him unsuccessfully for a full minute, a project I collaborated in by explaining that I would send the video to his aunt. But he refused to repeat any of his mother's multiple prompts, looking down, shaking his head, and eventually walking down the porch of the house away from her, me, and the camera. Through his silence and embodied distancing, Zacarías enacted a sustained resistance to his mother's project of cross-border communicative care.

Rosa waited until he had walked back to us, perhaps interpreting his return as a willingness to send a *saludo*. After unsuccessfully trying to prompt him one more time, she stated: "Decile pues. Si no, ya no te va a volver a hablar. No te va a hablar por teléfono." (Say it. If not, she won't call you anymore. She won't call you on the phone.) Zacarías responded to this threat by looking up at his mother for the first time in the interaction, indicating the profound impact of her words. And when his mother then urged him to face the camera and began again to prompt a *saludo*, he finally complied. Through a line-by-line format of prompt and repetition (see Excerpt 3.1), Rosa modeled and Zacarías learned the different components of the genre: the salutation, the articulation of emotional ties, and well-wishing.

Even as he learned the communicative norms of the *mandar saludos* genre, Zacarías was also being taught a great deal about transnational family, care, and cross-border communication. Rosa's threat is particularly weighty in this regard. She tells her son that if he does not produce the greeting, his aunt will stop calling him; because the family lacks the resources to make regular calls to the United States, this could effectively end Zacarías's relationship with his migrant aunt. Thus, the threat here involves disruption of the child's world, which helps to explain its immediate effectiveness in securing his cooperation. These words have evident emotional impact: although Zacarías follows

102 Living Together across Borders

Excerpt 3.1 Portillo Family Socialization to Saludos

1.	Rosa:	Hola tía Sere, decile.	Hello aunt Sere, tell her.
2.	Zacarías:	Hola tía Sere.	Hello aunt Sere.
3.	Rosa:	Le mando un saludo, decile.	I send you a greeting, tell her.
4.	Zacarías:	Le mando un saludo.	I send you a greeting.
5.	Rosa:	La quiero mucho.	I love you a lot.
6.	Zacarías:	La quiero mucho.	I love you a lot.
7.	Rosa:	Y cuídese.	And take care.
8.	Zacarías:	Y cuídese.	And take care.

his mother's prompts in sending a *saludo* to his aunt, and then to his migrant uncles, he eventually refuses to continue and begins to cry, at which point his mother lets him go: "Vaya para adentro pues. Ya no llorés." (Go inside. Don't cry anymore.) At the age of five, Zacarías may not be able to articulate his complex feelings, but these emotions nevertheless emerge in his embodied response to having to produce a *saludo*. Engaging in this form of cross-border communicative care came at an emotional cost not only for Zacarías but also for his mother. She clearly felt a great deal of pressure to be sure her son sent his *saludos*, as seen in her persistent prompting and ultimately, her threat of disconnection. Looking back at this encounter, it is clear to me that my presence—as well as that of my video camera—likely contributed to the intensity of this situation and may have amplified the emotional cost of this communicative practice. Nevertheless, the genre itself clearly packed an affective punch regardless of who was doing the recording: as with the *saludos* sent by the mothers Olivia Portillo and Rosario Mejía, the act of communicatively projecting oneself into the presence of distant kin simultaneously highlighted both love and loss. The cross-border communicative care enacted through *mandar saludos* was thus a form of emotional labor.

Moreover, this threat also taught Zacarías about the important role that *saludos* as communicative care were understood to play in transnational family life. The severing of this relationship between a child and his aunt would also involve a disconnection between a nonmigrant and a migrant. Recall that in dominant Salvadoran transnational imaginaries, cross-border kinship is envisioned as inherently tenuous, continually under a moral threat that will be realized when migrants forget their relatives back home and no longer call or send remittances (see Chapter 1). In her threat, Rosa implicitly draws on this broader imaginary, suggesting to Zacarías that his actions can cause such feared abandonment. If he does not enact communicative care by articulating his love for his aunt in this ritualized way, she will forget him and stop calling. *Mandar saludos* here is framed as a crucial care practice through which nonmigrants can ensure that their migrant relatives will remember them and continue to fulfill their care obligations toward them.

Thus, socializing children to *mandar saludos* also socializes them to a particular imaginary of transnational family life. Different individuals become members in the family largely through the care practices they enact toward one another, fulfilling asymmetrical relationships of obligation. Of course, these asymmetries are tied to the gendered and generational norms of kinship: Rosa's threat and prompting of Zacarías are influential because he is five and she is his mother. But socializing children to *mandar saludos* emphasizes another kind of differentiation, a primary distinction between migrant and nonmigrant members of the family. Zacarías must learn to send cross-border greetings, and take on the resulting emotional labor, because he is a nonmigrant and such communicative care work is his contribution to sustaining cross-border kinship. Socialization to this imaginary of transnational family life is therefore also socialization to a particular way of using language to enact care and forge *convivencia* across borders.

This larger context of socialization may help to explain why the children of migrants in the United States were not taught to *mandar saludos*, even to their siblings who remained in El Salvador. This disparity was part of a larger pattern in which the children of migrants were not actively socialized to engage in cross-border communicative care. While children in El Salvador participated in transnational conversations regularly, children in the United States did not. In part, this exclusion may have been due to a perceived language gap. While the children of migrants were all bilingual in English and Spanish, their proficiencies in the two languages varied. Moreover, they spoke US Spanish, a variety whose vocabulary and grammar are influenced by contact with English (Roca and Lipski 2011) and are often quite different from Salvadoran Spanish. Relatives in El Salvador thus reported that they did not understand the children and thought of them as non-Spanish speakers with whom they could not communicate.

Nevertheless, these differential patterns of socialization into communicative care reveal a great deal about how transnational families imagined their collective futures. If the children of migrants were not being socialized into the cross-border relationships of obligation that sustained the transnational family over time, who then is imagined to continue fulfilling these roles once current migrants age and eventually pass away? An answer to this question emerged in another *saludo*, this one sent by seventeen-year-old Kique Portillo, Zacarías's oldest cousin. He had at first attempted to prompt his two-year-old sister to send a *saludo*, and when she refused, his mother and grandmother

104 Living Together across Borders

Excerpt 3.2 Kique Portillo's Saludo

1. Hola tío Francisco,	Hello uncle Francisco,
2. Espero que esté bien.	I hope you are well.
3. Se encuentre bien con su familia, sus hijos.	That you are well with your family, your children.
4. Y, le mando saludos allí a todos.	And, I send greetings there to everyone.
5. Que se cuiden.	Take care.
6. Y que Dios los cuide.	And may God take care of you.
7. Y que sigan adelante y,	And may you all continue moving forward and,
8. algún día voy a llegar donde ustedes.	someday I am going to come to where you are.

encouraged him to *mandar saludos*. When he claimed not to know what to say, his grandmother teased him for his ignorance while his mother modeled a *saludo*: "'Hola tío Francisco,' decile. 'Espero que esté bien con sus niños.'" ("'Hello uncle Francisco' tell him. 'I hope you and your children are well.'") Kique then produced the following *saludo* (see Excerpt 3.2).

His *saludo* starts by closely following the model his mother has offered him, but after the usual salutations and well-wishing, he ends by saying that someday he hopes to join his migrant relatives in the United States. This statement is said with a smile in a joking tone of voice and is followed by brief laughter, all of which soften this otherwise weighty statement of future plans.

Here, Kique envisions his future as a migrant in the United States. This is a dream shared by many young people in poor Salvadoran communities like Cantón El Río (Abrego 2014; Dyrness 2012). And it is no accident that this statement comes on the heels of Kique's *saludo*. Prospective migrants rely on the help of relatives already living in the United States to migrate. Current migrants lend them the money needed for the journey and receive them upon their arrival in the United States, providing them with initial housing and often helping them find jobs. Maintaining relationships with migrants is thus crucial for young people hoping to migrate themselves. And communicative care—such as Kique's *saludo*—is the most potent resource that nonmigrant relatives have at their disposal for nurturing ties to migrant kin.

However, as demonstrated in this chapter, the genre of *mandar saludos* is not only a tool for individual relationships but rather a collective resource that works to sustain the transnational family form. While *saludos* help to maintain cross-border relationships from day to day, they also have longer-term consequences for the continuance of the transnational family across generations by socializing future generations into family life at a distance. This socialization is uneven: the children of migrants in the United States are not

Sending Greetings, Envisioning Family, and Grappling with Inequality   **105**

explicitly taught to participate in the transnational circulation of care, neither in the present nor in the future. That is not to say that children of migrants were not implicitly socialized into transnational family life; they of course observed their parents talking to relatives back home, sending them money, and discussing family life in El Salvador.[7] Rather, the emphasis is placed on the explicit socialization of children in El Salvador into cross-border family life. This is due, of course, to their current position as nonmigrants understood to be responsible for the communicative care work that maintains cross-border *convivencia*.

Nevertheless, this asymmetrical pattern of socialization implicitly enacts a vision of the future in which transnational family life will be sustained not by the children of migrants, but rather through new generations of migrants, individuals who were socialized into cross-border family care during their youth in El Salvador. This imaginary may well not be intentional on the part of those doing the socializing. Salvadoran parents are often quite aware of the dangers of an unauthorized journey to the United States and want to protect their children from having to migrate under these conditions. Nevertheless, the patterned practice of intensively socializing children in El Salvador into transnational care—all while largely excluding children in the United States from cross-border *convivencia*—has a cumulative effect. Socializing children to send *saludos* helps them to build and maintain ties with migrants, laying the foundation for the future migration of young people who have already been socialized to transnational kin care. Thereby, the genre of *mandar saludos* works to secure the existence of transnational relationships of obligation in the future, ensuring the survival of the cross-border family.

Attending to the socialization of *saludos* thus reveals how deeply transnational kinship is caught up with global inequity. Longer-term imaginaries of how the transnational family will survive across generations emphasize the continual one-way flow of migrants from El Salvador to the United States.[8] These imaginaries of family are premised on an understanding of inequities between Global North and South as enduring facts of life that families must continually navigate. The profoundly inequitable relationship between El Salvador and the United States remains unchanged. Making a life in El Salvador is still not possible, and the US economy continues to rely on the labor of undocumented Salvadoran migrants, a workforce whose exploitability is sustained by immigration policy that produces their illegality. *Mandar saludos* and socialization into this genre thus work to sustain from one generation to the next family forms that are inescapably shaped by these global inequities.

Resignifying and Reproducing Care Asymmetries

Video *saludos* lay out an asymmetrically reciprocal understanding of cross-border care, one in which migrants are responsible for economic care while nonmigrants enact communicative practices that are understood to sustain transnational *convivencia* not only from day to day and year to year, but also across the generations. However, this vision does not represent the full complexity of the role of communication in transnational kin care. Subsequent chapters of this book demonstrate that migrants participated actively in communicative care work as well, although always in ways that were informed by the divide between migrant and nonmigrant obligations. Here, I will illustrate this complexity with a continued focus on *mandar saludos*, turning to an exploration of how this genre was produced using a more reciprocal technology: phone calls. Unlike video recordings, phone calls allow for synchronous communication, meaning that interlocutors can respond to one another in real time. The synchronicity of phone calls had consequences for how *saludos* were sent and how they participated in cross-border care. In particular, examining phone calls demonstrates how migrants respond to *saludos* by themselves utilizing communication as a modality of care.

To exemplify this response, I analyze a representative example, taken from a transnational phone call between Luis, one of the migrant sons greeted above, and his mother, Rosario, at home in El Salvador (see Excerpt 3.3). When the video greetings discussed above were recorded, Luis's younger brother, Patricio, had been the primary remitter. Two years later, at the time of this phone call, Luis had started to send more money thanks to the assistance of his two recently arrived teenage sons, Adán and Beto. Reading these examples together highlights the flexibility of communication as a care strategy that can shift in response to the changing realities of family life, in this case the uncertain labor conditions and precarious lived realities of undocumented migrants in the United States.

The instance shown here appears toward the end of the conversation between Rosario and her migrant son; in fact, Luis seems eager to move on to talking to his nonmigrant brother, Fermín (line 14), with impatience coming through in his minimal responses and tone of voice. This may in part be due to the time limit on the long-distance calling cards that Luis purchased to make transnational calls.[9] It is also perhaps a manifestation of a particular mother-son relational dynamic. Regardless of its causes, Rosario's insistence on completing an elaborate greeting under these circumstances emphasizes the importance of this cross-border communicative care practice.[10]

Sending Greetings, Envisioning Family, and Grappling with Inequality   107

Excerpt 3.3 Saludos in a Mejía Family Phone Call[a]

1.	Rosario:	A pues, me les da saludos a los chamaquitos allí.	Well then, give my greetings to the kids there.
2.	Luis:	¿Ah?	Huh?
3.	Rosario:	Me les da saludes.	Give them my greetings.
4.	Luis:	A quién.	To whom.
5.	Rosario:	A Adán, a Beto, y a Inés.	To Adán, to Beto, and to Inés.
6.	Luis:	Okay mami. No pues yo les saludo de parte suya.	Okay mom. Of course I will give them your greetings.
7.	Rosario:	Sí. Y a toda la familia allí, me les da saludes.	Yes. And to the whole family there, give them my greetings.
8.	Luis:	Okay mami. Gracias.	Okay mom. Thanks.
9.	Rosario:	Sí.	Yes.
10.	Luis:	Ajá. Usted también se me cuida, que Dios me lo bendiga, y que,	Uh-huh. Take care of yourself too, may God bless you, and,
11.	Rosario:	Vaya pues.	Okay then.
12.	Luis:	Ajá.	Uh-huh.
13.	Rosario:	Vaya.	Okay.
14.	Luis:	No sé si hay tiempo [para que me pase un ratito a Fermín].	I don't know if there's time [for you to put Fermín on the phone for a minute].
15.	Rosario:	[También para ustedes también lo],	[Also for you also],
16.		Que Dios derrame bendiciones a ustedes,	May God pour blessings on you,
17.		porque, pues sí, están trabajando,	because, sure, you are working,
18.		pues para ayudarle a nosotros.	you know, to help us out.
19.		Imaginate que, [como te] digo, que uno aquí sin, ¿solo esperando?	Imagine that, [as I] told you, that one here without, only waiting?
20.	Luis:	[Sí]. Sí mami. Pero mira como le digo,	[Yes]. Yes mom. But look as I told you,
21.		mientras uno pueda pues uno hace el esfuerzo.	while one can well one makes the effort.
22.		No tiene que preocuparse.	You don't have to worry.
23.		Porque, yo me acuerdo que un tiempo pues,	Because, I remember that once well,
24.		usted y mi papá lucharon, sufrieron,	you and my dad struggled, suffered,
25.		por conseguir una [tor]tilla, un huevo.	to get us a [tor]tilla, an egg.
26.		Para darnos comida a nosotros.	To give food to us.
27.	Rosario:	[Sí].	[Yes].

[a] Spanish is transcribed as spoken, including the use of nonstandard forms ("saludes" in lines 3 and 7) and dialectal variation (the *voseo* as in "imaginate" line 19).

108 Living Together across Borders

Like its video counterparts, this phone *saludo* is explicitly situated within the family's cross-border circuit of care, as Rosario links her *saludo* to the fact that her migrant kin are fulfilling their care obligations by working to support the family back home (lines 17–18). Again, the *saludo* frames recognition of the debt that migrant remittances have placed on nonmigrants, thereby construing Rosario's communicative labor as a form of reciprocity, however insufficient. And once again, affect emerges through this genre. In a tired voice close to breaking, Rosario highlights the asymmetry of this exchange, pointing out how hard it is to simply wait for the funds migrants send (line 19). In response, Luis tells his mother not to worry about this current asymmetry (line 22), because he is simply reciprocating the hard-won care that his parents provided for him and his siblings when they were children during the Salvadoran civil war (lines 23–26). Luis uses communication as affective labor to reassure his mother, resignifying remittances as a form of generational reciprocity, insisting that his remittances are repaying the debt that younger generations owe to those who raised them. Here he draws on moral imaginaries that envision kin care as involving asymmetrical reciprocity enacted through an intergenerational contract (see Chapter 2). In this imaginary, it is he—and not Rosario—who is indebted, an understanding which she herself confirms (line 27). Here, the meaning-making capacity of language itself functions to enact care, as the resignification of remittances is used to assuage feelings of dependency. By interpreting asymmetrical cross-border care as motivated by generational indebtedness rather than political-economic inequality, mother and son resist the co-optation of their kin ties to capitalist logics. Here, a model of asymmetrical reciprocity is mobilized as a resource to reframe the significance of remittances, extricating kin care from neoliberal entanglements.

However, even as this conversation resignifies economic care, the interactional organization of this exchange functions to implicitly reaffirm an unequal division of communicative care work between migrants and nonmigrants. Greetings in general are understood to be reciprocal: uttering a greeting makes a matched response relevant from one's interlocutor, who is expected to provide a greeting in turn (Duranti 1997). However, as the foregoing sections have demonstrated, video *saludos* do not function in the same way for transnational families, as migrants are expected to reciprocate through remittances rather than through sending a *saludo* themselves. These genre conventions then raise the question of what happens when *saludos* are sent in the synchronous medium of phone calls.

In this instance, Rosario sends her *saludo* first to her grandchildren in the United States (lines 1, 3, 5) and then to the whole family. As with the videos, the *saludo* Rosario sends here is addressed to multiple distant relatives—her

Sending Greetings, Envisioning Family, and Grappling with Inequality **109**

grandchildren and the entire family in the United States. *Allí* (there) is appended to each term of reference, discursively emplacing these relatives in a distant realm and thereby reproducing the borders that separate them from Rosario. At the same time, Rosario reaches out to these distant relatives through the *saludo* by positioning Luis as an intermediary. Sending *saludos* projects Rosario as greeter into the distant world of her kin in the United States, envisioning a reality in which she is linked not only to her migrant son, but through him to her grandchildren as well as to the entire collective of migrant relatives.

Luis, for his part, does not respond symmetrically by sending a *saludo* to his many relatives in El Salvador. Nevertheless, his responses use communication to enact care in a more limited way, focused on his mother. He willingly takes up the communicative obligation she has placed on him, first clarifying who she is sending the *saludo* to (line 4) before promising to pass along the *saludos* (line 6) and thanking her (line 8). The most explicit form of reciprocation comes when Luis extends well-wishing to his mother (line 10), saying "Usted también se me cuida, que Dios me lo bendiga" (Take care of yourself too; God bless you). This response demonstrates his familiarity with the genre of *mandar saludos* which often includes such formulaic well-wishing. However, rather than extending those wishes broadly to all his relatives in El Salvador—including his father, siblings, nieces and nephews, and even his youngest son—Luis limits them to his mother. Adding this form has the effect of putting Luis more directly into the well-wishing, such that his mother is taking care of herself, and God is blessing her, for him. Through his response to his mother's *saludo*, Luis thus emphasizes their dyadic mother-son bond.

In response, Rosario extends her original *saludo*, adding well-wishing articulated in the same religious idiom Luis had used (line 16). However, her well-wishing contradicts the insistent dyadic focus her son had maintained; instead Rosario returns to the collective reference terms she had used at the outset, wishing God's blessing on all her migrant relatives.

Through this sequence of responses, Luis and Rosario thus articulate and enact radically different forms of cross-border relations; narrow dyadic ties are imagined between one migrant (Luis) and a specific nonmigrant relative (his mother), while an expansive web of connection is envisioned as connecting the nonmigrant (Rosario) to all her migrant kin. The articulation of these imaginaries is undergirded by a trenchant division of discursive labor in which *mandar saludos* remains a genre of communicative care located firmly within the purview of nonmigrants. Despite the synchronic pressure to produce matched sequential responses, both migrant and nonmigrant maintain this genre-based boundary in their contributions. This communicative

110 Living Together across Borders

division of labor profoundly shapes the interaction between mother and son, revealing how pervasively the migrant/nonmigrant divide shaped enactments of care in these families.

Communicative care practices at times thus work to reproduce hierarchy, mapping the global borders between migrants and nonmigrants onto conversational divides. In this instance, such reinforcement of inequality unfolds implicitly alongside a much more explicit resignification of economic care that resists neoliberal capitalist framings of transnational family life. Through such communicative care, the relationship between mother and son becomes more deeply entangled with the global inequities of the migrant and nonmigrant divide, even as communication provides a space to resignify care and reassert asymmetrically reciprocal relationships of obligation as the basis of social life. The communicative care of *saludos* thus works along multiple dimensions, producing deeply contradictory effects.

Conclusion

Transnational families take up a genre of indirect greetings (*mandar saludos*) that has long been used in Latin America to maintain social ties over space and time. They mobilize digital technologies to send *saludos* that discursively cultivate the relationships of obligation that are understood to undergird transnational *convivencia*. In so doing, they envision language as an essential form of care that can maintain cross-border relational ties. Here, phatic communication, rather than being empty small talk, constitutes a powerful form of social action with important consequences.

Even as *saludos* enact relational care and facilitate material care such as remittances, they simultaneously produce conceptualizations of cross-border kinship that make meaning by mobilizing imaginaries of transnational care and family life. *Saludos* participate in asymmetrically reciprocal relationships in which individual relatives participate in family life by enacting different kinds of care. These asymmetries are tied to gendered and generational kin hierarchies, but also to divisions between migrants and those in El Salvador.

Moreover, in these imaginaries, asymmetrical reciprocity not only shapes the daily distribution of kin care but also influences longer-term trajectories, envisioning particular familial futures. Asymmetrical socialization to *mandar saludos* lays out a specific imaginary in which new generations of migrants, rather than the children of migrants, will carry transnational relationships of obligation into the future. The locus of socialization into cross-border communication thus remains in El Salvador, with continued migration envisioned as the route by which such relationships of obligation move across borders. The transnational family form is therefore maintained under conditions of ongoing inequity between Global North and South.

Thus, *saludos* envision and enact an imaginary of kin care that is deeply impacted by global inequities, which shape both day-to-day distinctions between migrants and nonmigrants and understandings of the more durative intergenerational maintenance of the family. Here, as in state-endorsed imaginaries, cross-border care is motivated by enduring inequities between Global North and South. This vision emerges clearly in the radically different engagement of migrant and nonmigrant relatives with the genre of *mandar saludos*, as well as in the ways that greetings rank migrant kin to prioritize remitters. The force of this imaginary is clearly shored up by a political economy that concentrates wealth in the Global North that has been continually extracted from the Global South through hundreds of years of colonization and imperialism.

At the same time, however, *saludos* can be used to subtly resist dominant visions of cross-border care that emphasize unidirectional economic care from a male provider for his dependent relatives back home. Rather, in these greetings, care is envisioned and enacted as multidirectional; the communicative care of nonmigrant kin in El Salvador is understood as crucial to sustaining transnational family life. Moreover, migrants also bear responsibility for communicative forms of care, as when Camila requests that her migrant brother send pictures of his daughter and when Luis enacts communicative care toward his mother in their phone call. Through these engagements, families produce alternate imaginaries of cross-border care which depict asymmetrically reciprocal relationships of obligation as the foundation upon which *convivencia* can be built, not only from day to day but also from generation to generation. Thus, even as they bring global inequities into everyday family life by reproducing boundaries between migrants and nonmigrants, *saludos* simultaneously reproduce alternate models of care. They reconstitute kinship as the basis for social and economic exchange, emphasizing the maintenance of asymmetrical relationships of obligation despite separation over space and time. Seemingly insignificant forms of language use such as *mandar saludos* thus have profound and contradictory effects, and attending to these can lift up the collective wisdom that transnational families have developed as they navigate *convivencia* across borders.

4

Talking Remittances

The Conversational Temporalities of
Intergenerational Care

Consequential Conversational Temporalities

For many transnational families, remittances are a fundamental part of care and living-together across borders. When taken in the aggregate, funds sent home by migrants sustain the economies of many nations in the Global South (KNOMAD 2019). Remittances not only outpace development aid three to one, but they also constitute a much more stable external income stream for developing nations (World Bank Group 2016), demonstrating the role of global households as an aggregate macroeconomic actor (Safri and Graham 2010). However, while macrolevel analysis highlights the stability of remittance flows over time, for transnational families, remittances are a contingent accomplishment resulting from ongoing cross-border negotiations in which communication plays a vital role.

In the transnational phone calls I gathered, talk about remittances was pervasive. Not only were remittances the most frequent topic of conversation, but discussions about remittances took up the most time in these calls, a finding that resonates with research on transnational families around the world (Drotbohm 2010; Horst 2006; Primus Mbeanwoah Tazanu 2012). Moreover, conversations about remittances are charged and emotionally fraught, so these families tended to utilize subtle and indirect communicative strategies that necessitate the analytical tools of linguistic anthropology. This chapter therefore closely examines the linguistic details of remittance conversations. By tracing nuanced communicative practices, the analysis presented here develops insights into the behind-the-scenes labor that not only makes remittances possible but also makes them consequential for transnational family *convivencia* (living-together) in multiple ways.

Of course, conversations about remittances do not occur in a vacuum. Rather, they respond to and manage the complex realities of transnational families, whose everyday lives are fundamentally shaped by changing immigration policies and global political-economic regimes. While all immigrant

Living Together Across Borders. Lynnette Arnold, Oxford University Press. © Oxford University Press 2024.
DOI: 10.1093/oso/9780197755730.003.0005

communities are subject to these forces, unauthorized migrants are particularly vulnerable. For these transnational families, remittances are made precarious by factors such as the cost and uncertain outcomes of illicit journeys, the instability of employment, and the ever-present possibility of detention and deportation. Thus, through remittances, kin care becomes enmeshed with global political-economic inequities, which in turn interact with the gendered and generational norms that shape care labor within families.

Remittances constitute a crucial locus for negotiating gendered distributions of care work. When they are understood as a transnational form of provisioning, remittances become caught up with assumptions about masculine caregiving. Challenges to masculine identities may arise when male migrants find themselves unable to remit (Pribilsky 2012) or when women migrate and become breadwinners (Gamburd 2004; Parreñas 2005). As remittance practices change the distribution of care work within the family, they may provide opportunities for shifting gendered norms of kin care (Levitt 1998; Montes 2013). However, such negotiations do not necessarily result in more egalitarian divisions of labor and may in fact reinforce women's responsibility for the most burdensome care work (Fan and Parreñas 2018). In the case of Salvadoran transnational families, Abrego demonstrates that migrant mothers remit money more consistently than migrant fathers, despite earning significantly less than their male counterparts (2009, 2014); women, she argues, must compensate for being absent mothers through remittances, a pressure their male counterparts do not face due to different gendered expectations.

Moreover, as a form of intergenerational care, remittances respond to life course changes in both countries as nuclear families are formed, children are born and grow up, and elderly relatives ail and age.[1] Such intergenerational care responsibilities are often cited as the cause of migration, with parents seeking resources to provide for children or for their own aging parents. Remittances thus become part of asymmetrically reciprocal kin care, but migration can also change expectations and practices of intergenerational care. Same-generation care between siblings may assume increased importance (A. Flores 2018), and elders may become providers rather than recipients of care (Dossa and Coe 2017; Yarris 2017). Care through intergenerational cohabitation is often replaced by virtual care[2] and as a result, migrant remittances take on increased significance not simply as economic care but rather as a manifestation of love and affection.[3]

Taken together, these studies demonstrate that remittances must be understood as care that not only crosses space but also spans time. Existing scholarship highlights how remittances are connected to longer timescales, pointing to shifting intergenerational care over the life course, or highlighting how normative gendered and generational distributions of care labor respond to migration over time. However, the communicative approach I take in this chapter draws attention to the more immediate timescales of conversation. My analysis highlights two forms of conversational temporality. The first is the interactional timescale, in which each subsequent turn at talk shapes what can be said next. This incremental unfolding over interactional time constitutes the architecture of conversation, or what conversation analysts call sequence organization (Sacks, Schegloff, and Jefferson 1974; Schegloff 2007). Second, I highlight interdiscursive timescales that link conversations across time and produce patterns of regular communicative practices such as genres (Bauman 2004; Silverstein 2005).

I suggest that these interactional and interdiscursive timescales have profound consequences for cross-border care as transnational families repeatedly negotiate remittances in conversations over days, months, and years. Ultimately, I demonstrate that it is through such conversational temporalities that families navigate changing care needs and responsibilities, negotiate gendered and generational distributions of care work, and grapple with the effects of global political-economic forces on their lives. Transnational families produce *convivencia* across borders through interactional and interdiscursive timescales, thereby communicatively enacting the vision of asymmetrically reciprocal kin care that is articulated in their cross-border greetings (see Chapter 3). Conversational temporalities are thus a vital resource through which transnational families sustain living-together despite the powerful political-economic and discursive forces that work to tear them apart.

Communicative Labor in Remittance Conversations

Remittances do not happen without a great deal of communicative effort that is sustained over time. Of course, some of this work happens in face-to-face conversations between relatives in both El Salvador and the United States. But arguably the most charged remittance communication occurs in transnational phone calls that bring together remittance-sending migrants and relatives in El Salvador who rely on remittances to meet basic care needs such as housing and food, to provide education and healthcare, and to celebrate birthdays, graduations, and holidays. Such cross-border conversations must therefore bridge the deep asymmetries of transnational family economies in which nonmigrants depend on migrant remittances, with no end in sight to this unequal relationship. This chapter, therefore, explores how remittances are negotiated in such transnational conversations.

When migrants send money, they must minimally notify their relatives, specifying the amount of the transfer and the confirmation code needed for pickup. However, transnational conversations about remittances begin well before funds are sent, occurring even in cases where no remittances are ultimately forthcoming. Remittance communication generally begins with a request from a nonmigrant relative in El Salvador, which launches negotiations about how to spend the limited funds available to meet a range of expenses in both countries. How much money should be sent, and what will it be used for? Such conversations involve often tense and emotionally laden decision-making about which care needs should be prioritized and which are less urgent. This communicative undertaking therefore often mobilizes gendered and generational assumptions about who is obligated to care for whom, and who is entitled to receive what forms of care. Communication about remittances continues even once funds have been sent and received. Those in El Salvador provide reports and expressions of gratitude, sometimes using social media to send pictures of new clothes or home construction, or videos of family events funded through remittances.

Cross-border conversations about remittances thus involve a recurring cycle of communicative actions. Requests are made by those in El Salvador and elicit financial negotiations with migrants; if remittances are sent, communication continues with reports and gratitude that are seen as preconditions for future remittance. These conversations unfold over days, weeks, and sometimes months, and generally involve multiple individuals in both countries. Through the years of family separation, this cycle of conversation is repeated over and over, iteratively building the relational groundwork upon which future remittance negotiations will be enacted. Thus, these seemingly mundane conversations are vital to the ongoing maintenance of kinship and family economies across borders and through years of shifting intergenerational care needs.

This cycle of communication must navigate a veritable minefield of relational tensions produced by political-economic inequities between Global North and South. Because those in El Salvador depend on migrant remittances for survival, they are concerned with maintaining good relationships with their migrant relatives and work hard to avoid outright conflict that could threaten the relationships necessary for continued remittances. In addition, in order to convince migrants to send money, nonmigrants must design their requests to emphasize "legitimate consumption" (Tazanu 2018), stressing that they will be used to cover expenses such as health or education that migrants are likely to deem important. However, even such framings are sometimes doubted by migrants, who may request photos and videos as evidence of

116 Living Together across Borders

remittance spending. Nonmigrants themselves often anticipate this concern, and preemptively send such visual evidence to maintain trust. Underlying these tensions are migrant desires to have agency over their remittances. In part, this is because they work very hard to earn the money they send home, often through long hours in low-paying jobs with harsh conditions, all while living in crowded and poor-quality housing. They may feel resentment that their family back home is living an easy life at their expense, without truly understanding the sacrifices they are making (Katigbak 2015b). At the same time, however, remittances are an important way in which migrants care for loved ones across space and time, and they want to be sure it is done right. Remittance communication is thus emotionally fraught, especially in cases of illness or other serious care crises.

Indeed, existing research on remittances has demonstrated that, while increasing access to communicative technologies has provided a common "communication infrastructure" for talk about remittances (Couldry 2004, 357), this increased ability to negotiate remittances has profound and complex consequences for the relationship between migrants and nonmigrants.[4] This scholarship tends to rely on interviews, privileging people's reflections and after-the-fact analysis about remittance communication rather than investigating how it plays out in the moment. In this chapter, I move beyond interview accounts to instead examine how tensions emerge and are managed directly in remittance communication. While communication may manifest tensions and exacerbate conflict, in this chapter I focus on communicative practices that transnational families have developed to navigate the minefield of remittance negotiations in ways that sustain rather than fracture relationships.

A Birthday to Remember

To exemplify the complexity of the communicative labor that underpins remittances, I trace here one ongoing remittance negotiation within the Mejía family: how to celebrate the birthday of the patriarch of the family, David. Two of David's sons had migrated to the United States over a decade ago, having been joined in August by his two eldest grandsons, both in their late teens. That November, the family began to talk about how to celebrate David's birthday, which was still several months away. Remittance conversations began when David's last son remaining at home, Fermín, suggested to his migrant brother Luis that they send their parents on a pilgrimage to Esquipulas, Guatemala. Their parish in El Salvador was organizing a trip to commemorate the saint's day of the *Cristo Negro* (Black Christ) on January 15. Participating in this trip would fulfill a lifelong dream of their parents, who were both devout Catholics, and Luis was enthusiastic about the idea. He asked his brother to let him know the cost of the trip so that he and his fellow migrants could send the necessary funds. Like most cases of remittance negotiations, relatives in El Salvador made the request for funds and were also the ones tasked with verifying exact costs. This dynamic reveals an uneven distribution of communicative labor in which nonmigrants bear greater responsibility, a pattern that resonates with the role of the specific genre of *mandar saludos* (sending greetings) in cross-border circuits of family care (see Chapter 3). Once again, the inescapable economic asymmetry of transnational family life results in nonmigrants bearing a heavier communicative burden.

As the weeks passed, the care needs and resources of the Mejía family changed, as is their wont. In December, David suffered a sudden worsening of the chronic kidney disease he suffered from and had to be hospitalized for several days. The costs of this treatment, along with the expenses of Christmas and New Year's celebrations, significantly drained the migrants' economic resources. The family in El Salvador, however, forged ahead with birthday plans. On the first Sunday in January—when the family knew Luis would be home from work—his sister Teodora called him to report the cost of the trip to Esquipulas. Notably, although the initial idea for the trip had come from their brother Fermín, a woman in the family was ultimately responsible for verifying costs and communicating this information to migrant relatives. While Luis found the $20 transportation fee to be reasonable, he was outraged at the high cost of lodging ($80 a night per person). In no uncertain terms he told his sister that the trip was off: he and the other migrants in the family could not afford this expense at the moment. Luis told Teodora that they should think of a more affordable celebration, perhaps along the lines of a small party. Once they had a plan, they should call him back and the migrants would try to send at least some funds.

Remittance communication thus enacted and sustained the economic asymmetries of cross-border care, with migrants exercising greater decision-making power than their nonmigrant relatives. This pattern was repeated in a subsequent call, a week later, on Luis's next day off. His eldest sister Sara called and urged him again to fund the trip to Esquipulas. Luis once again rejected this plan and said the family in El Salvador had taken too long to find out the cost of the trip. If he and the other migrants had been informed earlier, he suggested, they might have been able to help, but not at this late date. He reiterated the plan for a small celebration "que tal vez no sea la gran cosa, pero para que él sepa que siempre nos acordamos de él" (it may not be

118   Living Together across Borders

a big deal, but it shows him that we always remember him). Luis's scolding of Sara and his sharp rebuttal to Teodora reveal that remittance communication reproduces not only economic but also gendered asymmetries of care. Just as when Teodora became responsible for concretizing the details of her brother's plan, here again men set the terms and women did the communicative work.

Luis was not the only migrant involved in ongoing negotiations about the birthday. His son Adán, a recent migrant, was excited about this opportunity to show care in this way for the grandfather who had raised him. Two weeks before the birthday, he called and asked David what he wanted as a gift. His grandfather was hesitant to make a request, citing the expense of his recent health crisis, but Adán insisted and David ultimately said he would like a new pair of shoes. At the same time, Adán had been busily coordinating with his aunts in El Salvador to set up a serenade by local musicians to surprise his grandfather on the morning of his birthday. Adán's enthusiastic involvement in planning this celebration demonstrated to his relatives back home how he intended to step into his new role as remittance-sender within the family.

Two days later, Teodora called again, and this time she spoke to her nephew Adán. As requested, she provided details of their new plan for the birthday celebration. In the morning, they would take David to the nearest town to choose new clothes and shoes. That afternoon, they would invite other elders from the village for a *rezo* (prayer service) with a local lay religious leader who would lead them in praying the rosary. Afterward there would be tamales and cake as well as a piñata for the children. Adán responded that the proposed cost—$250—was too expensive, but rather than leveling a flat "no" like his father had earlier, he said they would see what they could do. In his more mitigated response, the effect of generation is clear. Teodora is Adán's aunt, and the respect she must be afforded as an older relative offsets economic and gender hierarchies to some extent.

Later that evening, Luis sat down with his two sons to calculate who could send what: ultimately, each of them sent $100. Adán and his brother each chipped in an extra $50 to cover the cost of the serenade, which had been their idea. Ultimately, they sent more money than the family in El Salvador had ever requested—whether for the trip to Esquipulas or for the party— but they sent it on their terms. Cross-border conversations across months and weeks provided a space for migrants to exert their influence as the amount and purpose of remittance funds was actively negotiated.

Remittance conversations continued after the funds were sent. On the day of the birthday Adán was up early and called El Salvador to get an update before he went to work. The serenade had begun an hour ago, his aunt Teodora reported, and was still underway. David had danced for a while with some of his grandchildren and now was requesting that the musicians play all of his favorite songs. They reviewed the plans for the day, and Adán asked her to take pictures and video. He explained to both her and later to his aunt Sara how to make video recordings and how to send them through Facebook.

Notably, although his uncle Fermín had greater digital literacy than Sara or Teodora, Adán did not ask him to do this, again revealing gendered understandings of care work. Nevertheless, male migrants did take on affective communicative labor as part of these remittance conversations. At the end of the call, once the serenade was over, both Adán and his brother Beto talked to their grandfather to wish him a happy birthday. He reported having been woken up by the serenade and thanked them for organizing it. Although he said he felt happy, he also expressed concern that this might be his last birthday due to his illness. Adán and Beto comforted him, counseling him to have faith, follow doctor's orders, and trust that all would be well.

That evening at dinner, Adán showed everyone pictures that his aunts had sent of the birthday celebration, evidence of David's enjoyment of the events and also of how the remittances had been spent. This prompted his father Luis to text the family in El Salvador for updates, and later that evening, once the last party guests had left, David called on the phone. He spoke in turn to his grandsons and then his son, reporting on the day's events. They asked detailed questions about what clothing and shoes he had purchased and what refreshments the family had provided at the party. David responded to these questions, and also repeated to each of them a funny story about how his youngest two-year-old grandson had tried to hit the piñata with a stick bigger than he was, an account that the migrants received with laughter and additional joking. David also thanked each migrant for their help, reiterating how he and all the guests had had a good time. Luis responded, "Me alegra. Sabe que me siento tan feliz que, a pesar de estar largo pues, es como que estuviéramos cerca, pues hablando y con las fotos" (That makes me happy. You know that I feel so happy that, even though we are far apart, it is as if we were close, by talking and with the photos). Here, both the experiences that remittances facilitate and family communication about these events are articulated as benefits to migrants, as a way of experiencing *convivencia* across borders.

In these post-remittance conversations, economic and affective labor are interwoven. Migrant kin ask about how funds have been spent, while also sending well wishes and comforting nonmigrant relatives. For their part, relatives in El Salvador provide details about specific purchases made and the affective responses of those who benefit, including both appreciation and humorous narratives that serve as forms of communicative recompense similar

120 Living Together across Borders

to the cross-border greetings discussed in Chapter 3. Such accounts elicit affective responses from migrants, who may experience these conversations as bridging distance. While migrants may talk with one another about feeling resentment at the burden of constant requests for money, these complaints are silenced in cross-border phone conversations, which instead focus on the practicality of how to meet needs and the affective consequences of this engagement. Remittance communication is thus not just about making economic transfers. Rather, through such conversations, families work to build affective closeness, continually laying the relational foundation upon which the transnational family economy is built.

Crucially, male relatives—both migrants and nonmigrants—participate in these forms of emotional labor in remittance conversations. Following Montes (2013), we might then argue that migration creates opportunities for men to reflect on and change their affective relationships with kin. At the same time, however, these remittance conversations reveal a trenchant gendered asymmetry in the distribution of care labor. Women were still responsible for more onerous tasks like verifying and communicating costs or taking photos and videos and then sending them to migrant kin. Thus, remittance conversations evidence the contradictory nature of changes to gendered care distributions: while they may have created space for men to participate in emotional labor, they simultaneously reproduced an asymmetrical division of care work along the lines of gender. Remittance conversations thus navigate not only asymmetries between migrants and nonmigrants but also the ways that care is tied to gendered hierarchies.

These intersecting asymmetries had to be negotiated even as the family managed the complex temporal calculus of intergenerational care provision. Planned spending had to be adjusted both in response to sudden changes such as illness or due to seasonal expenses. Life course trajectories, such as aging or the transition of dependent children into new wage-earning members of the family also impacted these conversations. And even the temporality of migrants' work schedules and days off became consequential in remittance negotiations, often producing a lag between decisions made and their communication across borders.

As this account of David's birthday planning reveals, communication is central to how remittances participate in cross-border care and are experienced as meaningful by transnational families. Ongoing conversations manage shifting gendered and intergenerational care dynamics as relatives work to sustain living-together across borders. The rest of the chapter, therefore, takes a closer look at remittance communication in transnational phone calls, focusing on the heart of the matter: how remittances are requested.[5]

The Interactive Temporality of Requests

The requests through which nonmigrants make their needs known and the ways that migrants respond to these appeals are the essence of remittance communication. They must happen if money is to be sent. At the same time, such communicative negotiations highlight the durative asymmetry of transnational care, since nonmigrants are always the ones who ask their migrant kin for funds. This consistent inequality makes requests for remittances—and migrant responses to these requests—into high-stakes communicative encounters. Thus, requests and responses constitute a potent site for understanding how conversational timescales participate in the organization of intergenerational care across the life course.

In any context, requests are a powerful form of communicative action because they invoke relationships of obligation. To ask someone to do something for you is to perform your relationship as one in which you are entitled to expect obligation from the other (Ervin-Tripp 1976). Moreover, even as they solicit future actions, requests also work in the immediate moment to place interactional obligations on the interlocutor to respond in a particular way (Taleghani-Nikazm 2006). For instance, consider this illustrative example of a request in a transnational phone call, a request not for money but for a particular nostalgic food item. This example emerged in a phone conversation between Francisco Portillo, a migrant son, and his mother, Olivia Portillo, in El Salvador. She had mentioned that the *milpa* she had planted now has *jilotes* (baby ears of corn), which prompted Francisco to reminisce about a chicken and *jilote* soup his maternal grandmother used to make. He then went on to ask his mother to send him a more travel-ready nostalgic food item (see excerpt 4.1), *riguas* (fire-roasted cakes made from fresh corn).

Here, a migrant son asks his mother to send *riguas to* him and his family, a material reminder of the agricultural rhythms of home as well as a

Excerpt 4.1 Direct Request by a Migrant

1.	Francisco:	Oiga,	listen,
2.		Yo lo que, quiero que nos mande,	what I, I want you to send us,
3.		es riguas, pero riguas de allá.	is riguas, but riguas from there.
4.	Olivia:	Ah, ajá	Oh, uh-huh.
5.		Vaya,	Okay,
6.		voy a ver si en diciembre te los mando,	I will see if I can send them to you in December,
7.		cuando ya haiga elote,	when there is fresh corn,

122 Living Together across Borders

manifestation of the labor through which such sustenance is produced. While it might be possible for Francisco to purchase *riguas* where he lives in Los Angeles, given the city's large Salvadoran community, he emphasizes that he wants "riguas de allá" (*riguas* from over there, line 3), highlighting the symbolic meaning of this food as a stand-in for home and mothering. His request is articulated very directly as a statement of the actions he wishes his mother to take. Research suggests that this sort of bald request enacts a high degree of entitlement to place obligations on one's interlocutor.[6] Francisco's request also places an immediate obligation on his mother to respond to his request in their conversation. And indeed she does so, acquiescing to her son's request (line 5) and mentioning the contingency of needing to wait until the corn is ready to be harvested (lines 6–7).

This exchange is a clear example of what conversation analysts call an adjacency pair (Schegloff and Sacks 1973). Some pairs of communicative actions are closely tied to one another, such that uttering the first places significant constrains on the kind of communicative action that can follow. For instance, as an English speaker, I know that if an acquaintance says to me, "How are you?" I should respond with something along the lines of "Fine. How are you?" The first communicative action ("how are you") is known as the first-pair part, while the response ("fine, how are you?") is known as the second-pair part. Other common adjacency pairs include farewells, questions and answers, and requests. Adjacency pairs help organize how conversations unfold across interactional time, creating connections between communicative actions and their responses such that a break in this pattern becomes significant. For instance, if in response to the "how are you" question, I instead gave a longer response about how I was actually doing, this unusual response would be interpreted as meaningful and likely signifying something about my relationship with the interlocutor (Sacks 1975). In the case of a request (the first-pair part), the interlocutor is expected to respond in a way that acknowledges that a request has been made (the second-pair part), whether affirmatively, negatively, or seeking more information (Taleghani-Nikazm 2006). If an interlocutor responded to a request by ignoring it or changing the subject, this would suggest serious relational trouble. Adjacency pairs thus organize the temporal unfolding of conversation in ways that have important moral consequences (Duranti 1994b, 2009). Whether interlocutors follow or break the interactional expectations set up by adjacency pairs can lead to inferences being drawn about the ethico-moral status of individuals and of relationships.

In the context of remittance negotiations, the implications of adjacency pairs for ongoing relationships of obligation are incredibly weighty. Because communication is the primary form of transnational *convivencia*, small-scale interactional patterns such as these can powerfully shape the experience of living-together across borders. Investigating the specific linguistic design of these requests and their responses can thus shed light on how transnational families consistently utilize conversational practices to manage the durative inequalities of cross-border life, while also managing shifting intergenerational care needs.

Making Indirect Requests through Complaints

Although nonmigrants generally initiate conversations about remittances, their solicitations of help from migrant kin are seldom articulated as direct requests. Rather than directly asking, nonmigrants tend to complain about having care needs that they are unable to meet with the financial resources at their disposal. Migrants regularly respond to these economic complaints by offering to send remittances, or, if they cannot send funds, by helping their nonmigrant kin strategize about how to meet these needs. Remittances are thus solicited with more communicative delicacy than other transnational requests such as Francisco's request for *riguas*. This pattern reflects both of the higher-stakes nature of remittance requests and the fact that political-economic inequalities make such negotiations a permanent fact of transnational family life.

With the exception of requests made by children, all the remittance requests I gathered were formulated as complaints rather than direct solicitations of aid.[7] To demonstrate this practice, consider the two following examples, taken from phone calls in different transnational families. The first comes from another conversation between Olivia, this time with her teenaged daughter Serena, a recent migrant. Olivia had been reporting about her upcoming trip to Venezuela for cataract surgery. An arrangement between the Salvadoran FMLN (Frente Farabundo Martí para la Liberación Nacional) and the Venezuelan government would cover the cost of the trip and the surgery for former FMLN combatants such as Olivia. Serena asked if her mother was ready for the trip, and she responded: "Yo tengo todo mi papeleo ya, pero no tengo la ropa, ni nada comprado todavía, sí, no, no tengo dinero" (I already have all the paperwork, but I don't have the clothing, nor anything purchased yet, since I don't have any money).

In the second example, David Mejía had been speaking with his migrant grandson Beto. He had been reporting about recent medical visits and that the doctor wanted him to do a specific exam, and continued: "Está valiendo cuarenta dólares. El examen. Así es que tengo que hacerlo. . . . Pero estaba viendo que no me encuentro con ningún dinero, y cómo lo vamos a hacer" (It costs forty dollars. The test. So I have to do it. . . . But I was thinking that I don't have any money, and how are we going to do it). In both cases, the nonmigrant relative states a particular care need followed by a complaint about not having the funds to meet this expense.

Although both Olivia's and David's utterances look at first glance like complaints, they in fact do the work of requesting remittances. This can be seen in migrants' responses, which regularly treated such complaints as requests for money. When financial complaints were directed to them, migrants generally responded by offering to send remittances or explaining that they had no money to send and suggesting other ways to meet the need. Sometimes they first asked for more information about the precise needs and their associated costs, clearly gathering more information to shape their response. Even Serena, who was not working and was thus unable to send money, consistently treated her mother's continued complaints as requests for remittances, helping Olivia to strategize about which of her migrant sons (Serena's brothers) she could ask for money. In transnational conversations, economic complaints thus constituted a first-pair part of an adjacency pair. Although they were designed differently than Francisco's direct request, they nevertheless carried out the function of requesting and had the same effect of constraining interlocutors' responses, such that migrants needed to produce remittance-relevant responses.

Serena's brother Francisco was the one migrant who consistently responded to economic complaints from his mother in ways that did not fit this pattern, often changing the subject entirely. But this case is the exception that proves the rule. There had been a great deal of conflict between Francisco and his family back home over Serena's recent migration. He had made clear that because he felt forced to take responsibility for his younger sister until she was able to work, he would no longer be sending remittances home. When he consistently refused to treat complaints as requesting money, this action functioned to remind his family back home of his anger. Indeed, if complaints were not treated as remittance requests, Francisco's off-topic responses would not have had this immediate impact.

Why did nonmigrants choose to use complaints to replace straightforward requests for remittances? Long-standing anthropological scholarship (Feld 2012; Wilce 2009) has underscored the communicative power of complaint and other "rhetorics of grievance" (McLaren 2000). While some researchers separate ritual laments at funerals and weddings from conversational complaints such as Olivia's and David's, linguistic anthropological scholarship has suggested instead that they be understood along a continuum from more ritualized to more improvised complaints (Wilce 1998). Doing so allows researchers to trace the particular communicative forms and patterns through which rhetorics of grievance assume significant social force (Wilce 2006).

Around the world, such rhetorics are often a communicative strategy of the politically and socially disenfranchised. For instance, ritual lament can be used by women to challenge the powerful male-dominated institutions that control their societies (C. L. Briggs 1992; Holst-Warhaft 2002; McIntosh 2005). In medical contexts, patients use complaints in attempts to influence treatment plans and service provision.[8] The act of articulating grievance can thus be understood as resistance that simultaneously challenges inequalities even as it registers the difficult realities of life, be they illness, death, or lack of money. In addition, interactional research has demonstrated that complaints (Drew 1998; Schegloff 2005) and "troubles-talk" (Jefferson 1988) function in conversation to elicit empathetic responses. Requests are thus important sites for "the calibration of social distance" and provide opportunities "to shift the nature of a dyadic relationship from less intimate to more" (Hoey 2013, 15). Particularly in charged settings such as remittance requests, complaints can work to foster connection rather disconnection.

Ultimately, making complaints about economic shortfalls allowed relatives in El Salvador to bring their care needs into cross-border conversations without having to directly ask their migrant relatives for assistance. Direct requests are a high-stakes form of communicative action, since the person making the request places an explicit obligation onto their interlocutor (Brown and Levinson 1987; Ervin-Tripp 1976). The obligation can of course be refuted or denied, but communicatively negotiating entitlements to care in such an on-record way has the potential to do significant damage to the relationship between the interlocutors if things do not go smoothly. Avoiding direct requests is thus a common communicative concern, and around the world, speech communities have come up with different strategies for doing so.[9]

For transnational families, requests formulated as complaints served as a valuable communicative tool to protect kin ties in the face of continued economic inequalities that necessitated ongoing one-way requests. The conventionalized use of complaints to ask for remittances thus can be understood as a form of communicative care; this routine attended to transnational kin ties by delicately organizing the unfolding of conversation across interactional time in a particular way. Through such communicative care practices, families used everyday conversations to manage the challenges of asymmetrical cross-border care forced upon them by global political-economic inequalities.

126 Living Together across Borders

Intensifying Complaints with Reported Speech

While the adjacency pair of economic complaint followed by a remittance response was common across the families in my study, the Mejía family developed this interactional organization into an even more indirect means of requesting remittances. In the Mejía family, nonmigrant relatives regularly embedded their complaints within narratives (for more on complaints in narrative, see M. Goodwin 1990; and Ochs and Capps 1996). They told stories which involved an economic complaint as part of a conversation between relatives in El Salvador. Through this practice, they embedded indirect requests for remittances into another common conversational activity in transnational phone calls: reporting family news. These narratives often included accounts of conversations replayed word for word, and it was in such conversational reports that economic complaints would be embedded. Through this strategy, complaints were presented to migrants as reported speech, or repetitions of something that had been said already in another context.[10]

Reported speech mobilizes another form of conversational temporality known as interdiscursivity (sometimes also referred to as intertextuality). Interdiscursivity is a property of language in which any current utterance is inevitably situated vis-à-vis past communication (Bauman 2004; Silverstein 2005). These connections to past conversations can be more or less explicitly mobilized by speakers to carry out communicative actions in the present.[11] In reported speech, the interdiscursive connections to a specific previous conversation are made explicit (Holt and Clift 2007). Reported speech draws connections between the present moment and the previous time when the reported words were originally uttered, using this interdiscursive link to shore up the authority of the speaker's claims. For the Mejía family, reported speech was used to implicitly but powerfully support requests for money.

Consider for instance a conversation between a mother, Rosario Mejía, and her eldest son, Luis. In their conversation, Rosario had been discussing her husband David's health and all the medical tests the doctors had ordered for him. Luis commiserated with her, reminding her that at least the family could count on the medical expertise of Fermín, his youngest brother, who had just returned from Cuba, where he had completed medical school on a scholarship. Rosario built on this mention of Fermín to introduce a complaint about money, framing it as a report of something she had said to Fermín earlier.

> Le estaba diciendo yo a Fermín, o aquí a las bichas que, le digo yo, "Púchica, ahorita pues así estamos, así sin pisto. No tenemos para el gasto del examen y hay que pagar recibos del agua."

(I was telling Fermín, or to the girls here, "Darn it, right now that's the situation here, we have no cash. We don't have money for the test, and we need to pay the water bills.")

Rosario's complaint here is performed through reported speech: she quotes something she herself said earlier to another family member. This quote does not just draw on past experience but actively creates this conversation in El Salvador as a fact that can be reported to her migrant son.

The use of reported speech is common in the production of rhetorics of grievance around the world (Wilce 2005). For instance, Briggs (1992) shows how Warao women from an Indigenous community in Venezuela utilized reported speech in funeral laments in order to assert that the quoted events had taken place. They thereby claimed for themselves—as reporters of these events—the right to discursively intervene in the situation. Reported speech in laments allowed women to level accusations against powerful men in their community, denunciations that had immediate consequences and ultimately challenged the social dominance of men. This example demonstrates the interdiscursive power of reported speech in complaints. Not only does reported speech draw on past utterances to stake a claim in current discourse, but it is also deployed as a resource for shaping ongoing and future social relations. Here, Rosario draws on the past by recreating this purported previous conversation, which she then mobilizes to indirectly request remittances.

Re-creating the conversation draws Luis in, embedding the migrant listener into the daily life of their family members back home. Notably, the identity of Rosario's original interlocutor remains vague: it might have been Fermín (her son) or one of her daughters. What matters is the geographic location of her addressee as someone *aquí* (here) in El Salvador, to whom the need for funds is a cause for concern. Because this conversation happened in El Salvador, it therefore falls under the broad umbrella of family news to be shared with migrant relatives. Moreover, by using reported speech, Rosario adds another layer of indirectness to a request for remittances: not only is this request articulated as a complaint, but the complaint itself is not directly addressed to Luis. This reported complaint allows the mother to save face for herself and her son by embedding a request within different levels of indirectness. Reported speech thus provides additional communicative insulation to safeguard the mother-son relationship from the harm of ongoing asymmetries of care.

However, as the work of Briggs and others reminds us, indirectness is not all that reported speech accomplishes. By using reported speech, Rosario indirectly conveys her feelings about the family's economic situation. The first word of her reported speech is *púchica* (darn it), an interjection commonly

128　Living Together across Borders

used by women in rural El Salvador in place of more vulgar alternatives.[12] Like exclamations in general, this cry of *púchica* brings the hearer into the speaker's emotional experience, in this case providing Luis with a window into his mother's frustration. It is combined with the temporal adverb *ahorita* (right now) to signal the immediacy of the funding shortfall that Rosario laments. Reported speech thus amplifies the emotional appeal of the complaint, emphasizing the urgency of the family's need for economic assistance.

The efficacy of reported speech and interdiscursivity in making remittance requests is revealed in Luis's response. Even as Rosario completes a report of expenses—the medical exams, the water and phone bill, and the money owed to the local store for food purchased on credit—Luis insistently asks "cuánto es eso" (how much is that). Rosario then lists the specific amount of each of the expenses, to which Luis responds: "Mire, yo voy a ver si este fin de semana puedo poner algo de dinero" (Look, I'm going to see if I can send some money this weekend). Although he pursued his own line of questioning about amounts of expenses first, Luis here does provide the second part of the adjacency pair, a remittance response to match his mother's initial complaint.[13]

Luis clearly treats his mother's complaint narrative as placing obligations on him to help meet his family's needs, and by promising to send remittances, he accepts this care responsibility. However, his response remains vague as to the amount of money he will send. This fact is particularly noteworthy since he has just insisted on finding out the exact amount of each expense. This unspecified commitment thus asserts Luis's autonomy as a male migrant in the face of strong obligations to provide material care; he is the one who knows the contingencies he faces and decides what he can send. The questions also work to assert his control over how remittances will be spent. At the same time, the fact that he has asked detailed questions about the extent of these costs may implicitly suggest to his mother that he will attempt to cover these needs.

In this conversation, although there was no explicit request for remittances, a commitment to send remittances was nevertheless made. And this pattern repeated itself in most cross-border conversations about remittances within this family. All of the adult nonmigrant relatives used reported speech to formulate their complaints.[14] These narratives of economic shortfall were recounted to both established migrant relatives and to new migrants, who consistently provided a remittance response (see below for one significant exception).

The authorizing function of reported speech emerges clearly in the reported complaints the Mejía family used. The parents commonly quoted themselves, while siblings quoted their parents. Especially in health-related situations, the sisters also often quoted their brother Fermín (the doctor), though he never quoted them. Those who were subordinated in gendered and generational kin hierarchies thus quoted the utterances of individuals with more status in order to bolster their requests.

Thus, in the Mejía family, the more widespread adjacency pair of economic complaint followed by remittance-relevant response was modified such that reported complaints became the normative way of prompting a remittance response. The indirectness of reported complaints did not defuse their ability to make a request, but rather provided additional protection to kin relations in the context of sustained economic asymmetry while also allowing nonmigrants to increase the emotional and temporal urgency of their appeals.

At the same time, requests articulated as reported complaints provided an opportunity for migrants to demonstrate communicative care by responding appropriately to very indirect requests. When migrants responded to reported complaints by discussing remittances, they demonstrated their understanding of the communicative function of the complaint, thereby enacting their continued concern for family in El Salvador through conversational attentiveness. Through such responses, they indicated that they had not become selfish migrants who cared only for themselves but rather remained dedicated to their familial responsibilities. The strategy of reported complaints thus served as a multifaceted communicative resource for facilitating and enacting care across borders.

Creating and Breaking Communicative Norms

How did reported complaints become the primary means of requesting remittances in the Mejía family? How did the use of complaints more generally become the expected way to request remittances? Like all communicative norms, these practices are learned through language socialization. However, such subtle interactional patterns largely escape explicit awareness, and indeed, none of the participants in my study ever discussed how remittances were requested. Rather, individuals learned by observing and participating in frequent remittance conversations within their families. Recent migrants like Adán and his brother Beto had themselves grown up in a transnational family, surrounded by remittance-requesting conversations throughout their childhoods.

Communicative practices for negotiating remittance requests thus become normative through interdiscursivity. Here, interdiscursive relations are more implicit than in the case of reported speech. Rather than relying on explicitly articulating connections to other conversations, in this case interdiscursivity

130 Living Together across Borders

manifests through a regular pattern of discursive structure. This then makes complaints recognizable to interlocutors as instances of a particular communicative genre (Bauman 2004), a routinized way of doing things with words (see Chapter 3 for more on genre). Within the Mejía family, reported complaints become hearable as requesting remittances because of their consistent linguistic formulation: they are embedded within narratives about family life in El Salvador, involve grievances due to funding shortfalls, and begin with emotionally saturated expressions such as Rosario's cry of *púchica* or other terms that direct the attention of the interlocutor to what is to follow. In fact, the most common beginning to a reported complaint was the phrase *fíjese que* (lit.: take note or pay attention). It is this consistent linguistic structure that interdiscursively situates an individual reported complaint, making it recognizable as an instance of the genre of requesting remittances.

Thus, when nonmigrants requested remittances using complaints or reported complaints, and when migrants treated these accounts as solicitations of help, they drew on knowledge about patterned ways of communicating that had been developed over the weeks, months, and years of transnational separation. And, as demonstrated in Chapter 3, communicative practices used in transnational family life may build on long-standing communicative genres. The communicative practices of remittance negotiations were therefore not only organized in interactional time but also relied on interdiscursivity that continuously created linkages between current utterances and previous communication.

It is important to note that these interdiscursive relationships remained implicit. While some genres of grievance are named, or the uses of specific lament practices are debated (Wilce 2005), this was not the case here. I encountered no reflexive discussions about the use of complaints and reported complaints to make requests, suggesting that the continuance of this practice was due to implicit socialization (Ochs 1990); unlike *saludos*, these communicative practices were not explicitly named. Nevertheless, I regularly overheard migrants comment to one another that their relatives in El Salvador only called to ask for money. Later on, in listening to the recordings of these calls, I was struck to hear no direct requests but instead many complaints and reported complaints. Through their comments, migrants indicated their understanding of what actions such complaints worked to accomplish. Despite the lack of explicit discussion about complaints, the genre itself was nevertheless clearly recognizable to members of these transnational families.

Using complaints and reported complaints to request remittances thus became normative through such interdiscursive relations as families negotiated economic care provision across borders. Through the interweaving of interactional and interdiscursive temporalities, conversations became spaces in which families simultaneously navigated and worked to mitigate the effects of sustained economic asymmetries on their kin ties. The power of these conversational temporalities for cross-border care can be seen in an instance in which the adjacency pair of reported complaint followed by remittance response did not unfold as expected, the only such breach that appears in all the conversations I recorded within the Mejía family.

It was September, several months before David Mejía's birthday. Adán and Beto had only just arrived in the United States, and their grandfather David had been seriously ill. His family was working to get a diagnosis and treatment. Migrant relatives sent money, and those in El Salvador accompanied him to doctor's appointments, medical laboratories, and pharmacies. In transnational phone calls, relatives discussed the outcomes of tests and treatment options, while also coping with the affective and relational consequences of this reminder of David's mortality. On one afternoon, Beto called David to ask how he was doing. His grandfather answered "bastante mal" (quite bad) before launching into an extended account of the diagnostic test the doctor wanted him to do, a narrative that ended with the complaint discussed earlier: "pero estaba viendo que no me encuentro con ningún dinero, y cómo lo vamos a hacer" (but I was thinking that I don't have any money, and how are we going to do it). Rather than providing the expected remittance-relevant response, Beto instead provided a minimal acknowledgment ("ah") before repeatedly asking what his uncle Fermín recommended, given his greater medical expertise. Unlike Luis's request to his mother for further information, this line of inquiry never led to a remittance response. Beto thus did not provide the second part of the adjacency pair, ultimately failing to treat his grandfather's complaint as a request and disrupting the expected interactional organization of the conversation.

On the one hand, the absence of the expected response might signal Beto's lack of experience with these communicative norms. Beto was a recent migrant at that time, and as he was adapting to life as a migrant, he also needed to learn the forms of communicative care work that corresponded to his new role within the family. Although he had grown up in a transnational family, his experience up until two months earlier had been as a nonmigrant who depended on the remittances his migrant father and uncle sent. Now in the role of economic provider, he had to learn how to hold up the other side of remittance conversations, and his response here potentially signals a lack of interdiscursive familiarity with this communicative role.

On the other hand, recall that in the Mejía family, requests for remittances were overwhelmingly made through reported complaints: while David's complaint was indeed embedded in a narrative, he did not use reported speech. Beto's persistent questioning, "¿qué dice mi tío?" (what does my uncle say?), may have attempted to elicit such a reported complaint from his grandfather. Rather than showing a lack of knowledge, his response may thus potentially reveal deep familiarity with his family's particular way of negotiating remittances. He seems less savvy, however, about the differentiated usage of reported speech within the family. Beto's questions suggest that his grandfather needs to reinforce his complaint by incorporating the voice of Fermín, his doctor son; David's refusal to provide the reported complaint relies on his status as an elder, one who does not need to shore up his request with other voices in the same way as those who are more subordinate within the gendered and generational hierarchy of the family.[15]

Ultimately, then, this conversational rupture involved communicative actions by both individuals: David did not produce a reported complaint, and Beto did not provide a remittance response. Moreover, this exchange ignored both the interactional structure of the adjacency pair and the interdiscursive norms that guided remittance conversations in this family.

Understanding this serious breach requires attending to recent changes in intergenerational care. Only two months earlier, Beto had been a dependent teenager, living under the care of his grandfather David. Beto's sudden migration radically altered their care relationship to one another: the grandson became a migrant remittance-sender in his own right. At the same time, because of his illness, David depended more than ever on migrant remittances. In the face of this health crisis, Beto was one of the family members with access to the financial resources necessary for medical care. But Beto's new care obligations toward his grandfather went beyond the economic: David's occupation of the "sick role" (Parsons 1951) placed Beto in the role of caregiver. This position came with responsibilities for his grandfather's well-being, requiring relational and affective work of the kind discussed in the birthday example. At the same time, Beto was understandably worried about his grandfather's ill health, and this anxiety manifested clearly in their conversations. Moreover, despite all of these changes, David was still Beto's grandfather, an elder to whom he owed respect and deference.

In this cross-border conversation, then, grandfather and grandson struggled to navigate complex intersecting changes to their intergenerational relationship. The communicative breakdown in this instance emerged precisely at the height of the discussion: the moment of the remittance request. This rupture of interactional and interdiscursive organization thus reflects changes in intergenerational care. On the basis of this example, then, it might seem that conversational temporalities are simply mirrors of longer timescales, such that life course transitions cause disruption in communicative norms.

However, exploring the consequences of this breakdown reveals that conversational temporalities do not simply reflect shifting intergenerational care, but rather can be actively used to manage these transitions. Later in the call, Beto passed the phone to his father, Luis, who talked to David (his own father). Just one minute into their conversation, David once again complained about being unable to pay for necessary medical tests, saying that he had already told his grandsons about this financial shortfall. "Decía yo a los cipotes, a tus hijos, que 'yo no tengo pisto,' le digo yo. 'Y a saber cómo vamos a hacer con todo esto'" (I told the boys, your sons, "I don't have money," I said. "And who knows how we are going to handle all this"). Notably, David refers to his grandsons not by name or by their relation to him but by their relationship to Luis: they are "tus hijos" (*your sons*). By subtly highlighting that the boys are Luis's responsibility as he recounts their lack of response, David delicately holds Luis accountable. Luis seems to accept this premise, as he responds by insistently asking his father which of his two sons he had spoken to. He then promises to send money. That weekend, just days after the call, Luis and his sons sent funds to El Salvador to cover the costs of David's medical tests.

Conversational temporalities do not simply reflect life course changes but rather can be deployed to navigate shifting relationships of obligation. David here utilized interdiscursivity in the form of reported speech by quoting his previous conversation with Beto. Not only did this report register his economic shortfall with Luis, but it also produced the normative reported complaint that was the first-pair part of the family's adjacency pair used to request remittances. Rather than quoting a gendered or generational subordinate, David simply quoted himself, maintaining kin hierarchies even as he complied with interdiscursive norms. Luis's response restored the expected interactional adjacency pair by promising to send money. In producing conversational norms, interdiscursivity can also be used to hold individuals accountable to particular ways of acting; thus in this example, David complains about his grandson's lack of appropriate response in ways that reinforce particular relationships of obligation across generations and across borders. Here, conversational temporalities are used to forge the relational ground from which transnational care emerges.

One final example from the same phone call underscores the consequentiality of interactional and interdiscursive temporalities for managing shifting intergenerational care across borders. Here we return to the example that introduced this book, an affectively laden conversation between Beto and David, which is now transcribed in greater detail in excerpt 4.2. This example

134 Living Together across Borders

Excerpt 4.2 Affective Complaint and Response

1.	David:	Hoy no salgo para ninguna parte. Ayer hubo jugada en el campo. No voy.	These days I don't go out at all. Yesterday there was a game at the soccer field. I don't go.
2.	Beto:	Ah.	Oh.
3.	David:	Vieras cuando salgo, ando un gran dolor de los pies. No puedo.	You should see when I go out, I have huge pain in my feet. I can't.
4.	Beto:	Dile a mi tía que lo lleve en la bicicleta.	Tell my aunt to take you on the bicycle.
5.	David:	Acaso puede @@@@	As if she could @@@@.
6.	Beto:	@@	@@

comes from the same conversation described above, and happened after the communicative breakdown in remittance negotiations and before Beto passed the phone to his father. Here David issues another kind of complaint, this one concerned with physical health and well-being rather than with economic concerns.

David here complains about the social isolation resulting from his illness. Beto's joking response is telling. He draws on understandings of gendered norms in village life, painting a patently absurd picture of his aunt giving his grandfather a ride on her bike. David affirms his grandson's humor through his incredulous response, and they laugh together. Their laughter lightens a heavy situation, providing a moment of levity and distraction in the face of ongoing contemplation of serious illness. This moment of shared laughter, what Duranti calls intersubjective attunement (Duranti and La Mattina 2022), is also an instantiation of connection between grandfather and grandson. Through joint laughter, they stitch together a relationship frayed by separation and by the challenges of negotiating intersecting life course transitions.

In the course of conversational trial and error, Beto and David have hit upon a new way of communicatively caring across borders. Just as economic complaints receive remittance responses, so too does David's complaint about well-being elicit a caring response. Beto's response demonstrates the power of interactional and interdiscursive temporality: the widespread adjacency pair in which a complaint is treated as a request for remittances perhaps shaped Beto's care-ful response to this affective complaint by his grandfather. David's lament revealed the sadness he was experiencing due to his isolation, and it was this feeling that Beto's joking attended to. Although he failed to respond appropriately to David's request for remittances, here Beto demonstrated his attentiveness to other kinds of familial care needs.

This communicative way of caring for his grandfather became a consequential discovery for Beto. In subsequent conversations with David, he regularly used humor to lighten David's mood, thereby nurturing their ongoing relationship. The interactional success of this new adjacency pair—affective complaint followed by a humorous response—led to the development of a new interdiscursive pattern that allowed grandfather and grandson to continue to enact care in the face of changing intergenerational needs. Such relational forms of communicative labor in turn laid the groundwork for ensuing remittance conversations in which Beto consistently provided remittance responses to reported complaints. This discovery of new forms of cross-border care was made possible by conversational temporalities. The interactional and interdiscursive organization of communication therefore serves as a key resource for navigating the sustained asymmetries and intergenerational changes of transnational care.

Conclusion

This chapter has focused on the cross-border communicative labor that underpins remittances. The examples presented here draw attention to behind-the-scenes communicative work that remains largely unexamined in existing scholarship but is nevertheless crucial to transnational family economies. Not only are individual remittance transfers made possible by this communication, but these conversations also work to maintain the relationships within which ongoing remittance conversations unfold, thereby sustaining cross-border *convivencia*. It is through everyday conversations that families both maintain asymmetrical cross-border care circuits and manage the consequences of sustained inequities for kin ties.

My analysis builds on existing scholarship that highlights how gendered and generational care norms shape remittance practices. The chapter demonstrates that remittance conversations are not simply concerned with material considerations but allow family members—in particular men— in both countries to carry out emotional labor that attends to their family relationships. However, communication does not straightforwardly equalize the gendered distribution of care labor; the most thankless communicative care is still often relegated to women, as seen in the conversations about David's birthday celebration. Moreover, responsibilities for remittance provision are clearly understood by reference to norms of asymmetrically reciprocal care over the life course. As they discuss remittances, families work out the significance of life events—migration, illness, marriages, employment changes, births, and deaths—for continued intergenerational care. Thus, it is through such everyday communication that gendered and generational divisions of care are navigated in transnational family life.

In addition to negotiating these kin hierarchies, however, remittance conversations also manage the sustained economic asymmetry of cross-border care circuits. The continued reliance of those in El Salvador on their migrant relatives places a strain on relational ties: migrants are constantly reminded of their material obligations, and their patience with this arrangement can begin to wear thin. Similarly, those in El Salvador recognize that their access to remittances depends on staying in the good graces of their migrant relatives. These conditions put a great deal of weight on communication, which must perform complex relational work with profound consequences for ongoing cross-border care. Through practices of communicative care, transnational families nurture cross-border relationships, sustaining kinship despite the geopolitical and economic forces that push them apart. At the same time, however, these very same conversational strategies reproduce borders between migrants and nonmigrants within the family, creating distinct communicative roles for each. As a result, in their cross-border conversations, relatives must constantly inhabit the roles of migrant and nonmigrant, even as they navigate shifting intergenerational care needs and gendered expectations, thereby bringing durative global inequities into the heart of family life.

Examining conversations about remittances thus provides crucial insights into how transnational families confront the temporalities of care. This chapter has suggested that conversational temporalities—the utterance-to-utterance flow of interaction and the conversation-to-conversation linking of interdiscursivity—serve as crucial resources for such negotiations. These forms of conversational organization support the development of communicative practices that insulate kin ties against the corrosive effects of sustained economic asymmetry. Interactional and interdiscursive temporalities must therefore be understood as important tools that provide both consistency and flexibility for responding to the challenges of transnational care. As families regularly negotiate remittances, they develop patterned communicative coping skills, building interactional adjacency pairs that, through interdiscursivity, become normative communicative practices. These interdiscursive patterns are not hard and fast rules; existing patterns can always give rise to new ways of communicating. The temporalities of conversation can provide a flexible space of experimentation in which new ways of enacting care are developed and explored. In fact, as the case of Beto and his grandfather reveals, it is ultimately through such conversational temporalities that families implicitly construct what it means to care as a migrant or as a nonmigrant, incorporating affective practices attuned to intergenerational relationships.

This chapter thus reveals that conversation is crucial for understanding the asymmetrical temporalities of care—whether across the familial life course, in trenchant gendered ideologies of care, or within durative political-economic systems. For it is in these communicative moments that life course transitions are made sense of, that gendered distributions of care are negotiated, and that the effects of political-economic inequity are navigated. A complete account of care must therefore attend to these conversational time scales and their vital role in confronting the temporalities and asymmetries of care.

5

Communicative Memory

Defying Institutional Forgetting through Remembering as Care

¿Se Acuerda Cuando . . . ?
(Do You Remember When . . . ?)

It was a chilly November morning in Elizabeth, New Jersey. Adán had gotten up early to make coffee and was now waiting for his brother, Beto, and father, Luis, to get ready before they would leave for work where they would spend much of the day outside in the cold replacing tires. To fill the time, Adán decided to call his grandfather David in El Salvador—they talked often and liked to joke around together. Adán's early-morning phone call woke his grandfather up, and Adán teased him, "¡tan tarde y durmiendo!" (so late and still sleeping!). David protested that it was only 5 a.m., and he had another half hour before he needed to get up.

This exchange prompted Adán to remember when David had been on the other side of such conversations. When his grandsons had lived in El Salvador, David would often have to roust the two teens out of bed in the early morning so they could finish the day's work in the cornfield before they had to go to school in the afternoon. "¿Se acuerda cuando . . . ?" (Do you remember when . . . ?) he asked David, shifting the spatial and temporal reference point of the conversation back to when they lived together in El Salvador. "¿Se acuerda cuando levantó a Beto con un guacal de agua?" (Do you remember when you woke Beto up with a bucket of water?). After a brief pause, David laughingly responded, providing more details about the incident. Beto, he said, had reported that some people who had seen him emerge from the house afterward "decían que andaba ya bañado en orín" (said that he had wet the bed). This addition led to uproarious laughter from both Adán and David that lasted for five seconds, a significant duration in conversational time.

In this conversation, grandfather and grandson reminisced together about the past, reliving experiences from a time when they used to live together rather than separated across borders. As they discursively developed this

Living Together Across Borders. Lynnette Arnold, Oxford University Press. © Oxford University Press 2024.
DOI: 10.1093/oso/9780197755730.003.0006

shared account of the past, they simultaneously engaged in a conversational encounter in the present that was filled with laughter, creating a moment of communicative *convivencia* (living-together). This chapter focuses on such moments of shared reminiscence, seeking to understand what remembering together across borders accomplishes for transnational families.

As this book has so far demonstrated, remembering and forgetting are weighted with significance for transnational Salvadoran families. Memory is the linchpin of state-endorsed discourses of migration and family care in El Salvador. As Chapter 1 argues, these imaginaries depict migration as a rupture in familial care relations that creates divisions between migrants and their economically dependent nonmigrant relatives. Salvadoran migrants who remember their families are celebrated as national heroes, but the specter of the selfish migrant who has forgotten his family haunts this imaginary. These figurations of migration and family care mobilize memory, not as an internal psychological phenomenon but rather as an observable and highly consequential social action. The dedication of the migrant who remembers is demonstrated by the care he continually enacts toward his family back home, primarily in the form of consistent remittances and regular communication. This ongoing care, however, is perpetually threatened by the possibility of forgetting, which occurs when migrants become corrupted by the materialism of the United States, turning into selfish individuals who no longer remember their obligations to loved ones back home.

In the face of this dominant discourse that turns forgetting into a constant threat, transnational families have developed practices of collective remembering that are woven into cross-border care. Chapter 3 describes video greetings sent to the United States by relatives in El Salvador, demonstrating that these *saludos* prioritize those migrants who most remember their family, as demonstrated through their remittances. At the same time, these greetings remind migrants of their family ties and implicitly urge them not to forget their care obligations to those who remain behind. In addition, the indirect strategies families have developed for negotiating remittances also rely on memory, as described in Chapter 4. When migrants offer to send money in response to narratives of complaint articulated by their relatives back home, they demonstrate through their attentiveness to such indirect requests that they continue to remember their family. These practices implicitly resist narratives of inevitable migrant forgetting, instead reproducing social relations undergirded by continued collective remembering. Through these practices, transnational families envision and enact memory as the bedrock upon which asymmetrically reciprocal relationships of obligation are built and sustained across borders.

140   Living Together across Borders

To better understand the role of remembering in transnational family life, this chapter situates reminiscences like Adán and David's within their broader historical and cultural context. Specifically, I trace Salvadoran theorizations of memory that emerge in communicative memory practices, or repeated ways of using language to enact remembering. I begin by examining the role of naming in Salvadoran struggles for *memoria histórica* (historical memory) that make visible histories of violence and seek justice for victims. I then turn to meaning-making practices in Salvadoran traditions of Día de los Difuntos (Day of the Dead). Both cases demonstrate an understanding of remembering as a powerful collective social action that can resist forgetting. Moreover, attending specifically to communicative memory practices reveals remembering as a form of care that forges and sustains social relations. This grounded theorization of memory helps to elucidate the consequences of remembering together in cross-border phone calls. I ultimately suggest that for Salvadorans, communicative memory practices make meaning from the past in ways that work to suture a social fabric torn by violence, by war, and by transnational separation.

Institutional Forgetting and the Struggle for Memory

Silence about the past is a powerful force in El Salvador, woven into the weft of national imaginaries and shored up by institutional forgetting (Abrego 2017). In the face of the country's history of violence and dispossession, beginning with colonization and the theft of indigenous lands, state institutions have worked to erase and silence memories of past trauma. In 1932, when the military responded to a peasant uprising with a massacre that left tens of thousands of indigenous *campesinos* dead, these events were erased from official records and silenced (Gould and Lauria-Santiago 2008). Although memories of "La Matanza" (The Slaughter) would live on in individual and family trauma (Lovato 2020), it wasn't until sixty years later that the details of this violence began to be publicly discussed and investigated. This institutional forgetting is also at work in more recent silences about atrocities committed during the country's decade-long civil war. The UN-brokered peace accords that in 1992 put an end to the conflict included a general amnesty, establishing a postwar Salvadoran society constituted on the basis of institutionally mandated forgetting, rather than on processes of truth and reconciliation (Rivas Hernández 2016).

In the face of such deafening institutional silences, the consequences of memory are often negotiated in the court of public opinion in El Salvador

(Ching 2016). Partial accounts of past violence, rife with strategic forgetting, are mobilized to serve a range of political projects. For instance, dominant understandings of La Matanza focus on the role of communist organizing among peasants as the primary causal element. Such accounts were then mobilized to explain the civil war, allowing the right to portray themselves as defenders of democracy and the left to position guerrilla struggle as the vanguard protecting the interests of the people (Lindo-Fuentes, Ching, and Lara-Martínez, 2007). After the civil war, memories of wartime violence have become the interpretive framework by which Salvadorans understand continued violence. By comparison to the political violence of wartime, current "common" violence is seen as less predictable, and thus worse than the war (Moodie 2010).

Moreover, the consequences of these silences extend beyond the borders of the nation. When asked about the causes of widespread emigration, Salvadorans inevitably point to the violence of the war as the trigger that started the mass exodus that continues to this day (Anastario 2019). And yet, the reception of those fleeing violence in the United States silenced this knowledge by refusing to recognize Salvadorans as refugees, a refusal motivated by US support of the Salvadoran military. Today, the silence shaping past immigration policy has engendered collective amnesia within the United States that generates ongoing support for the continued criminalization and dehumanization of the Salvadoran diaspora (Abrego 2017).

Institutional forgetting is often accompanied by interpersonal forms of collective forgetting. During the civil war, remaining silent about violence observed or experienced was a survival strategy, one that refugees carried with them in their new lives outside El Salvador in order to protect their loved ones from traumatic memories (Cárcamo 2013, Lovato 2020). For rural populations who bore the brunt of the war's violence, practices of silence and intergenerational forgetting "permit survivors of violence to remake their everyday lives, particularly when justice is inaccessible" (Anastario 2019, 97).

However, not all survivors have chosen silence. Some have come together in organizations that work to uncover hidden truths about wartime violence, efforts directed toward the pursuit of justice for victims and survivors. These efforts often center on safeguarding and promoting *memoria histórica*, which is utilized throughout Latin America as a collective framework for confronting the consequences of past violence and seeking justice (Febres 2010). *Memoria histórica* works to counter the projects of forgetting that sustain a US-dominated regional system (Menjívar and Rodriguez 2005), and is grounded in the experiences of Latin American communities that have suffered the effects of violence. In El Salvador, as throughout Latin America, women are at the forefront of this movement, often mobilizing their moral authority as mothers to call the state to accountability for its violence (Bejarano 2002).

As a result of the consistent efforts of civil society organizations, in 2016, the Salvadoran Supreme Court overturned the 1992 "National Reconciliation Law" (Legislative Decree 147) (Malkin and Palumbo 2016). Originally enacted in 1992, just a week after the signing of the Peace Accords, this law mandated institutional forgetting by creating a broad amnesty for wartime violence. As part of the 2016 judicial decision, the legislative assembly was tasked with creating a new law for responding to war crimes, but a proposal they passed in 2020 was strongly opposed by civil society organizations, and was ultimately vetoed by President Bukele (Velásquez 2021). In October 2021, these community organizations presented their own transitional justice proposal that would center justice for victims, arguing that without such a law on the books, war crimes would remain in impunity (ARPAS 2021; MCIES 2020). But as of December 2023, the Commission on Justice and Human Rights of the legislative assembly, charged with studying this proposal, has made no progress in doing so or in developing a new proposal, despite continued community pressure (García 2023). Indeed, although the 2016 court decision allowed for the first trials of wartime crimes on Salvadoran soil, efforts to convict the intellectual authors of this violence remain stalled due to interference by powerful institutions and individuals opposed to justice (Chacón Serrano et al. 2021; Cornejo 2023; *Prensa Latina* 2023). Even as silences about past violence are being broken in El Salvador, and partial truths are being challenged by the accounts of survivors, the forces that have long sustained institutional forgetting remain strong.

Remembering has thus always been a political act in El Salvador. Struggles for *memoria histórica* and postwar justice mobilize collective memory or "knowledge about the past that is shared, mutually acknowledged, and reinforced by a collectivity" (Savelsberg and King 2007, 191). For Salvadoran survivors of violence, as for subjugated groups around the world, collective memory is mobilized as a resource for resisting marginalization by claiming a "right to historicity" (Trouillot 1991, 19). The use of memory as resistance is thus not unique to El Salvador. However, this chapter suggests that attending closely to how Salvadorans use communicative memory practices reveals that remembering enacts a more subtle but nevertheless consequential form of resistance that actively repairs social ties through the continued labor of care.

Naming the Dead to Preserve *Memoria Histórica*

As it is enacted in Salvadoran struggles for justice, *memoria histórica* understands memory not primarily as an internal individual experience but rather as a powerful form of political and collective social action. *Memoria histórica* insists that "the past is not history."[1] Rather, memories of the past are collectively produced in the present, to address current concerns, and to shape future directions (DeLugan 2019). As demonstrated in a recent special issue of the journal *Realidad* (Lara Martínez 2019), research in El Salvador has consistently highlighted the discursive dimensions of *memoria histórica*. Especially for rural communities which, like Cantón El Río, were resettled after the war, discourses of *memoria histórica* serve as vital tools for organizing community life and enacting participatory local politics (Alas 2019; Lara Martínez 2018; Silber 2011, 2022). Within such communities, the discursive work of *memoria historica* is socialized across generations, so that those born after the war nevertheless mobilize collective memories of the war in their life history narratives, using these to take up political and ethical stances (Chacón Serrano 2020). And just as silences about the war travel transnationally, so do discourses of *memoria histórica*, inspiring new generations of Salvadoran American scholars (Abrego 2017) as well as the emergence of organizations like Our Parents' Bones (https://ourparentsbones.com/). Led by Salvadoran Americans whose parents were disappeared during the civil war, this group is based on the belief that "only when we tell our stories and lift up models of truth and reconciliation, will we be able to resurrect our collective historical memory and heal our collective trauma" (Our Parents' Bones 2014). The centrality of discourse to *memoria histórica* is clear here; telling stories about the past is key to healing shared trauma.

In this chapter, I draw on such scholarship on Salvadoran *memoria histórica* to highlight the consequentiality of the discursive aspects of memory work, doing so by understanding communicative memory practices as crucial forms of social action. With this analytical approach, I bring together different types of communicative memory work, moving from the more ritualized practices often discussed in existing scholarship to less examined forms of everyday reminiscing such as the conversation between Adán and his grandfather. I suggest that drawing out the grounded theory of memory that is enacted by ritualized practices can shed new light on the consequences of transnational conversations that may otherwise be dismissed as mundane and unimportant.

I begin by focusing on a communicative practice that is central to *memoria histórica*: naming the victims of violence. Ricouer suggests that "forgetting boils down to a forgetting of the victims. It then becomes the task of memory to correct this systematic forgetting" (Ricoeur 2011, 480). Naming is one way to counter such silences. Remembering the names of the victims of the war was a crucial goal of civil society groups whose decade-long struggle resulted in the inauguration of the *Monumento a la Memoria y la Verdad* (Monument to Memory and Truth) in 2003. This eighty-five-foot, black granite wall,

144   Living Together across Borders

located in Parque Cuscatlán in the center of San Salvador, is inscribed with the names of more than 25,000 civilian victims of the war, a fraction of the 75,000 lives lost in the conflict. The monument also bears an inscription dedicated to the anonymous victims of the war (RM 2009). Below an image of a cornfield with two faces superimposed, the inscription reads "A ellos y a ellas está dedicado este espacio, como homenaje de respeto y admiración. Su nombre es patria" (This space is dedicated to them, as an homage of respect and admiration. Their name is homeland). Although individual names are missing, these lives lost to war are collectively christened "homeland"; in so doing, naming converts anonymous deaths into a representation of the nation as a whole. This identification of nameless victims and the monument itself constitute a public act of remembering; through naming, war victims are reanimated, their lives made to speak as evidence of violence that must be accounted for. Their deaths are thus given meaning as evidence of the need for postwar justice that counteracts institutional forgetting.

The victims of wartime violence are also named on other occasions, particularly in gatherings held to commemorate the assassinations of prominent religious figures. For instance, an annual vigil held at the Jesuit Universidad Centroamericana commemorates the assassination of six Jesuit priests and their two Salvadoran housekeepers on November 16, 1989. The vigil begins with a candlelit procession in which participants carry small crosses made from wood or cardboard, each cross inscribed with the name of an individual who died in the civil war. Such commemorations expand the communicative work of the monument; not only do they increase the visibility of the lives lost to war, but they also make this act of remembering more collective, shared by every participant who carries an inscribed cross. When I attended this vigil, I wondered about the person whose name I was carrying: who were they in life? When and where and why were they killed? Who were the loved ones they left behind? Carrying this cross made the violence of the civil war much more present by connecting it with a specific victim.

Through my involvement with Cantón El Río's church choir, I attended many such commemorative gatherings over the years that I spent in El Salvador. I repeatedly noticed a widespread practice of naming: the ritual of *los presentes* (those who are present). One by one, a speaker reads aloud the names of those who have died, and the crowd responds after each name with shouts of ¡*Presente!* (present). "Monseñor Romero—¡Presente! Padre Octavio Ortiz—¡Presente! Hermana Silvia Arriola—¡Presente!" As with the monument, even those whose names were not known could be brought into presence through this ritual. On one occasion, the choir attended a religious service at a neighboring rural community, where a mass grave had recently been discovered, providing evidence of a wartime massacre that had been institutionally silenced and forgotten. Exhumation had just been completed and none of the victims had yet been identified. But the number of bodies of children, women, and men were read out, to responses of "¡Presentes!" shouted by *campesino* survivors of violence, often with tears running down their faces. Name upon name, death upon death, the ritual of *los presentes* insists on remembering the cost of the war and the lives lost to violence. For those who participate in this ritual, hearing and responding to these names are communicative actions that quite literally break the silence of institutionalized forgetting through collective cries of *¡Presente!*

Naming as a practice of *memoria histórica* turns remembering into a collective form of resistance through communication. The crucial actions of speaking, inscribing, hearing, and reading the names of the dead function as acts of remembering. Through naming, their lives are made meaningful, their deaths lifted up as consequential, not only for understanding the past, but also for building a nation founded on justice. Naming resists projects of institutionalized forgetting, but at the same time, it also forges social relations, building the connections needed to fuel ongoing struggles. Walking and chanting in unison binds participants as they quite literally act together. These communicative practices forge the collective action necessary for shared justice struggles. As these rituals nourish the collective strength of survivors, movements for justice are simultaneously supported through the palpable presence of the deceased who have been summoned through the collective voicing of their names.

Thus, it is precisely the communicative dimensions of naming that allow this practice to serve as a form of care that nurtures the social relations undergirding all struggles for collective memory. Indeed, scholars of language and social life contend that close attention to meaning-making practices is crucial for understanding the social function of memory (French 2012; Lempert and Perrino 2007; Wertsch 2009). This is particularly true for socially marginalized groups, as Mendoza Denton (2008b) demonstrates in her work on memorialization among gang-affiliated Latina youth. She shows how these young women use communicative practices—specifically, the creation of poems and drawings that are circulated through their social networks—to construct a shared past that upholds and sustains their collective identity in the face of continual persecution by school and societal authorities. Attention to communicative dimensions of memory work is therefore crucial to understanding how remembering as care becomes a consequential form of social action. For Salvadorans, communicative memory practices are central to the ways that remembering resists institutional forgetting and participates in struggles for justice.

Making Meaning in *Día de los Difuntos* Rituals

The importance of remembering as communicative care can also be seen in a less immediately political domain, that of traditions around the Day of the Dead, celebrated every November 2 and known in El Salvador as el Día de los Difuntos. Like its counterparts in other Latin American countries, the contemporary celebration of this holiday emerged from a syncretic blending of Catholic doctrine and local indigenous traditions. In El Salvador, families travel across the country to get to the cemeteries where their loved ones are interred, bringing with them bouquets and wreaths for the graves, as well as candles in glass jars often bearing images of religious figures. Women generally take the lead in organizing these preparations, as well as in carrying out the hard work of cleaning the graves. This is a laborious process particularly in rural areas, where cleaning involves using a machete to cut back weeds and vines that have run rampant during the rainy season that is just drawing to a close. Then the cement structures of the sepultures themselves must be washed to get rid of dirt and cobwebs, often using water carried in from relatives' homes in large jugs balanced on heads and shoulders. In some years, new paint is applied to refresh the façade. Only once this work has been completed does the family put flowers on the graves of their loved ones, light the candles they have brought, and say prayers for their spirits.

Previous linguistic anthropological scholarship has demonstrated that the ritual practices associated with the Day of the Dead in Latin America constitute powerful social actions that can be taken up by local communities to advance social change and political critique (Faudree 2013, 2015). Like practices of *memoria histórica*, these traditions understand remembering not primarily as an act of internal reflection, but rather as collective social action. In El Salvador, the emphasis is on the publicly visible actions of cleaning and *enflorando* (decorating with flowers). In these labor-intensive traditions, remembering loved ones involves embodied practices of care through which relatives tend to the memory of their loved ones. Unlike the naming rituals discussed above, these practices are less obviously communicative. However, cleaning and *enflorando* produce changes in the material world that are consistently treated as signs from which meaning can be read. A sepulture that has been cleaned of weeds, washed, and covered with flowers and candles signifies remembrance of the living for their relatives who have passed on. By contrast, untended graves become signs of forgetting, of relatives who do not care for their dead, of ruptured familial relations. Thus, the traditions associated with Día de los Difuntos are treated as meaning-making memory practices that communicate about the past and present realities of family care.

The communicative dimensions of these practices are particularly clear within transnational families. Migrants regularly designated a portion of their remittances in late October to be used by their relatives for purchasing candles and flowers when they went to *enflorar*. In El Salvador, remittances are generally understood as a sign of migrants' continued remembrance of their relatives (Chapter 1), and in Día de los Difuntos, this memory work was extended to include those loved ones who had passed away. Migrant remittances could be used to purchase more elaborate and durable flower arrangements made of paper and plastic. These flowers, when left at graves, served as signs of transnational remembrance and care, as compared with the live flowers that were cut from flowering shrubs and gardens by those with fewer resources. Migrants were attuned to the meaning-making potential of flower arrangements, and often discussed extensively with nonmigrant relatives which flowers should be purchased. Through these conversations, they sought to ensure that these arrangements would appropriately materialize their remembrance of and care for the deceased. For their part, nonmigrants regularly documented their efforts to care for the memory of the dead by taking photos or videos of the tomb once their labors were complete. These images were then sent to migrant kin, making visible the remembrance of their relatives in El Salvador and their adequate use of migrant remittances. Such images were also sometimes posted more publicly on social media by both migrants and nonmigrants, amplifying the communicative reach of these signs.

For transnational families, then, celebrating Día de los Difuntos involved the combination and layering of distinct communicative practices—sending remittances, cleaning, *enflorando*, and taking and circulating pictures—each of which signified memory and care for the dead. Moreover, this joint production of cross-border remembering had crucial consequences for cross-border kin ties. Just as the gang-affiliated youth in the study by Mendoza Denton (2008a) used communicative memory practices to produce a shared identity in the face of discrimination, so too the communicative memory practices of Dia de los Difuntos served as a collective project through which transnational families could forge belonging across borders. Through these actions, both migrants and nonmigrants demonstrated their memory and care for the family, working together to combat political-economic and discursive forces that produced fissures between migrants and nonmigrants. The memory practices of Día de los Difuntos become an opportunity for reconstituting ties to a shared past that simultaneously reinforces connections across borders, thereby serving as relational care.

My understanding of these traditions as communicative care emerged from events I observed within the Portillo family. Magda, a migrant living in

148   Living Together across Borders

Los Angeles, was not sure that her siblings in El Salvador would care for her mother's tomb. She refused to send remittances to pay for flowers, as previous experience had led her to believe that her siblings would not spend the money as she requested. Instead, she purchased and lit a candle in memory of her mother, but she still worried. A few days later, her husband Francisco called his mother, Olivia, in El Salvador, who recounted how the family had gone to clean and *enflorar* the tomb of her mother, his grandmother. He asked whether she had seen anyone attending to the grave of Magda's mother, buried in the same cemetery. Someone had gone, she reported, because there were flowers on the grave, but the tomb had not been cleaned. She emphasized the limits of the memory work done by Magda's siblings. "Solo un ramo de flores" (just one bouquet) she said. "Solo habían ido a dejarlo quizás" (maybe they just went to drop it off), since there was no evidence of greater care in cleaning, candles, or prayer. The state of the grave was thus read as a sign of insufficient care for the deceased and of fragmented familial ties.

Concerned by this report, Francisco recounted that, although she was far away, his wife had lit a candle for her mother. Olivia reassured him, saying, "Si prende una candela, uno encomienda todas las ánimas a Papá Chus" (If one lights a candle, one entrusts all souls to Jesus).[2] Continuing in her reassurances, Olivia articulated the consequences of memory.

> Ellos ya no están en esta tierra, pero en la persona de uno siempre viven. Porque en la mentalidad de uno, las personas nunca, durante uno esté vivo, siempre existen, viven. . . . Mi mamá siempre vive en el corazón de nosotros. Y en la presencia de la memoria de nosotros, mi mamá siempre vive.
>
> (They are no longer on this earth, but they are always alive in one's self. Because in your mind, people never, as long as you are alive, they always exist, they live. . . . My mom always lives in our hearts. And in the presence of our memory, my mom always lives.)

Olivia's words underscore the full significance of remembering. Practices of cleaning and *enflorando* and lighting candles maintain connections with deceased loved ones: those who have passed away will remain with those who remember them. Memory here sustains ties, breathing life into social relations that might otherwise seem to have ended. Remembering as care has power that can overcome even the seemingly final end to social life brought by death.

Like the communicative memory practices of *memoria histórica*, then, the traditions of Día de los Difuntos turn remembering into care that produces and nurtures social relations. Through these traditions, remembering is understood and enacted as a consequential form of social action that can forge relational ties even beyond death. Given the long history of violence in El Salvador, this relational dimension of remembering serves as a potent—but often unrecognized—form of resistance. Memory as collective communicative labor resists the silences of institutional forgetting and heals the seemingly irreversible social ruptures of death. In light of these powerful functions of communicative memory practices in El Salvador, we might then ask: what is it that remembering keeps alive for transnational families? How might it serve as a form of resistance for them? To answer these questions, I turn now to an exploration of transnational conversations in which families reminisce together about the past.

Remembering Together across Borders

Just as institutionalized silences threaten remembrance of past violence, forgetting is seen as a constant threat for transnational families in El Salvador. Migration—like death—is understood as a source of social rupture. Dominant discourses suggest that migrants will forget their families back home upon arrival to the United States. In this context, remembering becomes a charged communicative practice, carrying a great deal of significance, even when the topics being discussed seem quite trivial.

Let us return to where we began the chapter, with Adán and David reminiscing together about a humorous incident that happened before they were separated by migration. In this conversation, grandfather and grandson engaged in joint remembering, a communicative practice in which individuals collaboratively reminisce about the past. Research has demonstrated that joint remembering is often structured by the needs and purpose of ongoing talk in the present moment (Bietti 2010; Edwards and Middleton 1986; Fivush and Hudson 1990; Middleton and Edwards 1990; Middleton 1997). Reminiscing often carries out important relational work and tends to privilege emotional responses over chronologically focused accounts (Edwards and Middleton 1986). As with struggles for *memoria histórica* in El Salvador, joint remembering reveals that memory is never just about the past, but has implications for the current moment while also shaping future possibilities through the social relations it forges.

The centrality of affect to remembering is clear in David and Adán's conversation. Laughter threaded through their words, sometimes bubbling up in short chuckles that layered over speech, and at other times erupting in extended shared laughter. Remembering together allowed grandfather and grandson to bond, creating a space for affective connection that brought them

150 Living Together across Borders

together despite the miles and months that separated them. Joint remembering here became a means of nurturing relationships and bridging transnational separation. Remembering the past (re)produced ties in the immediate conversational moment, forging closeness that strengthened the connections between grandfather and grandson and carried their relationship into the future.

Existing scholarship highlights the role of memory in constructing and maintaining cross-border communities (Fortier 2000; Goldring 1996; Halilovich 2013; Maj and Riha 2009), revealing how discursive practices like narrative are crucial to transnational remembering (Bauer and Thompson 2004; Bletzer 2013; Chamberlain and Leydesdorff 2004; Watkins 1999). Here, I focus on the collaborative communication involved in joint remembering, suggesting that in these instances, memory becomes a resource for cross-border care. To understand how this communicative memory practice functions requires attending closely to the specific discursive strategies through which shared remembrances are collaboratively constructed. This analysis reveals how remembering is put to work as a resource for care that nurtures and sustains family relationships, even as it resists dominant narratives that depict transnational ties in ways that actively harm cross-border connections.

Connecting Past and Present through Stance Alignment

Adán's conversation with his grandfather did not end with remembering the past. Rather, their collaboratively produced reminiscence was explicitly brought into the immediate moment. Right after their laughter, once he had caught his breath, Adán again shifted the temporal and spatial reference of the conversation, this time through the place adverb *aquí* (here). This is a deictic term that points to his location in the United States, bringing grandfather and grandson back from the memory of past co-presence into the current here-and-now of cross-border separation. "Aquí, si no me levanto yo, no se levanta él tampoco" (Here, if I don't get up, he doesn't get up either), Adán tells his grandfather. As the eldest brother, he must get up first, a responsibility evidenced in the fact of this early-morning phone call itself: Adán got up before Beto to make them coffee, and thus had time to call his grandfather while waiting for his brother to get ready for work. Here, Adán draws a parallel from the past to the present, making their memory of the water-bucket incident relevant for understanding their experience of transnational kinship.

Communicative Memory   151

Excerpt 5.1 Así es él (*That's How He Is*)

1.	Adán:	Aquí, si no me levanto yo, no se [levanta] él tampoco.	Here, if I don't get up, he doesn't [get up] either.
2.	David:	[@@]	[@@]
3.		Sí vos@. **Así** es él, @@@	Yes you@. He's like that, @@@
4.	Adán:	**Sí.** [Si]-	Yes. [If]-
5.	David:	[dor]milón. @@	[slee]pyhead. @@
6.	Adán:	Es burro. [@@@@]@	He's stubborn. [@@@@]@
7.	David:	[**Así** es]. @@@@	[That's how he is]. @@@@
8.	Adán:	**Sí.**	Yes.

This spatiotemporal shift would seem to end the possibility of grandfather and grandson constructing an account together. David had never visited his grandsons in the United States, and thus would seem to have no information to add to a discussion of Adán and Beto's life there. And yet, as shown in Excerpt 5.1, their conversation about the present continues and expands the discursive collaboration seen in their joint remembering. David agrees with Adán's statement, a claim that is not based on firsthand knowledge of his grandsons' lives in the United States but rather, on deep knowledge of Beto himself: "así es él" (that's the way he is). David suggests that Beto continues to be the same person he was before he migrated, using the present tense to indicate that his knowledge of his younger grandson is current information. Through this contribution, David cements the parallel between past and present that Adán has initiated, confirming that memory of the past is relevant to their current reality.

Moreover, in collaboratively constructing this conversational bridge from past to present, David and Adán continue to forge connection with one another. In under ten seconds, grandfather and grandson use no less than five explicit markers of agreement (*sí*—"yes" and its adverbial form *así*, all bolded in Excerpt 5.1), each concurring with the statements made by the other. In this short stretch, David and Adán work and rework a strong discursive alignment in which they position themselves as agreeing in their evaluation of Beto.

The analytical tool of stance can help to unpack how this alignment is built through their talk. In conversation, participants take a stance when they describe an object, person, or experience in a way that expresses their relationship or attitude to whatever is being evaluated (Englebretson 2007; Kockelman 2004; Jaffe 2012). Here, Adán and David both evaluate Beto, describing him as a stubborn sleepyhead, the kind of person who has a hard time getting up in the morning. But these stances are not just about Beto. Rather, when each one evaluates Beto, they are also evaluating their interlocutor's stance toward him. In this case, they take stances of strong alignment, concurring over and over again, that despite his migration, Beto has not changed, and remains the kind of person who has a hard time getting up in the morning. Stance-taking is thus an important resource for communicatively building intersubjective relations (Du Bois 2007).

Thinking through the lens of stance reveals the consequentiality of this conversation in new ways. While joint remembering here clearly does relational work that nurtures the bond between Adán and his grandfather, it also has more profound implications for their current reality of cross-border life. By aligning their stances, grandfather and grandson collaboratively build discursive linkages across the space and time of transnational separation. The past can be used to understand the present because Beto has remained the same despite migration. The repetitive alignments of grandfather and grandson here insist on continuities rather than change, pushing back against the dominant understanding of migration as a rupture that fundamentally changes migrants and thus their relationships with their family. The conversational engagements of grandfather and grandson here thus serve as interactional resistance that insists on the continuity of family life despite migration. Through remembering, they not only care for their personal relationship but also for the continuity of family life from past premigration times into the present reality of cross-border separation.

Motivations for Remembering

The consequentiality of joint remembering as a form of resistance against negative stereotypes of migrants is underscored by a consistent pattern: recent migrants—those who had been in the United States for shorter periods of time—initiated the vast majority of such instances. While in their conversation, both David and Adán participate in the joint remembering, it was Adán, the recent migrant, who launched their reminiscences. Moreover, engagements in joint remembering did not display the gendered division that shaped the distribution of many forms of communicative care. That is, both men and women recent migrants initiated this highly affective form of communicative labor, although as this chapter shows, they tended to do so primarily with same-gender interlocutors. Perhaps such same-gender conversations provided greater interactional insulation for the deeply affective work of joint remembering. Why was it that young recent migrants—rather than their nonmigrant relatives or indeed their more established migrant counterparts—were the ones to most consistently initiate remembering?

One might be tempted to think that this simply comes down to the fact that new migrants had more recent memories of El Salvador than their more established counterparts who had been in the United States for at least a decade. It may thus have been easier for them to recall incidents—like the water-bucket wake-up call—that could launch collaborative reminiscences. But of course, people often remember salient interactions like this one for decades. And migrants who had been separated from their families for long periods of time might arguably come to rely more on such stand-out memories. Clearly, more complex answers are needed.

One such resolution emerged in an interview I conducted with Adán and Beto less than six months after their arrival in the United States. Recall from the "Introduction" that in this interview Beto stated: "Recién venido, como que a uno le daba desesperación por estar allá, por convivir con ellos" (Recently arrived, it was like you were desperate to be there, to live together with them). The expressed desire to *convivir* (live together) with family back home signals a yearning to once again participate with loved ones in El Salvador in the care practices of everyday life: working together, eating together, spending time together. Underlying this desire is an idealization of former *convivencia* that ignores the fact that Beto used to regularly complain about his life together with his grandparents before he migrated (see Chapter 2).

I asked Beto if phone conversations with relatives in El Salvador helped with this longing, and building on the statement quoted in the Introduction, he reported:

> Sí ayudaba en algo porque estábamos hablando y teníamos la comunicación. Se sentía uno ya relajado, cuando uno se recordaba de lo pasado, las cosas buenas que vivió allá.
>
> (It did help somewhat because we were talking and we had communication. You felt relaxed then, when you remembered the past, the good things that one lived there.)

So, while communication helped in some way to assuage this longing, remembering together in conversation was especially restorative, particularly when such reminiscing focused on happy memories. This perspective puts the stance alignment of David and Adán's conversation in a new light. It is not simply that conversation allows separated families to remember what it was like to live together. Rather, for these transnational families, remembering together becomes a form of *convivencia,* a way of living-together with distant loved ones, even if only in the interactional time of conversation. The closeness forged through such communicative exchanges becomes increasingly significant, as it must stand in for the *convivencia* that co-present families build by living-together every day. As Beto states, recent migrants may feel the loss of former *convivencia* more intensely than their more established counterparts, and may therefore more actively seek out conversational forms of living-together such as joint remembering. From this perspective, the idealization of life before migration can be understood not simply as a result of nostalgia, but rather as a means to communicatively enact *convivencia* to bridge separation.

However, recent migrants not only have a unique experiential relationship to migration processes; they also are positioned differently within dominant Salvadoran imaginaries of transnational family care. Recall the figure of the *migrante desobligado* (the selfish migrant) who shadows the footsteps of the heroic migrant in Salvadoran migration discourse. In this imaginary, migrants are expected to become corrupted by the allure of easy money into forgetting their families. The actions of recent migrants are thus subject to heightened scrutiny, with nonmigrant relatives readily interpreting their actions as revealing this expected change. In other words, this imaginary puts recent migrants in the position of constantly having to demonstrate that they have not changed, that they remain the same family-oriented individuals they were when they lived in El Salvador. The recent migrants in my study were well aware of these imaginaries: all of them had grown up in families where fathers or older brothers had already migrated. Dominant discourses about migration and family care had thus necessarily shaped their own understanding of the implications of migration, imaginaries that they brought with them when they themselves became migrants.

Under these conditions, the practice of joint remembering provides recent migrants with a key resource through which to resist the implications of this dominant imaginary of migration and family care. What better way to demonstrate that you remain committed to family connection than by initiating reminiscences of former experiences of *convivencia*? Through joint remembering, recent migrants opened up conversational spaces within which to continually develop relational ties to loved ones back home, demonstrating their ongoing dedication to and belonging in the family. Stance alignment in instances of joint remembering was thus a powerful care practice through which relatives separated across borders could nurture their relationships and collectively forge understandings of transnational family life that pushed back against dominant imaginaries that made family disintegration seem an almost inevitable consequence of migration.

Dialogic *Convivencia* and Imagined Togetherness

So far, we have seen how joint remembering mobilizes the past to do crucial work in the present moment of cross-border conversations. However, in addition to creating connections between the past and the present moment, joint remembering could also be used as the ground upon which imagined scenarios of family togetherness could be built. These discursively created alternative realities that consequentially shaped ongoing cross-border relationships.

For instance, consider this phone call between a recent migrant, Serena Portillo, and her older sister Perla. In their conversation, Perla complained about having spent all weekend washing her three children's clothes, a labor-intensive process that involved scrubbing and rinsing each item by hand, and then hanging them to dry. Serena responded to her sister saying "como ya ves que ya no estoy yo para ayudarte" (now you see I am no longer there to help you), but then broke into peals of laughter, signaling that her statement had been a joke. And indeed, her sister joined in this extended laughter, suggesting that even if Serena had remained in El Salvador, she likely would not have been participating in this form of care work. Perhaps inspired by this counterfactual claim, Perla then launched into an imagined account of her own, one in which she envisioned her sister remaining involved in family life in El Salvador in a different way.

> Así dije yo hoy a mi mami. "Estuviera la Serena," le digo yo,
> "solo jugando con la Ursulina pasara," le dije. "Como ella decía," le digo yo, "que si era niña la iba a cuidar, pero si era niño no." Y de allí mi mami, "Sí. Ella feliz pasara," me dice ella, "tirado hasta allí en el piso con ella."
>
> (That's what I said to my mom today. "If Serena were here," I tell her, "she would just play with Ursulina," I told her. "Because she used to say," I tell her, "that if it was a girl, she would take care of her, but if it was a boy, she wouldn't." And then my mom says, "Yes. She would be happy," she tells me, "even down on the ground with her.")

If Serena had not migrated, Perla suggests, she would spend her time playing with her niece Ursulina. Perla had been pregnant with Ursulina when Serena had migrated. She only knew her two-year-old niece through photos and had, in fact, never had the opportunity to play with her as Perla imagines here.

This hypothetical scenario is grounded in the past in two ways. Firstly, Perla presents the account to Serena as a report of a recent conversation between herself and their mother, Olivia. This account of a previous family conversation in El Salvador supports the imagined scenario the sisters construct. In addition, this imagined togetherness is figured as emerging from the sisters' shared experiences, as Perla cites Serena's expression of gender preference

156 Living Together across Borders

Table 5.1 Diagraph of Serena and Perla's Conversation

	Speaker		Utterances				
1.	Perla		solo	jugando	con	la Ursulina	pasara	
2.	Serena		solo		con	ella	pasara	
3.	Perla (voicing Olivia)	ella feliz		{tirado hasta allí en el piso}	{con	ella}	pasara	
4.	Serena		solo	jugando	{con	ella}	pasara	{de seguro}

during Perla's pregnancy. Although Perla did indeed give birth to the girl that Serena so desired, in the current situation of cross-border separation, Serena has not been able to get to know her little niece. By tying the memory of this more distant past conversation into the hypothetical scenario she is constructing, Perla extends the basis of this imagined togetherness back into the time when the family lived together. Both recent and more distant past are used to anchor this imagined scenario, justifying Perla's account.

Furthermore, this imagined togetherness is not produced by Perla alone. Serena ratifies each of Perla's statements: she agrees that she would play with Ursulina if she had the chance, and laughingly confirms that she had indeed expressed a preference for a niece. Just as with David and Adán's conversation, the sisters engage in collaborative stance-taking through which they align with one another through the shared evaluation of past events. However, in this instance, the sisters' discursive *convivencia* is strengthened through a more subtle form of communicative alignment as they take up and recycle one another's words in their own utterances. The extent of this uptake is illustrated in table 5.1, which aligns several sentences from this conversation. In this diagraph representation, the sentences are presented in chronological order, and each semantic chunk of the sentence is assigned its own column in order to reveal resonances across utterances.[3]

As the table shows, as the sisters discursively construct this imagined scenario of togetherness, they heavily take up and recycle one another's words. Their conversation thus mobilizes a particular form of interdiscursive relations (see Chapter 4) known as dialogism. Drawing on Bakhtin's theorization of dialogism in literary analysis (1981), scholars of language and social life have demonstrated the pervasiveness of such repetitions, which produce particular kinds of engagement between interlocutors and can create important relational meanings (C. Goodwin 2018; M. H. Goodwin 1990; Jakobson 1968; Moore 2012; Silverstein 1984; Tannen 1987). Dialogism creates resonance between utterances and their speakers, strengthening stance alignments and deepening discursive forms of *convivencia*.

One means of analyzing dialogic relations in speech is that of dialogic syntax (Du Bois 2014; Du Bois and Giora 2014), which focuses analysis on how speakers repeat not only one another's words but also entire syntactic structures. The syntactic parallelisms created by dialogic syntax simultaneously draw out similarities and highlight differences between speakers' utterances. In this conversation between Perla and Serena, the four utterances shown in table 5.1 each share the same core phrase "con ella pasara" (with her I/you would be). Through repetition and maintenance of the imperfect subjunctive, the sisters employ dialogism to emphasize the hypothetical nature of the scenario and the importance of Serena being together with her niece. As the conversation continues, the utterances expand on this imagined scenario. Perla voices their mother Olivia (line 3) and references the affective and embodied aspects of Serena's experience: she would be happy down on the floor playing with her niece. In summing up the interaction (line 4), Serena confirms this imagined togetherness, saying "de seguro" (surely).

The intensive dialogism of this conversation creates discursive alignment through which the sisters interactionally nourish their relationship, creating a form of communicative care that can withstand cross-border separation. The imagined scenario they collaboratively constitute extends this belonging, envisioning a joyful and co-present version of family life as grounded in everyday *convivencia*. In particular, this scenario emphasizes Serena's familial role as Ursulina's aunt rather than her status as migrant. Their consistent use of dialogic repetition reinforces this emphasis, insisting on the importance of such relational ties. This scenario of imagined togetherness thus pushes back against dominant discourses of migration and family that emphasize distinctions between migrants and nonmigrants as the defining factor of transnational life. Here, Serena and Perla insist that migrants remain first and foremost family members, using memories of both the recent and distant past as the foundation upon which both imagined togetherness and interactional alignment can be built. Once again, as in David and Adán's conversation, joint remembering becomes a tool of everyday resistance to the political, economic, and discursive forces that push transnational families apart.

The Future of the Past

Conceptualizing joint remembering—and the imaginary scenarios it grounds—as a form of care suggests that this discursive practice is

158 Living Together across Borders

fundamentally future-oriented. Just as with practices of naming in *memória historica* and the ritual of *los presentes*, as well as in the traditions of the Day of the Dead, remembering across borders nurtures relationships in order to sustain them into the future. One final example serves to make clear the future consequences of communicative memory practices.

In this conversation, Serena Portillo called her mother, Olivia. Serena had been asking her mother about the family home in great detail: was the clothesline still where it used to be? Were the coconut and guava trees giving fruit? And what had her mother done with the few items that Serena left behind when she migrated? In their conversation, Serena drew upon a highly detailed memory of the space of home including particular items and their location. Through the interaction she sought to update her mental model of what the family home looked like now, two years after she left. Eventually, their talk turned to the furnishings of the home, and Olivia complained to her daughter about the state of her few pieces of furniture. The bed creaked every time she moved, and the legs were ready to fall off. Serena laughingly warned her mother to be careful: "Al rato va a amanecer en el suelo" (someday you are going to wake up on the floor). Olivia did not immediately align with her daughter's evaluation of the situation as funny, and instead continued to elaborate on what was wrong with the bed.

Serena responded by launching an imagined scenario in which she returned to the theme of the broken bed falling down. "Ya imagina si las dos durmiéramos allí, ya nos hubiéramos caído" (Imagine if we both slept there, we would have already fallen). As with the hypothetical scenario built by Serena and Perla, this imagined co-presence was anchored in the past. Serena and her mother did indeed share that same bed before she migrated, in the practice of bed sharing that is common among families in the village. Shared memory can thus be relevant to conversational labor even when not explicitly articulated. Olivia then extended this imagined scenario: "Ya la hubiéramos quebrado fíjate. ¡En el suelo durmiéramos!" (We would have broken it already you know. We would be sleeping on the floor!) Mother and daughter then laughed uproariously together for several seconds about their imagined predicament.

Thus far, this instance seems much like the preceding two, with collaborative remembering of the past providing space for discursive alignment and relational nurture. But then, emerging right out of their shared laughter, Olivia stated, "Yo tengo la esperanza que cuando vos trabajés, me vas a mandar para una cama" (I hope once you are working, you will send me [money] for a bed). Although it would seem that Olivia imposed this obligation, Sara readily accepted it, saying "Sí. Para que ya no duerme en el suelo" (Yes. So you no longer sleep on the floor). Serena's agreement here uses dialogism to link the motivation for her acquiescence to the hypothetical scenario she and her mother have constructed. In this instance, the temporal work of dialogism is quite clear in the ways that the "sleeping on the floor" construction is taken up and put to new uses. Table 5.2 shows these utterances again in diagraph form, highlighting that while the prepositional phrase "en el suelo" (on the floor) and the semantic domain of the verb (sleeping and waking) remain constant, the tense and mood of the verbal phrase shift with each utterance from the periphrastic future (line 1) to the imperfect subjunctive (line 2) to the present indicative (line 3) and finally the infinitive (line 4).

This temporal variation reveals how the phrase is being repurposed. What began as a vision of Olivia's future with the broken bed changes into a scenario of imagined togetherness grounded in the past. Finally, in the last two instances, the phrase is tied to a much more concrete vision, one that imagines mother and daughter connected in the future through remittances. Here, the relational implications of remembering and imagining are made explicit. It is not only that language practices foster cross-border relationships, but that these communicatively invigorated ties may ultimately sustain transnational care within cross-border families—in this case economic ties. It might seem that this claim to future ties fits the family back into a vision of transnational family life as primarily one between remittance-sending migrants and nonmigrant recipients. However, the fact that this commitment to provide economic care emerges from and is grounded in communicative *convivencia* reveals that, once again, memory is being used to resist divisive dominant narratives. Economic relations of dependency between migrants and nonmigrants are not foundational, but rather emerge as a consequence of familial obligation that predate migration and will survive separation.

Conclusion

In El Salvador, remembering is a crucial social practice that undergirds struggles for survival. As with traditions of collective memory around the world, remembering can be used to explicitly forge accounts of the past that include the experiences of survivors in order to build a more just society. However, this chapter has demonstrated that attending specifically to the communicative dimensions of memory practices reveals a more subtle but equally consequential dimension of resistance in which memory functions as care that forges social relations. Communicative memory practices stitch together a social fabric that has been torn by war,

160 Living Together across Borders

Table 5.2 Diagraph of Serena and Olivia's Conversation

Speaker			Utterances			
1.	Serena	al rato	va a amanecer	al		suelo
2.	Olivia		{durmiéramos}	en el		suelo
3.	Serena	para que	ya no duerme	en el		suelo
4.	Olivia	para	ya no dormir	en el	puro	suelo

working to make the dead present in the continued struggles of the living. It is through memory that those who have been lost are kept alive, whether through cleaning and *enflorando* tombs every year on Día de los Difuntos, or in the recitation of victims who are called into presence through the ritual of *los presentes*.

For transnational families, communicative memory practices work in a similar way to bridge absence and separation. In particular, I have suggested that remembering across borders creates discursive space in which new forms of togetherness can be forged. Through stance-taking— both explicit agreement and the more subtle alignments of dialogic syntax—family members build interactional closeness, creating a form of conversational *convivencia*. In the context of transnational family life, David and Adán can no longer work the *milpa* together. Serena cannot play with her niece, nor can she share a bed with her mother. These forms of *convivencia*, of interweaving individual actions with one another in some collaborative project, are no longer possible across borders. Instead, members of transnational families use talk, interlacing communicative actions to accomplish a new form of discursive *convivencia* that can span across borders.

Such communicative togetherness is of course fleeting, but through joint remembering, transnational families use memories of the past to construct lasting visions of unified family life that push back against dominant discourses that emphasize distinctions between migrants and nonmigrants. In remembering together, transnational families refuse the imaginaries imposed upon them: their experiences cannot be understood through a lens that posits a heroic migrant and his dependent nonmigrant relatives, nor have they been abandoned by their selfish migrant kin who have forgotten them. Rather, as they remember together, families imagine, enact, and sustain cross-border kin ties. Through these conversations, remembering becomes a potent form of care through which transnational families nourish their collective resilience in the face of both political-economic and discursive forces that would sever their ties.

Conclusion

Social Change through Communicative Care

A Miracle?

In June 2014, a year after his diagnosis with chronic kidney disease, David Mejía was granted a ten-year, multiple entry visa that would allow him to visit the United States. His migrant sons Luis and Patricio were overjoyed. They had not seen their father in over a decade, and his diagnosis with chronic kidney disease the year before had led them to fear that they might never see him again. Luis reported "es como un milagro" (it's like a miracle) to be able to see his father again and spend time together. But this miracle, and the transformations in transnational family life that it produced, was brought about by concerted collaborative efforts. And communication played a vital role not only in arranging the visa but more fundamentally in helping to build and maintain the relationships that made visa-solicitation not only possible but also desirable.

Luis himself had initiated this process. From talking to other Salvadoran migrants, he knew that elderly relatives were often granted tourist visas to visit their migrant relatives, but that their visa application needed to be sponsored by a relative with legal standing. US immigration law treats the family ties of undocumented migrants—like Luis' ties to his father—as if they did not exist. So Luis used Facebook to find his half-sister, David's older daughter from a previous relationship, who he knew had obtained legal permanent residency in the United States. She had no relationship with David but agreed to write the invitation letter with the understanding that Luis and Patricio would pay for all the expenses associated with the visa process and travel for a chance to see their ailing father.

The next year, expanding on the success of this partial reunification, Patricio and Luis pooled funds to pay for a visa appointment for their mother, Rosario, who was ultimately granted a similar multiple entry visa linked to David's original paperwork. In April 2015, she and David visited the United States again, just in time to celebrate the first birthday of Luis's son, their youngest grandson. Patricio posted a photo of him and his mother on Facebook, his

Living Together Across Borders. Lynnette Arnold, Oxford University Press. © Oxford University Press 2024.
DOI: 10.1093/oso/9780197755730.003.0007

162 Living Together across Borders

arms around her shoulders, their faces so close they were almost touching. The photo garnered twenty-five comments, all excepting mine from other migrants originally from Cantón El Río, commenting on how wonderful it was to see mother and son together again. One poster asked Patricio if he was happy and he responded, "siii amiga, ¡no sabes cuánto! Ya eran varios años sin verla" (Yeees friend, you don't know how much! It's been several years without seeing her). The congratulatory responses by fellow migrants validated the efforts that Patricio and his family had undertaken to make this visit a reality. At the same time, these comments also held up such in-person reunions as an accessible future of transnational family life worth striving toward.

The new cross-border mobility of the Mejía parents changed the entire family's experience of transnational life. Long-term physical separation was now punctuated with regular visits for some members of the family, giving migrant sons the chance to see their aging parents and allowing grandparents to connect with their US-based grandchildren. Those who did not travel to the United States saw photos and talked about the visits, which shifted the dynamics of the family's cross-border communication in the time between visits. Such conversations were vital to the organization and planning of visits, which became a new topic of complex negotiations about who would travel where, when, and how long they would stay.

However, the partial family reunions that emerged through these visits were only possible because the Mejía family had sustained their cross-border connections during more than a decade of separation. And maintaining such transnational relationships would not have been possible without communicative care practices such as greetings, remittance negotiations, and joint remembering. Through these everyday care practices, families enacted transformative work, forging communicative *convivencia* across borders, nurturing relationships across space and time, and ultimately working to change the conditions of their collective lives.

* * *

Through a close investigation of cross-border conversations, this book has argued that communication functions as a vital form of care through which transnational families work to sustain *convivencia* and continue to live together at a distance. While communication in this setting bears a particularly heavy weight, the insights about communication and care developed in this book have much broader significance beyond the transnational family.

Care is entangled with communication wherever it occurs. This fact became newly apparent to many during the COVID-19 pandemic, which often disrupted existing forms of care by pushing them online and into socially distanced interactions. But engaging in care with others has always inevitably involved communication. Whether among medical staff working in a hospital unit or clinic, between home care workers and their elderly clients, in community organizations providing social services, or among kin networks, navigating care relies on communication. Through these quotidian conversational negotiations, relationships are established and continually reworked as particular ways of doing care emerge and are consolidated. This is not to say that the relational work of communication will always be the same as that traced in this study. Varying institutional regulations and organizational models, the economic aspects of paid care work, and kinship norms all shape language use, producing different communicative care practices—and relationships of obligation—in each setting.

Thus, how care is enacted and made meaningful through communication will also be specific to the particular contexts in which care is being carried out. For care workers employed in biomedical settings, which actions count as enacting care—and which are made invisible—is likely to be shaped by more explicitly formulated norms than in familial settings. However, research shows that even in more formalized care settings like the NICU (newborn intensive care unit) or a dementia hospital, the implicit and unspoken ethico-moral orientations of hospital staff consequentially shape how care practices unfold and the meanings that are drawn from them (Svendsen et al. 2018). Therefore, despite more overt regulation of care in institutional settings, collective care inevitably involves communication that builds the relational foundations of care as well as often implicit communicative negotiations about how care is carried out, by whom, and what their different actions mean.

A communicative approach thus provides a capacious yet detailed lens that can shed new light on how people navigate care together in a range of different settings. While this book has focused on care-at-a-distance in transnational families, where communication bears a particularly heavy weight, the lessons learned from this work can inform studies of many other kinds of care. In what follows, I outline three key insights from this book, highlighting the interdisciplinary potential of a communicative approach to care. I conclude with a call to action that urges readers to become accomplices in struggles for transnational *convivencia* and justice for cross-border families.

Thinking Communication and Care Together

By closely tracing the entanglements of language and care, this book draws attention to materiality, multifunctionality, and temporality to understand how

164 Living Together across Borders

seemingly mundane communicative practices become consequential forces for care. In what follows, I outline each of these three areas in turn, drawing out contributions for those who study language, care, migration, family, and their intersections. Ultimately, I suggest that these insights reveal the ways in which communicative care can be mobilized as a consequential form of transformative work.

First, a communicative care perspective highlights the profound entanglements of language and materiality. While work on language materiality is a well-established area of research (Cavanaugh and Shankar 2017), this book demonstrates that examining language as care can reveal the specific practices through which communicative labor builds the largely taken-for-granted relational infrastructures that undergird political-economic systems. In particular, the book has demonstrated how transnational families use everyday conversations to navigate global neoliberalism by continually forging relationships of obligation that span space and time. This approach thus suggests that a broader range of communicative practices should be understood as relevant to political-economic structures, while also providing a grounded approach for such analyses.

Often, such communicative practices reinforce unequal economic relationships both interpersonally and institutionally. Within transnational families, the norms that shape how different relatives participate in communicative care consistently rely on distinctions between migrant and non-migrant relatives, as shown in greeting rituals (Chapter 3) and remittance negotiations (Chapter 4). Such bifurcated communicative practices—repeated time and again over the months and years of family separation—continually reproduce boundaries within the family, mapping geopolitical borders onto kin ties. Often, these borders are reproduced in ways that intersect with gendered and generational inequalities, as when male relatives in El Salvador shift the most difficult remittance communication to the women in the family (see Chapter 2). Through such communicative practices, the gendered and generational hierarchies of everyday family life become inextricably entangled with political-economic inequities between Global North and South.

Moreover, at the aggregate level, communicative care continues to make migration succeed as a strategy for familial—and national—economic sustenance. By maintaining the cross-border relationships of obligation that keep remittances flowing, communicative care supports the provisioning of El Salvador, allowing the government to adopt neoliberal policies that push care onto individual citizens while largely avoiding mass protest. As communicative care sustains relationships and keeps remittances flowing, it makes migration seem like a viable solution to global inequality, thereby ensuring that Salvadorans continue to make unauthorized journeys north. Ultimately, then, communicative care works in tandem with powerful political-economic forces that continually push more families into lives of cross-border separation to provide the cheap and exploitable labor force required by capitalism.

However, to say that communicative care only reinforces structural violence would be a gross oversimplification. The analysis presented in this book has demonstrated that as communicative care forges relational ground, it functions as a consequential form of transformative work. Much like the kin work of the African American women Mullings (1996) writes about, communication in transnational families enacts transformation not only by maintaining collective continuity but also by incrementally transforming the conditions under which they struggle for survival. This is not to say that transformative work is necessarily only positive; Mullings (2005) reminds us of the costs of transformative work for those who engage in it. And indeed, this book has underscored the inequitable and labor-intensive nature of communicative care, and pointed to the stresses that it may cause for migrants and nonmigrants alike.

Moreover, as they enact transformative work in their everyday conversations, transnational families mobilize the multifunctional and temporal dimensions of language. Beginning with multifunctionality, I have shown that language facilitates nonlinguistic care such as remittances even as it enacts care, sustaining the relationships of obligation upon which asymmetrically reciprocal care is founded. At the same time, language can signify care, valorizing particular actions carried by specific people, while eliding or condemning others. While it is analytically useful to separate these three functions, they are often produced simultaneously in the same stretch of conversation. For instance, Chapter 3 shows that video greetings sent across borders enact relational ties between the sender and the migrant relatives they greet, articulating love and care across the miles. Simultaneously, these greetings lay out visions of family life, implicitly ranking kin by prioritizing those blood relatives who are primary remitters; by highlighting these individuals, the greeters valorize particular kinds of provision by migrants and elide others, thereby signifying care. Through this enactment and signification, transnational families conceptualize the act of sending greetings as a communicative form of care that facilitates ongoing remittance flows.

In such multifaceted engagements of language and care, not all communicative care functions necessarily work together toward the same end. Thus, even as greetings are framed as relational care that sustains transnational family ties, they simultaneously enact kin hierarchies that may weaken ties to those individuals envisioned as more peripheral. Implicit enactments of care

166 Living Together across Borders

through communication may be at odds with explicitly articulated meanings, even as the nonlinguistic forms of care facilitated by communication may reproduce hierarchical norms that communicative care at times works to undermine.

I suggest that this multifunctionality underpins the contradictory consequences of communicative care for transnational families. Care scholarship has often pointed to this puzzle, highlighting how care is simultaneously vital to human life even as it serves to reproduce multiple social inequities (Arnold and Aulino 2021). Rather than simply taking this paradox as an essential property of care, a communicative approach delves deeper, seeking to understand how these conflicting consequences emerge from the everyday practices that produce care. Attending closely to the multifunctionality of communication sheds light on how specific care practices themselves—when approached ethnographically and understood in their sociopolitical context—may contribute to contradictory consequences. Moving beyond language, this finding encourages scholars of care to examine the multifunctionality of care practices in all their diversity, considering how particular practices might work in ways that are consonant or at odds with one another.

The simultaneity of enactment and signification is of particular importance to such efforts. Care scholarship at times mobilizes a clear distinction between enactments of care on the one hand and reflexive meaning-making on the other (cf. Black 2018), but a communicative care approach demonstrates that these two aspects of care are not easily separated. Of course, language does lend itself to explicit meaning making, such as when Luis tells his mother that he sends remittances to reciprocate the care she provided him and his siblings in childhood. But the meaning-making power of language goes far beyond such reflexive accounts, most often emerging implicitly in the patterned ways through which communicative practices enact care.

The communicative care practices used by transnational families demonstrate the power of this simultaneity for transformative work. Families use language to implicitly shift the meaning of the pervasive boundary between migrants and nonmigrants, resignifying this divide as a matter of agentively enacted familial obligation rather than as a manifestation of political-economic inequity. For instance, in remembering together across borders, families deemphasize migration-based distinctions and instead insist on the continued primacy of familial relationships despite cross-border separation (Chapter 5). Thus, implicit significations of care are a vital resource by which families work to communicatively transform the conditions of their collective lives. Through communicative care, transnational families enact subtle but profound resistance to the powerful forces that seek to sunder or co-opt their cross-border care work. The meanings that families produce through their communicative care practices reject dominant state-endorsed visions of unidirectional economic provision from migrants to dependent relatives in El Salvador (see Chapter 1), instead envisioning cross-border care as involving asymmetrically reciprocal engagements in which the relational and affective labor of communication constitutes an important contribution. Through everyday communication, transnational families implicitly reject a capitalist framework, insisting instead that all aspects of human life—including economic dimensions—are grounded in relationships of asymmetrical obligation that connect people across the generations. Through everyday conversations, transnational families consistently regenerate themselves over space and time, lifting up kin ties and affirming connection despite separation.

Furthermore, the book has demonstrated that the temporal properties of language are also vital to its transformative potential. Here I build on linguistic anthropological scholarship on scale (Carr and Lempert 2016), which contends that the spatiotemporal domains of social life are not fixed entities established a priori but are discursively produced and negotiated. Scalar discourses often elevate certain aspects of our collective lives—migration, state discourses—as large scale and therefore important, while dismissing others—family, everyday conversation—as small scale and inconsequential. My analysis suggests that the interweaving temporalities of everyday conversations make communicative care into a powerful scalar resource, one that transnational families use in an implicit yet constant resistance that insists upon the far-reaching political consequences of kin care (cf. Thelen and Coe 2017).

Everyday conversations operate simultaneously within and across multiple timescales, with effects that powerfully reach far beyond the immediate moment in which they are enacted. Each utterance is interdiscursively linked to other instances of language use, past or future. Patterned linguistic exchanges—such as indirect remittance requests and responses—can become expected ways of carrying out communicative action, exerting normative force across conversations. The book shows that through these interdiscursive ties and the development of communicative genres, language becomes a vital part of the repeated rhythms of care labor through which families sustain themselves from day to day, year to year, and, ultimately, generation to generation. As illustrated in language socialization practices around greetings (Chapter 3), communication shapes who engages in cross-border kin care and how they participate; communicative care therefore works intergenerationally to maintain the family over time, sustaining collective continuity.

168 Living Together across Borders

At the same time, the interactional and interdiscursive organization of communication also provides opportunities for change, openings through which individuals can work to incrementally shift the conditions within which care is navigated. For instance, women's greater normative responsibility for communicative labor can provide them with opportunities to maneuver within patriarchal care norms, just as young people can use their greater technological literacy to insert their perspectives into care conversations among their elders (Chapter 2). Thus, communicative care may provide opportunities for transforming the gendered and generational ground upon which family survivance is enacted. The moment-to-moment, day-to-day, and year-to-year unfolding of communication thus has profound consequences for the futures of transnational families.

A communicative care approach therefore reveals how complex temporalities—interactional and interdiscursive, life course and intergenerational—are integral to the unfolding of sociohistorical processes like global migration. This insight resonates with recent work on raciolinguistics (Rosa and Flores 2017; Smalls 2020), which argues that contemporary language use must be understood as having deep historical roots in global histories of colonialism. By examining communicative care, scholars can trace how histories of colonialism and neocolonialism play out in everyday life through experiences of migration. This approach reveals the falsity of widespread scalar discourses that tend to treat interactional and interdiscursive dimensions as "small scale" while dismissing intergenerational and life course dimensions as "private," thereby rendering both irrelevant to more important and "larger" sociopolitical concerns. Rather, this book demonstrates that immediate interactions are not only situated within but also sustain such sociohistorical processes. The communicative care practices enacted in everyday conversations do not simply respond to the sociopolitical landscape, but rather reconstitute and at times incrementally transform these global processes from moment to moment and across the years.

Of course, these care-based transformations often operate primarily at a relational level, rather than directly advancing structural change. However, in thinking through the implications of these changes, we must not fall prey to assumptions about "larger" scales as inherently more consequential. As the transnational families in this book insist time and again through their everyday communicative enactments of care, without such relationality, there is no social life. Therefore, transformative work that functions at the scale of interpersonal relationships is profoundly consequential, operating as it does on the very foundation of society. Nevertheless, around the world, neoliberal capitalism, restrictive immigration policy, and xenophobic rhetoric continue to separate families. In this context of ongoing structural violence, the everyday transformative work carried out by transnational families needs greater support and amplification.

A Call to Accompany as Accomplices

I therefore end with a direct call to you, my reader. Through this book, I hope you have learned something new about the ways that transnational families continue to live together across borders, as well as about the powerful forces arrayed against them. Here, I urge you to use what you have learned as the basis for action in solidarity with families like the Mejías and the Portillos. For readers who are themselves migrants or members of transnational families, I hope this call to action resonates with your experiences. I will suggest specific actions that can be taken to support migrant communities, suggestions that emerge from the stories told in this book and from my own twenty years of accompanying transnational families. I also lay out an approach for this work that calls us all to become accomplices in migrants' struggles for a more just world.

Accompaniment is an approach to collective social transformation that involves individuals from different backgrounds working together as equals in a shared struggle (Justice Power 2020, Tomlinson and Lipsitz 2013). This approach is rooted in the work of Salvadoran Archbishop Óscar Romero, who was ultimately assassinated at the behest of the country's elites for his work to accompany poor communities (López Vigil 2000). Yet his legacy of accompaniment lives on, as I saw through my involvement with community organizations in El Salvador, which taught me how change can emerge by working together across difference. Accompaniment emphasizes the processual nature of social change work and the importance of social relations in these journeys.

As I discuss elsewhere (Arnold 2019b), accompaniment as a model for community engagement can be strengthened by combining it with recent calls from social movements for more committed forms of participation as accomplices (Indigenous Action 2014; Jackson 2016). Drawing on Martin Luther King, Jr.'s "Letter from Birmingham City Jail" (1963), the call for accomplices in social justice struggles "urges progressives to avoid the deceptive comfort of allyship, and, instead, to pursue complicity with criminalized communities" (Gomberg-Muñoz 2018, 36), including migrants and their families. Accompliceship begins with recognizing the ways in which we are all already complicit with unjust laws and instead moves us to "becoming complicit in a struggle towards liberation" (Indigenous Action 2014,

2). The accompliceship model complements accompaniment by clarifying how to best conduct this work. First, accompanying as accomplices means developing a critical understanding of individuals' different positionalities with regard to oppressive structures, through which accomplices "find creative ways to weaponize their privilege" (Indigenous Action 2014, 6). Moreover, accomplices understand the urgency of taking action together with others to dismantle oppressive systems, while also balancing this sense of urgency with careful attention to relationships by cultivating mutual accountability and responsibility.

Accompanying as accomplices is a skill, something we must learn how to do and continually cultivate. If we ourselves are not migrants or members of transnational families, accompliceship must begin by building and maintaining relationships with migrant communities that sustain cross-border lives. Migrants may be our coworkers, our neighbors, people who are part of our faith communities or social circles. For teachers and professors, many of our students may also belong to transnational families. Depending on our own positionality, migrants may also be the people who care for us and our loved ones as nannies and home care aids, housecleaners, gardeners, and farmworkers, since this intensive and often undervalued labor is increasingly carried out by migrants in many parts of the world (Batalova 2023; Kumar et al. 2022). Building relationships between nonmigrants and migrants directly undermines the segregation of many receiving societies and the ways that care is co-opted under neoliberal capitalism to reproduce political-economic inequalities. This relationship building, if undertaken as a form of accompliceship, has a great deal of radical potential through which we can begin to enact the equitable social relations we ultimately wish to see in the world even as we work for change. And as the transnational families in this book have taught us, communicative care is central to this relational work.

Beyond building relationships, what does accompanying as accomplices look like? One way to answer this question is by following the lead of those most impacted. In my interviews with transnational families, I always ended by asking them what changes could be made to improve their collective cross-border lives. Many of them wished for the ability to easily make video calls to their loved ones across borders. While increasing access to smartphones has gone some way toward making this a reality, significant barriers remain. High-speed internet is often inaccessible for migrant and nonmigrant relatives alike, forcing them to rely on cellular data which limits access to video calls. In addition, these services are often costly, and may be quite unpredictable, leading to challenges for family budgeting. Creating global access to high-speed and low-cost internet connectivity through community broadband networks in sending and receiving countries would significantly improve the ability of transnational families around the world to sustain their long-distance connections. Expanding technological access must also be accompanied by efforts to foster digital literacy for all segments of the population; in particular, this book shows that the elderly may be disempowered in cross-border communication due to their lack of digital literacy. Greater individual ability to use a broader range of digital technologies creates space for all family members to participate more equitably in communicative care.

Scholars of language can use our disciplinary training to support family members in building and/or maintaining the communicative skills needed to participate in transnational conversations. Many receiving societies have educational structures that ignore or actively eradicate the home languages used by the children of migrants. We must work to change existing language education policy, which all too often functions as a tool of state-sponsored family separation by pushing the children of migrants towards monolingualism in dominant languages like English. Supporting bilingual education is crucial for ensuring that children of migrants can maintain their family's mother tongue so that they can communicate with relatives back home. To be most effective, these programs must develop culturally sustaining pedagogies that build on the funds of knowledge that children bring from home (Paris and Alim 2017; Vélez-Ibáñez and Greenberg 1992). This move will require reorienting the curricular focus of many contemporary bilingual programs, which tend to cater to elite interests in ways that ignore or actively push out immigrant families (Flores, Tseng, and Subtirelu 2021). Instead, the communicative needs of migrant communities must guide pedagogical and curricular choices, thereby supporting the children of migrants in developing the communicative competencies valued in their transnational communities. Specifically, such programs must valorize the diverse linguistic varieties—often including stigmatized dialects like Salvadoran Spanish—that are used within immigrant communities. In addition, these bilingual curricula must attend to the technologically mediated forms of communication that are so vital in these communities, supporting the development of bilingual digital literacy.

However, while increasing access to cross-border communication is vital, such policies do not address the powerful forces that continually work to tear transnational families apart. As this book has demonstrated, one such force is discursive, appearing in state and media discourses about transnational family ties. In the United States, the transnational relationships of these families are legally erased even as they are discursively stigmatized as criminal or as threats to the nation. In El Salvador, cross-border family ties are co-opted to nation-building projects, thereby elevating some forms of transnational connection while ignoring or demonizing others. These damaging discourses call for a communicative response, as transnational families teach us through their everyday conversations. By sustaining connection and well-being over space and time, transnational families insist on the value of their cross-border connections and their deep rooting in intergenerational reciprocity and relationships of obligation. Thus, through everyday acts of communicative care, transnational families consistently produce a potent counter-discourse through which they attribute their own meaning and significance to cross-border ties. This vital message must be amplified if it is to be heard over the deafening din of xenophobia and harmful state rhetoric. This book seeks to contribute to this counter-discursive project, and I urge you to consider how you might do so in your own life. At minimum, all of us can pay attention to immigration news—even (or perhaps especially) when supposedly pro-immigrant politicians hold local and national offices—and continue to educate ourselves, our families, and our friends about the realities of migration beyond the fearmongering headlines.

Dominant migration discourses about transnational families are one tool of the regimes of (im)mobility that push families apart and keep them separated. These political-economic systems incite individuals to continue to migrate, despite the increasingly hazardous conditions that these same forces create. Neoliberal capitalism compels migrants to risk their lives for a chance at familial survival. And even if migrants arrive safely at their destination, their families often become trapped apart, with migrants unable to travel or to request visas for their relatives to come visit them. Economic inequities make cross-border family separation the only viable option for collective survival. Companies and nations in the Global North continue to enrich themselves through family separation, as they have since their founding. It is clear that as long as these inequitable global systems remain in place, transnational families will continue to suffer.

More systemic change is ultimately necessary to create a world where all families have full self-determination over their own *convivencia*. By accompanying families like the Mejías and the Portillos and working to become an accomplice in their struggles, I have ultimately come to believe that abolition—dismantling borders, the state, and global capitalism (Bradley and De Noronha 2022; Wilson Gilmore 2022)—is the path toward such a world. While the goals of abolition may seem like an impossible dream, Latin American social justice movements like the Zapatistas remind us that "otro mundo es posible" (another world is possible). Similarly, in their call for accomplices, Indigenous Action (2014, 6) urges their readers not to give in to

Social Change through Communicative Care 173

paralysis: "you wouldn't find an accomplice resigning their agency or capabilities as an act of 'support.'" For academics like myself and many of my readers, Indigenous Action (2014, 5) suggests: "An accomplice as academic would seek ways to leverage resources and material support and/or betray their institution to further liberation struggles. An intellectual accomplice would strategize with, not for and not be afraid to pick up a hammer."

In my own journey over the past two decades, I have worked to accompany as an accomplice by participating in struggles for social justice led by migrant communities. I have attended protests for immigrant rights, supported struggles to end immigrant detention, and gotten involved in campaigns to do away with xenophobic policies locally and nationally. Beyond organized protests, I have also worked directly with families. I have helped them locate relatives picked up by immigration officers or police, and have helped locate legal representation for those fighting deportation. At other times, I have informally accompanied individuals through our labyrinthine immigration system. Those looking for more formal accompaniment options can participate in court accompaniment programs (Justice Power). There is always work to be done to raise funds to bail people out of immigrant detention centers or pay attorney fees (Black Immigrants Bail Fund, https://www.blackimm igrantsbailfund.com; National Bail Fund Network, https://www.community justiceexchange.org/en/nbfn-directory). I invite fellow scholars to consider volunteering their time and knowledge by writing expert testimonies to support asylum cases (Billingsley 2022; Rodriguez 2022).

How might you accompany migrant communities and become an accomplice in their struggles? What kinds of relationships—with whom—will you build as you engage in this social change work? As this book has shown, if we attend carefully to the ways that transnational families make cross-border lives, we can begin to see glimmers of insight into how everyday care practices—including communication—can move us toward these goals through ongoing transformative work. Indeed, abolitionist organizers are increasingly working toward these changes through mutual aid, which recognizes everyday acts of mutual care and support as critical form of resistance under contemporary conditions, where multiple intersecting systematic crises create ever deeper and more widespread vulnerability for so many (Spade 2020). Of course, mutual aid as resistance is not new: it has always been key to human survival and has particularly deep roots in organizing within Black and Indigenous communities (Chiles 2015, Indigene Community 2021). But in the face of overwhelming forces that work to tear them apart, transnational families need more accomplices to accompany their struggles. Through acts of collective

174 Living Together across Borders

care, we can find ways to enact and live out liberatory social relations, ones founded on justice and collective survival, even as we work to dismantle systems of oppression (Big Door Brigade 2021). Transnational families show us that care through communication is inescapably a way of maintaining relationships, of continually regenerating social life, and ultimately of making worlds. What kind of world will you create with your communicative care?

Notes

Introduction

1. All individual and family names are pseudonyms. I also use pseudonyms for smaller locales, such as the Salvadoran village that is the hub of this research, but not for larger cities such as Los Angeles.

2. A note on the terminology used throughout this book. I generally use the term "migrant" when referring to those individuals who have traveled to the United States, avoiding narrower terms like "immigrant," "emigrant," or "refugee"; while each of these might be appropriate at times, the term "migrant" more broadly captures the fluid and ongoing nature of migration processes and is in keeping with the terminology used in contemporary studies of global mobility (Basch et al. 1994; Berg 2016; Dick 2018). I also use the term "nonmigrant" to refer to family members who were in El Salvador at the time of the events being described. Of course, these categories are not static—indeed, over the course of my research, three nonmigrant individuals became migrants. Nevertheless, these terms are useful shorthand references that capture a consequential divide within transnational families between those living in El Salvador and those in the United States.

3. Lynn Stephen (2007) has suggested a change to "transborder" instead of "transnational," as a means of indicating the many kinds of borders—regional, class, ethnic—traversed, in particular by Indigenous migrants. I will use the term "transnational family" throughout this book, both because it is the term most commonly used in the literature and because it emphasizes the powerful influence of states on the experiences of these families.

4. My understanding of family separation builds on conceptualization of the "necropolitics of reproduction" by Leith Mullings (2021). This framework links the "accumulation of wealth through the dispossession of racialized people" (Mullings et al. 2021, 676) to government policies that "determine who will live and who will die" (Mullings 2021, 107), a dynamic that has become undeniably clear during the COVID-19 pandemic, but also underpins the forces that push people to migrate.

5. Because I approach language not primarily as a structured grammatical system but as a means of acting in the world, I use the terms "language" and "communication" interchangeably through the book. For more on linguistic anthropological approaches to language, see Duranti (2011); Ochs (2012); and Silverstein (2004).

6. Dick 2018, 2011; Paz 2018, 2016; Perrino 2020; Perrino and Wortham 2018.

7. Relatedly, linguistic anthropologists have taken up Bahktin's concept of the chronotope to analyze the spatiotemporal workings of language. For more detail on scholarly debates around these two terms, see Blommaert 2015, De Fina and Perrino 2020.

8. Dick 2010; Karimzad and Catedral 2021; Perrino 2011; Perrino and Kohler 2020; Pritzker and Perrino 2021.

9. In 1980, there were 94,447 in the United States, and by 1990 this number had grown to 565,081 (Menjívar 2000).

176 Notes

10. Silber (2022, 2011) describes a similar process in another rural community she studied in the immediate years postwar. She attributes this shift to the ways that national reconstruction projects left many rural poor out of the equation, pushing them to turn to migration to fulfill their dreams of "una vida digna" (a dignified life). In addition, the demographic pressures created by an unusually high rate of births from 1992 to 1997 made it increasingly difficult for rural families to sustain collective well-being.

11. This chronic family stress has been shown to negatively impact children's development (Dreby 2012; Landale et al. 2015; Suárez-Orozco et al. 2011).

12. These realities are documented in greater detail by a well-established literature on the experiences of Salvadoran migrants (e.g., Coutin 2000, 2007; Hallett 2012, 2013; Hamilton and Chinchilla 1991; Menjívar 2000; Menjívar and Abrego 2012).

13. See work on the transnational dynamics of Salvadoran migrants' lives (e.g., Abrego 2009, 2014, 2019; Baker-Cristales 2004; Padilla 2012).

14. While work across these subfields is not new (see Kuipers 1989; Wilce 2009), current scholarship at this intersection is burgeoning (Black 2019; Briggs and Mantini-Briggs 2016, 2004; Buchbinder 2010; Carr 2010; Corwin 2012, 2014, 2021; T. S. Harvey 2013; Marsilli-Vargas 2016; Parkin 2013; Pritzker 2014; Shohet 2007, 2018).

15. Glenn 2010; Kroger 2009; Parreñas 2001; Vora 2015.

16. E.g., Cavanaugh and Shankar 2017; Gal 1989; Irvine 1989; Rossi-Landi 1983; Shankar and Cavanaugh 2012; Voloshinov 1929; Williams 1977; Woolard 1985; Urciuoli 1995.

17. See for instance Baldassar et al. 2020; Fan and Parreñas 2018; Merla 2012; Yarris 2017. This multigenerational approach to cross-border family care resonates with scholarship on kinwork (Di Leonardo 1987; Stack and Burton 1993). While this approach was developed with nontransnational families, it is productive for understanding cross-border care because it emphasizes efforts to sustain families that extend beyond the co-present household (Dossa and Coe 2017).

18. The use of care practices to create kin relations that extend beyond biological delimitations is well-documented in Latin America (Gálvez 2011; Peña 2011; Pérez 2014; Smith 2006). While often referred to as "fictive kinship" in anthropological studies, this distinction reifies biological kinship as normative (Sahlins 2013; Schneider 1984). Here I follow queer theorists who instead use terms like "chosen family" to theorize kinship in broader terms that make clear the political nature of these debates (for recent iterations, see Chávez 2017b; Mizielińska et al. 2018; Silver 2020).

19. M. Goodwin 2015, M. Goodwin and Cekaite 2018; Perrino 2020.

20. For more on affect and language, see, e.g., Besnier 1990, 1992; Bucholtz et al. 2018; Du Bois and Kärkkäinen 2012; Irvine 1990; McElhinny 2010; Ochs and Schieffelin 1989.

21. Ahlin 2017; Berg 2016; Francisco-Menchavez 2018; Madianou and Miller 2012b.

22. Baldassar et al. 2016; Francisco-Menchavez 2015; Madianou 2012; Uy-Tioco 2007.

23. This raises the question of whether formal interpretation may be understood as a form of communicative care, and indeed, linguistic anthropological work suggests that at least some interpreters may understand their work as care labor (Rao 2021).

24. Scholars working on language and intimacy have made similar arguments about how intimacy is simultaneously enacted within and across different temporal scales (Perrino and Pritzker 2019; Pritzker and Perrino 2021). Similarly, interdisciplinary approaches to intimacy contend that while such feelings of closeness are often relegated to the "private" domain, in reality they "shape and are contoured by historical residues, socio-cultural norms,

Notes **177**

state-centric policies and global economic dynamics" (Barabantseva, Mhurchú, and Peterson 2021, 344).

25. I follow Zigon and Throop (2014), and other scholars of language and migration (Dick 2017), in not making a clear distinction between ethics and morality. Although scholars sometimes distinguish between morals as habitual actions and ethics as post hoc reflexive accounts, communication blurs this divide, allowing for ethico-moral signification that is at times fully implicit in actions, at times explicitly formulated through reflexive accounts, and at times presented via intermediate and less coherent reflection (Black 2018, 81). To capture this blurring, I use the term "ethico-moral" throughout the book.

26. Such communicative resistance has also been traced in face-to-face interactions. For instance, young children may use embodied actions with speech to resist their parents' attempts at everyday care routines (M. Goodwin 2006). Care recipients can also use language to shape longer-term care trajectories, such as when children in a pediatric cancer ward strategically ask questions in order to participate more fully in discussions about their treatment (Clemente 2015).

Chapter 1

1. More specifically, migration discourse can be defined as "talk and writing that summon up or presuppose the figures of personhood, rhetorical themes, forms of spatial reference, or logical propositions that people associate with the causes and consequences of migration" (Dick 2018, 10).

2. While related to Anderson's notion of the imagined community, the concept of the imaginary provides a more nuanced framework for exploring the contested processes through which national belonging is continually reconstituted (Dick 2018, 12).

3. Crapanzano 2004; Dave 2012; Mittermaier 2011; Salazar 2013.

4. I use the term "national belonging" to refer to the many ways that individuals are able to claim membership in the nation-state. This inclusion is fundamentally tied to the kinds of people they are imagined to be and the sort of social space they are deemed deserving to occupy (Dick 2018, 46).

5. Abrego 2009, 2014; Mahler 1999; Padilla 2012; Zentgraf 2002.

6. Another example of this extension can be seen in the figure of the entrepreneurial returnee who lives the "Salvadoran dream" by providing for their family in their home country (Arnold 2023).

7. Here, I am inspired by on work on "citizenship variegation" that examines how people are formally incorporated into the nation by being produced as marginal to it (Biolsi 2005; Ong 1999; Paz 2018; Stack 2012; Stephen 2007). I use the term "belonging" rather than "citizenship" because I am focused on visions of inclusion that extend beyond political participation, though of course these two are often deeply connected.

8. Migrants themselves are attuned to the ways these exclusions are articulated in such imaginaries. They often understand their designation as *hermanos lejanos* to be a form of marginalization (Baker-Cristales 2004). They have sought to shape understanding of migrants' role in Salvadoran society through discursive struggles, such as attempts to change the name of the Hermano Lejano monument (Arnold 2015; Marroquín Parducci 2009). One proposed name, *hermano cercano* (nearby brother) gained some level of circulation (Aparicio 2022), but although the monument was officially renamed *Hermano*

178 Notes

Bienvenido a Casa (Brother Welcome Home), it is still most often referred to with its original name. This example reveals the power of state-endorsed migration discourses to set the terms within which migration is understood.

9. As with all typification in figures of personhood and imaginaries, this is a partial representation that actively erases the fact that many migrants find love and familial attachment in the United States, often by forming new partnerships and having children of their own.

10. As shown in table 1.1, another depiction of failed migration is that of the victimized migrant, who emerges from transnational moral panics about the dangers of the unauthorized journey, particularly for women and children (for more discussion of this figure, see Arnold 2023).

11. Between 1996 and 2005, the United States deported an average of 4,686 Salvadorans per year, double the average number from 1980 to 1995 (Coutin 2007, 24). This drastic increase resulted from the 1996 Illegal Immigration Reform and Immigrant Responsibility Act, which expanded the list of deportable offenses. This change was applied retroactively, and in conjunction with the Anti-Terrorism and Effective Death Penalty Act (also passed in 1996), it led to many more deportations.

12. In this figuration, the deportee is depicted as a gang member whose criminal involvement with groups like the Mara Salvatrucha (MS-13) had led to his removal from the United States. Such depictions stoked widespread fear of the deportee as a new criminal figure in Salvadoran national imaginaries (Zilberg 2004, 15).

13. Andrade-Eekhoff 2003, 2006; Hammock et al. 2006; Menjívar 2000; Miyares et al. 2003.

Chapter 2

1. For a review of how language produces kin relations, as well as relationlessness, see Ball (2018).

2. Salvadoran Spanish, particularly in rural areas, does not traditionally use the informal *tú* form (e.g., ¿lo conoces?). Many other varieties of Spanish, including that spoken in the United States, use *tú* rather than *vos*, converting the use of *vos* forms into a marker of Central American identity among the Latinx diaspora in the United States (Rivera-Mills 2011; Woods and Rivera-Mills 2012). Varieties of Spanish also differ in terms of which form is the default form of address—in many varieties it is the informal form (whether *tú* or *vos*) rather than *usted*. Latin American Spanish does not maintain these formality distinctions in the second-person plural (you all), although peninsular Spanish does.

3. This was not an idiosyncratic language ideology. In fact, many couples in rural El Salvador—especially those of older generations—use *usted* rather than *vos* with one another as a means of enacting and signaling the seriousness of their relationship.

4. Officially, more than 30 percent of Salvadoran families are multigenerational (FUSADES 2015), but this statistic is very likely an undercount, as it relies on a residential definition of the household and thus does not include multigenerational families like the Mejías that function as extended households.

5. There are long-standing debates within anthropology about the distinction between households and families. Households are generally assumed to be defined on the basis of co-residence, though anthropological scholarship has also included cases of separate but proximate dwellings (Dorjahn 1977; C. B. Stack 1975). Moreover, households also share ongoing daily engagements in care, working to provide for the collective (Yanagisako 1979).

Notes 179

6. Feminist philosophers have argued that asymmetrical reciprocity is central to the ways that relationships between individuals are constituted and maintained (Caze 2008; Huntington 2016; Young 1997). This work has been foundational to the theorization of how transnational family relationships are enacted through cross-border care (Baldassar and Merla 2013; Coe 2016; Cole and Durham 2007; Cole and Groes 2016).
7. Aulino 2019; Bourdieu 1977, 1984; Buch 2018; Csordas 1993.
8. Nonheteronormative sexuality is generally only mentioned in the context of disparaging remarks, and LGBT individuals often suffer immense social stigma and pervasive discrimination, a reality that forces many to flee the country and seek asylum in the United States (Balaguera 2018).
9. Marriage as such is rare, particularly in rural areas; about 60 percent of partnerships nationwide are long-term common-law marriages based on cohabitation (Fussell and Palloni 2004)
10. Gracious personhood can thus be understood in contrast to imaginaries of autonomous liberal personhood, which emphasize individual characteristics and individual accomplishments.
11. Indeed, Flores's work (2018, 2021) with Latinx immigrant youth in the United States highlights the importance of sibling care as a means of managing the precarity that migration policy produces for mixed status families.
12. See for instance Alber and Drotbohm 2015; Boris and Parreñas 2010; Cancian and Oliker 2000; Hanlon 2012; Nakano Glenn 2010; Zimmerman, Litt, and Bose 2006.
13. Following this analysis, this example is an instance of "on record off-record-ness," meaning that while it is formulated as off the record, the meaning is easily retrievable from context (P. Brown and Levinson 1987, 212). For an in-depth review of indirectness in discourse, see Lempert (2012).

Chapter 3

1. Scholarly dismissal of phatic communication is likely a manifestation of a broader tendency to negatively evaluate ways of speaking associated with women (Lakoff 2004). Early research in language and gender studies demonstrated that, at least in some contexts, women bear greater responsibility for the phatic effort of keeping conversations going (Fishman 1978; Maltz and Borker 1983). More recent scholarship has suggested that, regardless of actual practice, women are often understood to be responsible for such phatic communication, part of the architecture of gendered language ideologies that shore up patriarchy (Cameron 2014; Philips 2014).
2. Indeed, although it is not used among the families in my study, Chavez's work (2017a) shows that a related term, *saludado*, names a separate genre of poetic greetings used in the transnational networks he studies.
3. For a more in-depth discussion of remembering in the lives of transnational families, see Chapter 5.
4. Rosario consistently uses an alternate form of the term (*saludes* rather than *saludos*). This form has the same meaning and is widely used in El Salvador, although in some circles it may be stigmatized as archaic.
5. In light of this analysis, it would be interesting to see the ranking of greetings in a family where a woman was the primary remitter, a dynamic which did not manifest among the families in my study, though other research suggests it is quite common (Abrego 2009).

180 Notes

6. Bhimji 2005; De León 1998; Demuth 1986; Iwamura 1980.
7. The children of migrants were also all under the age of twelve when this research was conducted, and thus their imagined and actual involvement may well shift as they grow up.
8. Although these visions implicitly suggested that aging migrants would need to be relieved from their remitting obligations, there was no clear vision of what their futures would hold. In part, this may be because the migrants in these families were still quite young, but it is likely also a manifestation of the social invisibility of aging individuals in discussions of transnational migration (Dossa and Coe 2017, 3). Like the dominant Salvadoran imaginary laid out in Chapter 1, migration discourse around the world tends to figure migrants as individuals in the prime of life, erasing the important contributions that the elderly make to transnational care, as well as the reality that many elderly migrants may need care and are often unable to receive government benefits because they remain undocumented.
9. This concern with cost was ever-present in transnational calls, regardless of whether migrants purchased calling cards and initiated the calls, or whether relatives in El Salvador purchased minutes—using money sent by migrants—and made the calls themselves.
10. Spanish is transcribed as spoken, including the use of nonstandard forms ("saludes" in lines 3 and 7) and dialectal variation (the *voseo* as in "imaginate" line 19).

Chapter 4

1. Åkesson 2009; Coe 2011; Krause and Bressan 2018; Pauli and Bedorf 2018.
2. Ahlin 2017; Baldassar et al. 2016; Merla 2012a; Parreñas 2005.
3. Cole and Groes 2016; Groes-Green 2014; Hannaford 2016; Katigbak 2015a; McKay 2007.
4. Ahlin 2017, 2019; Baldassar et al. 2016; Cole 2014; Hernández-Carretero 2015; Madianou 2012; Madianou and Miller 2011b.
5. I have no record of families making remittance requests in other mediums such as in texts or video recordings like those in Chapter 3. Since the time of my research, as smartphones have become more common, more transnational communication may be happening asynchronously. For instance, my *comadre* Sara and I communicate consistently using voice memos, and among other topics, she has used this medium to request remittances for health and educational expenses.
6. Curl and Drew 2008; Heinemann 2006; Stevanovic and Peräkylä 2012.
7. Children living in El Salvador tended to ask their migrant kin more directly for what they wanted. This pattern supports the argument by Berman (2018) that different communicative norms for children are a means of constituting age as a socially meaningful category in societies around the world. In this case, making direct requests may be a way that children enact themselves socially as children.
8. Buchbinder 2010; Chua 2012; Clemente 2015; Griffith 2008.
9. Curl and Drew 2008; Félix-Brasdefer 2005; Fox 2014; García 1993; Gill, Halkowski, and Roberts 2001; Lindström 2005; Rossi 2012; Ruzickova 2007; Taleghani-Nikazm 2006.
10. I use the term "reported speech" since it is the most widely used term for this phenomenon; however, in understanding this linguistic practice, I draw on Tannen's conceptualization of this practice as "constructed dialogue," which highlights the fact that such reproductions are "primarily the creation of the speaker, rather than the party quoted" (1989, 99).
11. Becker 1979; C. L. Briggs and Bauman 1992; M. Goodwin 1990; M. Goodwin and C. Goodwin 1987.

12. "Púchica" is used throughout Latin America but is particularly associated with Central American varieties of Spanish. Like other terms (*pucha, puya*), the word is derived from the much stronger exclamation "puta" (lit. *whore*).

13. In conversation analytic terms, this line of questioning about precise amounts can be understood as an insert expansion that intercedes between the two pair parts. Specifically, this is a pre-second expansion, which makes important clarifications that then shape the second-position responding action, determining how Luis will respond to his mother's indirect request.

14. As with requests made through direct complaints, children did not make use of this even more subtle form of requesting remittances.

15. For another instance of this, see Rosario's complaint above, in which a mother (David's wife and family matriarch) quoted herself rather than another family member.

Chapter 5

1. Here I quote the title of a 2015 documentary "El pasado no es memoria," which focuses on wartime memories of campesinos living in Chalatenango, El Salvador (Duffy, Goldwater, and Pearce 2015).

2. Papá Chus is a name for God used in rural areas of El Salvador (Chus is a diminutive derived from Jesús).

3. The analytical tool of the diagraph was formalized by Du Bois (2007, 2014). Curly brackets are used here to mark off semantic elements that have been moved into a different order than that in which they were originally spoken.

References

Abrego, Leisy J. 2009. "Economic Well-Being in Salvadoran Transnational Families: How Gender Affects Remittance Practices." *Journal of Marriage and Family* 71, no. 4: 1070–85.

Abrego, Leisy J. 2014. *Sacrificing Families: Navigating Laws, Labor, and Love across Borders.* Stanford, CA: Stanford University Press.

Abrego, Leisy J. 2017. "On Silences: Salvadoran Refugees Then and Now." *Latino Studies* 15, no. 1: 73–85. https://doi.org/10.1057/s41276-017-0044-4.

Abrego, Leisy J. 2019. "Relational Legal Consciousness of U.S. Citizenship: Privilege, Responsibility, Guilt, and Love in Latino Mixed-Status Families." *Law & Society Review* 53, no. 3: 641–70. https://doi.org/10.1111/lasr.12414.

Achiume, E. Tendayi. 2019. "Migration as Decolonization." *Stanford Law Review* 71, no. 6: 1509–74.

Acosta, Tony, dir. 2013. *Musica de El Salvador *Hermano Lejano**. https://www.youtube.com/watch?v=7xyL-8rfStI.

Ahlin, Tanja. 2017. "Only Near Is Dear? Doing Elderly Care with Everyday ICTs in Indian Transnational Families." *Medical Anthropology Quarterly* 32, no. 1: 85–102. https://doi.org/10.1111/maq.12404.

Ahlin, Tanja. 2019. "Frequent Callers: 'Good Care' with ICTs in Indian Transnational Families." *Medical Anthropology* 39, no. 1: 69–82. https://doi.org/10.1080/01459740.2018.1532424.

Åkesson, Lisa. 2009. "Remittances and Inequality in Cape Verde: The Impact of Changing Family Organization." *Global Networks* 9, no. 3: 381–98.

Alas, Adriana. 2019. "Sensaciones a través del tiempo: El dolor en las negociaciones de posguerra de El Salvador." *Realidad: Revista de Ciencias Sociales y Humanidades*, 153 (June): 135–61. https://doi.org/10.5377/realidad.v0i153.9475.

Alber, Erdmute, and Heike Drotbohm, eds. 2015. *Anthropological Perspectives on Care: Work, Kinship, and the Life-Course.* 1st ed. New York: Palgrave Macmillan.

Alonso, Ana Maria. 1994. "The Politics of Space, Time and Substance: State Formation, Nationalism and Ethnicity." *Annual Review of Anthropology* 23: 379–405.

Alvarez, Sonia E. 1990. *Engendering Democracy in Brazil: Women's Movements in Transition Politics.* Princeton, NJ: Princeton University Press.

Anastario, Mike. 2019. *Parcels: Memories of Salvadoran Migration. Latinidad: Transnational Cultures in the United States.* New Brunswick, NJ: Rutgers University Press.

Andrade-Eekhoff, Katharine. 2003. *Mitos y Realidades: El Impacto Economico De La Migracion En Los Hogares Rurales.* San Salvador: FLACSO-El Salvador y FUNDAUNGO.

Andrade-Eekhoff, Katharine. 2006. "Migration and Development in El Salvador: Ideals versus Reality." *Migration Information Source.* http://www.migrationpolicy.org/article/migration-and-development-el-salvador-ideals-versus-reality.

Aparicio, Javier. 2022. "Fotos: Llegan nuestros hermanos cercanos." *La Prensa Gráfica*, December 9, 2022. https://www.laprensagrafica.com/elsalvador/Fotos--Llegan-nuestros-hermanos-cercanos-20221208-0090.html.

Arévalo, Mariana. 2019. "La historia de tres migrantes salvadoreños que fueron deportados y ahora emprenden en su país." *La Prensa Gráfica*, October 28, 2019. https://www.laprensagrafica.com/elsalvador/La-historia-de-tres-migrantes-salvadorenos-que-fueron-deportados-y-ahora-emprenden-en-su-pais-20191027-0626.html.

184 References

Arispe-Bazán, Diego. 2021. "Disreputable Spaniards Versus Middle-Class Limeños: The Coloniality of Speech in Lima, Peru." *Journal of Linguistic Anthropology* 31, no. 1: 43–63. https://doi.org/10.1111/jola.12298.

Arnold, Lynnette. 2015. "The Reconceptualization of Agency through Ambiguity and Contradiction: Salvadoran Women Narrating Unauthorized Migration." *Women's Studies International Forum* 52: 10–19. https://doi.org/10.1016/j.wsif.2015.07.004.

Arnold, Lynnette. 2019a. "Language Socialization across Borders: Producing Scalar Subjectivities through Material-Affective Semiosis." *Pragmatics* 29, no. 3: 332–56.

Arnold, Lynnette. 2019b. "Accompanying as Accomplices: Pedagogies for Community Engaged Learning in Sociocultural Linguistics." *Language and Linguistics Compass* 13, no. 6: 1–20. https://doi.org/10.1111/lnc3.12329.

Arnold, Lynnette. 2020. "Cross-Border Communication and the Enregisterment of Collective Frameworks for Care." *Medical Anthropology* 39, no. 7: 624–37. https://doi.org/10.1080/01459740.2020.1717490.

Arnold, Lynnette. 2021. "Communication as Care across Borders: Forging and Co-Opting Relationships of Obligation in Transnational Salvadoran Families." *American Anthropologist* 123, no. 1: 137–49. http://dx.doi.org/10.1111/aman.13517.

Arnold, Lynnette. 2022. "Data Management Practices in an Ethnographic Study of Language and Migration." In *Open Handbook of Linguistic Data Management*, edited by Andrea L. Berez-Kroeker, Bradley McDonnell, and Lauren B. Collister, 249–56. Cambridge, MA: MIT Press.

Arnold, Lynnette. 2023. "National Heroes or Dangerous Failures: Mobilizing Gender in Salvadoran Migration Discourse to Create Relational Neoliberal Personhood." *Gender and Language* 17, no. 4: 412–32. https://doi.org/10.1558/genl.22687.

Arnold, Lynnette, and Felicity Aulino. 2021. "A Call to Care." *Anthropology News* website, June 23. https://www.anthropology-news.org/articles/a-call-to-care/.

Arnold, Lynnette, and Steven P. Black. 2020. "How Communicative Approaches Enrich the Study of Care." *Medical Anthropology* 39, no. 7: 573–81. https://doi.org/10.1080/01459740.2020.1814285.

Arnold, Lynnette, and Hilary Parsons Dick. 2018. "From Distant Brother to Dangerous Animal: A Transnational Participation Framework of Migrant Interpellation." Politics of Participation, Helsinki, Finland.

ARPAS. 2021. "Presentan nueva propuesta de ley de justicia transicional." October 8, 2021. https://arpas.org.sv/2021/10/presentan-nueva-propuesta-de-ley-de-justicia-transicional/.

Aulino, Felicity. 2016. "Rituals of Care for the Elderly in Northern Thailand: Merit, Morality, and the Everyday of Long-term Care." *American Ethnologist* 43, no. 1: 91–102. https://doi.org/10.1111/amet.12265.

Aulino, Felicity. 2019. *Rituals of Care: Karmic Politics in an Aging Thailand*. Ithaca, NY: Cornell University Press.

Backhaus, Peter. 2017. *Care Communication: Making a Home in a Japanese Eldercare Facility*. Routledge Studies in Sociolinguistics 14. New York: Routledge.

Baker-Cristales, Beth. 2004. *Salvadoran Migration to Southern California: Redefining El Hermano Lejano*. New World Diasporas. Gainesville: University Press of Florida.

Bakhtin, M. M. 1981. *The Dialogic Imagination: Four Essays*. Trans. Michael Holquist. Austin: University of Texas Press.

Balaguera, Martha. 2018. "Trans-Migrations: Agency and Confinement at the Limits of Sovereignty." *Signs: Journal of Women in Culture and Society* 43, no. 3: 641–64. https://doi.org/10.1086/695302.

Baldassar, Loretta, and Laura Merla, eds. 2013. *Transnational Families, Migration and the Circulation of Care: Understanding Mobility and Absence in Family Life*. Routledge Research in Transnationalism 29. New York: Routledge.

References 185

Baldassar, Loretta, Mihaela Nedelcu, Laura Merla, and Raelene Wilding. 2016. "ICT-Based Co-Presence in Transnational Families and Communities: Challenging the Premise of Face-to-Face Proximity in Sustaining Relationships." *Global Networks* 16, no. 2: 133–44.

Baldassar, Loretta, Raelene Wilding, and Shane Worrell. 2020. "Elderly Migrants, Digital Kinning and Digital Home Making Across Time and Distance." In *Ways of Home Making in Care for Later Life*, edited by Bernike Pasveer, Oddgeir Synnes, and Ingunn Moser, 41–63. Health, Technology and Society. Singapore: Springer. https://doi.org/10.1007/978-981-15-0406-8_3.

Ball, Christopher. 2018. "Language of Kin Relations and Relationlessness." *Annual Review of Anthropology* 47, no. 1: 47–60. https://doi.org/10.1146/annurev-anthro-102317-050120.

Barabantseva, Elena, Aoileann Ní Mhurchú, and V. Spike Peterson. 2021. "Introduction: Engaging Geopolitics through the Lens of the Intimate." *Geopolitics* 26, no. 2: 343–56. https://doi.org/10.1080/14650045.2019.1636558.

Barba, Maribel, Concha Martínez, and Maria Morales, eds. 1996. *Like Gold in the Fire: Voices of Hope from El Salvador—War, Exile, and Return 1974-1999*. Translated by Maureen Russell and Jacky Shipton. Nottingham, UK: Russell Press.

Basch, Linda, Nina Glick Schiller, and Cristina Szanton-Blanc. 1994. *Nations Unbound: Transnational Projects, Postcolonial Predicaments and Deterritorialized Nation-States*. Langhorne, PA: Gordon and Breach.

Basso, Keith H. 1970. "'To Give up on Words': Silence in Western Apache Culture." *Southwestern Journal of Anthropology* 26, no. 3: 213–30.

Batalova, Jeanne. 2023. "Immigrant Health-Care Workers in the United States." Migration Policy Institute. April 6. https://www.migrationpolicy.org/article/immigrant-health-care-workers-united-states.

Bauer, Elaine, and Paul Thompson. 2004. "'She's Always the Person with a Very Global Vision': The Gender Dynamics of Migration, Narrative Interpretation and the Case of Jamaican Transnational Families." *Gender & History* 16, no. 2: 334–75.

Bauman, Richard. 1999. "Genre." *Journal of Linguistic Anthropology* 9, no. 1–2: 84–87. https://doi.org/10.1525/jlin.1999.9.1-2.84.

Bauman, Richard. 2004. *A World of Others' Words: Cross-Cultural Perspectives on Intertextuality*. Malden, MA: Blackwell.

Bauman, Richard. 2009. *Let Your Words Be Few: Symbolism of Speaking and Silence among Seventeenth-Century Quakers*. Tucson, AZ: Wheatmark.

Bauman, Richard, and Charles L. Briggs. 2003. *Voices of Modernity: Language Ideologies and the Politics of Inequality*. Studies in the Social and Cultural Foundations of Language 21. Cambridge: Cambridge University Press.

Becker, Alton L. 1979. "Text Building, Epistemology, and Aesthetics in Javanese Shadow Theater." In *The Imagination of Reality: Essays in Southease Asian Coherence Systems*, edited by Abram Yengoyan and Alton L. Becker, 211–43. Norwood, NJ: Ablex.

Bejarano, Cynthia L. 2002. "Las Super Madres de Latino America: Transforming Motherhood by Challenging Violence in Mexico, Argentina, and El Salvador." *Frontiers: A Journal of Women Studies* 23, no. 1: 126–50.

Benavides, Blanca Mirna, Xenia Ortíz, Claudia Marina Silva, and Lilian Vega. 2004. "Pueden Las Remesas Comprar El Futuro? Estudio Realizado En El Cantón San José La Labor, Municipio de San Sebastián, El Salvador." In *Desarollo Económico Local En Centro América: Estudios de Comunidades Globalizadas*, edited by Guillermo Lathrop and Juan Pablo Pérez Saínz, 139–80. San José, Costa Rica: Flacso.

Benítez, José Luis. 2006. "Transnational Dimensions of the Digital Divide among Salvadoran Immigrants in the Washington DC Metropolitan Area." *Global Networks* 6, no. 2: 181–99.

Berg, Ulla D. 2016. *Mobile Selves: Race, Migration, and Belonging in Peru and the U.S.* New York: New York University Press. https://doi.org/10.18574/nyu/9781479803460.001.0001.

186 References

Berman, Elise. 2018. *Talking like Children: Language and the Production of Age in the Marshall Islands*. Oxford Studies in Anthropology of Language. New York: Oxford University Press.

Besnier, Niko. 1990. "Language and Affect." *Annual Review of Anthropology* 19: 419–51.

Besnier, Niko. 1992. "Reported Speech and Affect on Nukulaelae Atoll." In *Responsibility and Evidence in Oral Discourse*, edited by Jane H. Hill and Judith T. Irvine, 161–81. Cambridge: Cambridge University Press.

Bhimji, Fazila. 2005. "Language Socialization with Directives in Two Mexican Immigrant Families in South Central Los Angeles." In *Building on Strength: Language and Literacy in Latino Families and Communities*, edited by Ana Celia Zentella, 60–76. New York: Teachers College Press.

Bietti, L. M. 2010. "Sharing Memories, Family Conversation and Interaction." *Discourse & Society* 21, no. 5: 499–523. https://doi.org/10.1177/0957926510373973.

Big Door Brigade. 2021. "What Is Mutual Aid?" 2021. https://bigdoorbrigade.com/what-is-mutual-aid/.

Billingsley, Krista. 2022. "Teaching Anthropology under Oath: Establishing Expertise in Asylum Hearings through Anthropological Training, Research, and Publications." *Fieldsights*. December 6. https://culanth.org/fieldsights/teaching-anthropology-under-oath-establishing-expertise-in-asylum-hearings-through-anthropological-training-research-and-publications.

Biolsi, Thomas. 2005. "Imagined Geographies: Sovereignty, Indigenous Space, and American Indian Struggle." *American Ethnologist* 32, no. 2: 239–59.

Black, Steven P. 2018. "The Ethics and Aesthetics of Care." *Annual Review of Anthropology* 47, no. 1: 79–95. https://doi.org/10.1146/annurev-anthro-102317-050059.

Black, Steven P. 2019. *Speech and Song at the Margins of Global Health: Zulu Tradition, HIV Stigma, and AIDS Activism in South Africa*. New Brunswick, NJ: Rutgers University Press.

Blegen, Theodore Christian. 1955. *Land of Their Choice: The Immigrants Write Home*. Minneapolis: University of Minnesota Press. http://www.aspresolver.com/aspresolver.asp?IMLD;S161.

Bletzer, Keith V. 2013. "Mexican Trans-Migrants and Their Experience on Both Sides of the Border: Intimacy and Distance Through Use of Deictic Referents." *Open Anthropology Journal* 6: 1–10.

Blommaert, Jan. 2015. "Chronotopes, Scales, and Complexity in the Study of Language in Society." *Annual Review of Anthropology* 44, no. 1: 105–16. https://doi.org/10.1146/annurev-anthro-102214-014035.

Bloomfield, Brian P., Yvonne Latham, and Theo Vurdubakis. 2010. "Bodies, Technologies and Action Possibilities: When Is an Affordance?" *Sociology* 44, no. 3: 415–33.

Blum, Larry, Marcia Homiak, Judy Housman, and Naomi Scheman. 1980. "Altruism and Women's Oppression." In *Women and Philosophy: Toward a Theory of Liberation*, edited by Carol C. Gould and Marx W. Wartofsky, 222–47. New York: Putnam.

Boehmer, Elleke. 2005. *Stories of Women: Gender and Narrative in the Postcolonial Nation*. Manchester, UK: Manchester University Press. https://doi.org/10.2307/j.ctt155j4ws.

Boris, Eileen, and Rhacel Salazar Parreñas, eds. 2010. *Intimate Labors: Cultures, Technologies, and the Politics of Care*. Stanford, CA: Stanford Social Sciences.

Bourdieu, Pierre. 1977. *Outline of a Theory of Practice*. Translated by Richard Nice. Cambridge Studies in Social and Cultural Anthropology. Cambridge: Cambridge University Press. https://doi.org/10.1017/CBO9780511812507.

Bourdieu, Pierre. 1984. *Distinction: A Social Critique of the Judgement of Taste*. Translated by Richard Nice. Cambridge, MA: Harvard University Press.

Bradley, Gracie Mae, and Luke De Noronha. 2022. *Against Borders: The Case for Abolition*. London: Verso.

References   187

Briggs, Charles L. 1992. "'Since I Am a Woman, I Will Chastise My Relatives': Gender, Reported Speech, and the (Re)Production of Social Relations in Warao Ritual Wailing." *American Ethnologist* 19: 337–61.

Briggs, Charles L., and Richard Bauman. 1992. "Genre, Intertextuality, and Social Power." *Journal of Linguistic Anthropology* 2: 131–72.

Briggs, Charles L., and Clara Mantini-Briggs. 2004. *Stories in the Time of Cholera: Racial Profiling during a Medical Nightmare.* Berkeley: University of California Press.

Briggs, Charles L., and Clara Mantini-Briggs. 2016. *Tell Me Why My Children Died: Rabies, Indigenous Knowledge, and Communicative Justice.* Critical Global Health: Evidence, Efficacy, Ethnography. Durham, NC: Duke University Press.

Briggs, Charles L., and Paja Faudree. 2016. "Communicating Bodies: New Juxtapositions of Linguistic and Medical Anthropology." *Anthropology News* (blog). May 6. http://linguistica nthropology.org/blog/2016/05/06/an-news-communicating-bodies-new-juxtapositions-of-linguistic-and-medical-anthropology-by-charles-l-briggs-u-california-berkeley-and-paja-faudree-brown-u/.

Briggs, Laura. 2020. *Taking Children: A History of American Terror.* Oakland: University of California Press.

Brody, Jill. 2000. "'Spatilab'il Sk"ujol' 'Tell Them "hey" for Me': Traditional Mayan Speech Genre Goes Multimedia." *Texas Linguistics Forum* 43: 1–14.

Brown, Penelope, and Stephen C. Levinson. 1987. *Politeness: Some Universals in Language Usage.* Studies in Interactional Sociolinguistics 4. New York: Cambridge University Press.

Brown, R., and A. Gilman. 2003. "The Pronouns of Power and Solidarity." *Sociolinguistics: The Essential Readings,* edited by Christina Bratt Paulston and G. Richard Tucker, 156–76.

Brown, Wendy. 2003. "Neo-Liberalism and the End of Liberal Democracy." *Theory & Event* 7, no. 1. https://doi.org/10.1353/tae.2003.0020.

Buch, Elana D. 2018. *Inequalities of Aging: Paradoxes of Independence in American Home Care.* New York: New York University Press.

Buchbinder, Mara. 2010. "Giving an Account of One's Pain in the Anthropological Interview." *Culture, Medicine and Psychiatry* 34, no. 1: 108–31. https://doi.org/10.1007/s11 013-009-9162-2.

Bucholtz, Mary, Dolores Inés Casillas, and Jin-Sook Lee, eds. 2018. *Feeling It: Language, Race, and Affect in Latinx Youth Learning.* New York: Routledge.

Cameron, Deborah. 2000. "Styling the Worker: Gender and the Commodification of Language in the Globalized Service Economy." *Journal of Sociolinguistics* 4: 323–47.

Cameron, Deborah. 2014. "Gender and Language Ideologies." In *The Handbook of Language, Gender, and Sexuality,* 2nd ed., edited by Susan Ehrlich, Miriam Meyerhoff, and Janet Holmes, 281–96. Malden, MA: Wiley Blackwell.

Cancian, Francesca M., and Stacey J. Oliker. 2000. *Caring and Gender.* Lanham, MD: Rowman & Littlefield.

Cárcamo, Jennifer A., dir. 2013. *Children of the Diaspora: For Peace and Democracy.* Syracuse University and Centro de la Memoria Histórica Salvadoreña. https://childrenofthediasp ora.com/.

Carothers, Thomas. 1991. *In the Name of Democracy: U.S. Policy toward Latin America in the Reagan Years.* Berkeley: University of California Press.

Carr, E. Summerson. 2010. *Scripting Addiction: The Politics of Therapeutic Talk and American Sobriety.* Princeton, NJ: Princeton University Press.

Carr, E. Summerson, and Michael Lempert, eds. 2016. *Scale: Discourse and Dimensions of Social Life.* Oakland: University of California Press. https://doi.org/10.1525/luminos.15.

Carsten, Janet. 2000. *Cultures of Relatedness: New Approaches to the Study of Kinship.* New York: Cambridge University Press.

188 References

Castañeda, Heide. 2019. *Borders of Belonging: Struggle and Solidarity in Mixed-Status Immigrant Families*. Stanford, CA: Stanford University Press.

Caton, Steven C. 1986. "Salam Tahiyah: Greetings from the Highlands of Yemen." *American Ethnologist* 13, no. 2: 290–308.

Cavanaugh, Jillian R., and Shalini Shankar, eds. 2017. *Language and Materiality: Ethnographic and Theoretical Explorations*. 1st ed. Cambridge University Press. https://doi.org/10.1017/9781316848418.

Caze, Marguerite La. 2008. "Seeing Oneself through the Eyes of the Other: Asymmetrical Reciprocity and Self-Respect." *Hypatia* 23, no. 3: 118–35. https://doi.org/10.1111/j.1527-2001.2008.tb01208.x.

Chacón Serrano, Fernando. 2020. "Estamos en guerra." *ECA: Estudios Centroamericanos* 75, no. 763: 71–96. https://doi.org/10.51378/eca.v75i763.3284.

Chacón Serrano, Fernando, Cristian Fabián Rodríguez, Jacqueline Escobar Pacheco, Daniela Marroquín Salamanca, Andrea Aparicio Silis, and Flavio Menjívar Cartagena. 2021. "Abusos de la memoria por el Gobierno salvadoreño y las prácticas de resistencia desde las nuevas generaciones." *Revista Estudios Psicosociales Latinoamericanos* 4, no. 1: 97–115. https://doi.org/10.25054/26196077.3155.

Chamberlain, Mary, and Selma Leydesdorff. 2004. "Transnational Families: Memories and Narratives." *Global Networks* 4, no. 3: 227–41.

Chávez, Alex E. 2017a. "From Potosi to Tennessee: Clandestine Desires and the Poetic Border." In *Sounds of Crossing: Music, Migration, and the Aural Poetics of Huapango Arribeño*, 232–77. Refiguring American Music. Durham, NC: Duke University Press.

Chávez, Alex E. 2017b. "Intimacy at Stake: Transnational Migration and the Separation of Family." *Latino Studies* 15, no. 1: 50–72. https://doi.org/10.1057/s41276-017-0045-3.

Chiles, Nick. 2015. "8 Black Panther Party Programs That Were More Empowering Than Federal Government Programs." *Atlanta Black Star*, March 26. https://atlantablackstar.com/2015/03/26/8-black-panther-party-programs-that-were-more-empowering-than-federal-government-programs/.

Ching, Erik Kristofer. 2016. *Stories of Civil War in El Salvador: A Battle over Memory*. Chapel Hill: University of North Carolina Press.

Chua, Jocelyn Lim. 2012. "The Register of 'Complaint':" *Medical Anthropology Quarterly* 26, no. 2: 221–40. https://doi.org/10.1111/j.1548-1387.2012.01202.x.

Clemente, Ignasi. 2015. *Uncertain Futures: Communication and Culture in Childhood Cancer Treatment*. Blackwell Studies in Discourse and Culture 7. Chichester, West Sussex, UK; Malden, MA: Wiley Blackwell.

Coe, Cati. 2011. *Everyday Ruptures Children, Youth, and Migration in Global Perspective*. Nashville, TN: Vanderbilt University Press. http://site.ebrary.com/id/10456990.

Coe, Cati. 2016. "Orchestrating Care in Time: Ghanaian Migrant Women, Family, and Reciprocity." *American Anthropologist* 118, no. 1: 37–48. https://doi.org/10.1111/aman.12446.

Cole, Jennifer. 2014. "The *Téléphone Malgache*: Transnational Gossip and Social Transformation among Malagasy Marriage Migrants in France: Gossip and Social Transformation." *American Ethnologist* 41, no. 2: 276–89. https://doi.org/10.1111/amet.12075.

Cole, Jennifer, and Deborah Lynn Durham. 2007. "Age, Regeneration and the Intimate Politics of Globalization." In *Generations and Globalization: Youth, Age, and Family in the New World Economy*, edited by Jennifer Cole and Deborah Lynn Durham, 1–28. Tracking Globalization. Bloomington: Indiana University Press.

Cole, Jennifer, and Christian Groes, eds. 2016. *Affective Circuits: African Migrations to Europe and the Pursuit of Social Regeneration*. Chicago: University of Chicago Press.

Cornejo, Iliana. 2023. "Nuevas órdenes de captura en caso El Mozote 'promueven fines ajenos a la justicia', dice acusación particular." Diario El Mundo. December 23, 2023. https://dia

References   189

rio.elmundo.sv/nacionales/nuevas-ordenes-de-captura-en-caso-el-mozote-promueven-fines-ajenos-a-la-justicia-dice-   acusacion-particular.

Corwin, Anna I. 2012. "Let Him Hold You: Spiritual and Social Support in a Catholic Convent Infirmary." *Anthropology & Aging* 33, no. 4: 120–29. https://doi.org/10.5195/aa.2012.29.

Corwin, Anna I. 2014. "Lord, Hear Our Prayer: Prayer, Social Support, and Well-Being in a Catholic Convent." *Journal of Linguistic Anthropology* 24, no. 2: 174–92. https://doi.org/10.1111/jola.12047.

Corwin, Anna I. 2020. "Care in Interaction: Aging, Personhood, and Meaningful Decline." *Medical Anthropology* 39, no. 7: 638–52. https://doi.org/10.1080/01459740.2019.1705297.

Corwin, Anna I. 2021. *Embracing Age: How Catholic Nuns Became Models of Aging Well*. Global Perspectives on Aging. New Brunswick, NJ: Rutgers University Press.

Couldry, Nick. 2004. "Liveness, 'Reality,' and the Mediated Habitus from Television to the Mobile Phone." *The Communication Review* 7, no. 4: 353–61. https://doi.org/10.1080/107144 20490886952.

Coutin, Susan Bibler. 1998. "From Refugees to Immigrants: The Legalization Strategies of Salvadoran Immigrants and Activists." *International Migration Review* 32, no. 4: 901–25.

Coutin, Susan Bibler. 2000. *Legalizing Moves: Salvadoran Immigrants' Struggle for U.S. Residency*. 1st ed. Ann Arbor: University of Michigan Press.

Coutin, Susan Bibler. 2007. *Nations of Emigrants: Shifting Boundaries of Citizenship in El Salvador and the United States*. Ithaca, NY: Cornell University Press.

Coutin, Susan Bibler. 2011. "Re/Membering the Nation: Gaps and Reckoning within Biographical Accounts of Salvadoran Émigrés." *Anthropological Quarterly* 84, no. 4: 809–34. https://doi.org/10.1353/anq.2011.0058.

Crapanzano, Vincent. 2004. *Imaginative Horizons: An Essay in Literary-Philosophical Anthropology*. Chicago: University of Chicago Press.

Csordas, Thomas J. 1993. "Somatic Modes of Attention." *Cultural Anthropology* 8, no. 2: 135–56.

Curl, Traci S., and Paul Drew. 2008. "Contingency and Action: A Comparison of Two Forms of Requesting." *Research on Language & Social Interaction* 41, no. 2: 129–53. https://doi.org/10.1080/08351810802028613.

Dave, Naisargi N. 2012. *Queer Activism in India: A Story in the Anthropology of Ethics*. Durham, NC: Duke University Press.

De Bremond, Ariane. 2007. "The Politics of Peace and Resettlement through El Salvador's Land Transfer Programme: Caught between the State and the Market." *Third World Quarterly* 28, no. 8: 1537–56. https://doi.org/10.1080/01436590701637391.

De Fina, A. 2013. "Top-Down and Bottom-Up Strategies of Identity Construction in Ethnic Media." *Applied Linguistics* 34, no. 5: 554–73. https://doi.org/10.1093/applin/amt026.

De Fina, Anna, and Sabina Perrino. 2020. "Introduction: Chronotopes and Chronotopic Relations." *Language & Communication* 70 (January): 67–70. https://doi.org/10.1016/j.lang com.2019.04.001.

De León, Lourdes. 1998. "The Emergent Participant: Interactive Patterns in the Socialization of Tzotzil (Mayan) Infants." *Journal of Linguistic Anthropology* 8, no. 2: 131–61.

De León, Lourdes. 2011. "Language Socialization and Multiparty Participation Frameworks." In *The Handbook of Language Socialization*, edited by Alessandro Duranti, Elinor Ochs, and Bambi Schieffelin, 81–111. Malden, MA: Wiley Blackwell.

DeLugan, Robin Maria. 2012. *Reimagining National Belonging: Post-Civil War El Salvador in a Global Context*. Tucson, AZ: University of Arizona Press.

DeLugan, Robin Maria. 2019. "La guerra civil, la memoria social y la nación: algunas consideraciones teóricas y éticas." *Realidad: Revista de Ciencias Sociales y Humanidades*, no. 153 (June): 9–21. https://doi.org/10.5377/realidad.v0i153.9458.

Demuth, Katherine. 1986. "Prompting Routines in the Language Socialization of Basotho Children." In *Language Socialization across Cultures*, edited by Bambi B. Schieffelin and Elinor Ochs, 51–79. New York: Cambridge University Press.

190 References

Deumert, Ana. 2014. *Sociolinguistics and Mobile Communication*. Edinburgh Sociolinguistics. Edinburgh, Scotland: Edinburgh University Press.

Di Leonardo, Micaela. 1987. "The Female World of Cards and Holidays: Women, Families, and the Work of Kinship." *Signs* 12, no. 3: 440–53.

Díaz, Juan Carlos. 2019. "Migrante que perdió un pie al caer de tren solicita ayuda." *La Prensa Grafica* (blog). August 12. https://www.laprensagrafica.com/elsalvador/Migrante-que-per dio-un-pie-al-caer-de-tren-solicita-ayuda-20190811-0428.html.

Dick, Hilary Parsons. 2010. "Imagined Lives and Modernist Chronotopes in Mexican Nonmigrant Discourse." *American Ethnologist* 37, no. 2: 275–90. https://doi.org/10.1111/j.1548-1425.2010.01255.x.

Dick, Hilary Parsons. 2011. "Language and Migration to the United States." *Annual Review of Anthropology* 40, no. 1: 227–40. https://doi.org/10.1146/annurev-anthro-081309-145634.

Dick, Hilary Parsons. 2017. "Una Gabacha Sinvergüenza (A Shameless White-Trash Woman): Moral Mobility and Interdiscursivity in a Mexican Migrant Community." *American Anthropologist* 119, no. 2: 223–35. https://doi.org/10.1111/aman.12884.

Dick, Hilary Parsons. 2018. *Words of Passage: National Longing and the Imagined Lives of Mexican Migrants*. 1st ed. Austin: University of Texas Press.

Dick, Hilary Parsons, and Lynnette Arnold. 2017. "Multisited Ethnography and Language in the Study of Migration." In *Routledge Handbook of Migration and Language*, edited by Suresh Canagarajah, 397–412. New York: Routledge.

Dick, Hilary Parsons, and Lynnette Arnold. 2018. "From South to North and Back Again: Making and Blurring Boundaries in Conversations across Borders." *Language & Communication* 59: 17–27. https://doi.org/10.1016/j.langcom.2017.02.005.

Dorjahn, Vernon R. 1977. "Temne Household Size and Composition: Rural Changes over Time and Rural-Urban Differences." *Ethnology* 16, no. 2: 105–27. https://doi.org/10.2307/3773381.

Dossa, Parin Aziz, and Cati Coe, eds. 2017. *Transnational Aging and Reconfigurations of Kin Work*. Global Perspectives on Aging. New Brunswick, NJ: Rutgers University Press.

Dreby, Joanna. 2012. "The Burden of Deportation on Children in Mexican Immigrant Families." *Journal of Marriage and Family* 74 (4): 829–45. https://doi.org/10.1111/j.1741-3737.2012.00989.x.

Drew, Paul. 1998. "Complaints about Transgressions and Misconduct." *Research on Language & Social Interaction* 31, no. 3–4: 295–325. https://doi.org/10.1080/08351813.1998.9683595.

Drotbohm, Heike. 2010. "Gossip and Social Control across the Seas: Targeting Gender, Resource Inequalities and Support in Cape Verdean Transnational Families." *African and Black Diaspora: An International Journal* 3, no. 1: 51–68. https://doi.org/10.1080/175286 30903319839.

Du Bois, John W. 2007. "The Stance Triangle." In *Stancetaking in Discourse*, edited by Robert Englebreton, 139–82. Philadelphia, PA: John Benjamins.

Du Bois, John W. 2014. "Towards a Dialogic Syntax." *Cognitive Linguistics* 25, no. 3: 359–411.

Du Bois, John W., Susanna Cumming, Stephan Schuetze-Coburn, and Danae Paolino. 1992. "Discourse Transcription." In *Santa Barbara Papers in Linguistics: Vol. 4*, edited by Sandra A. Thompson, 1–72. Santa Barbara: University of California Press.

Du Bois, John W., and Rachel Giora. 2014. "From Cognitive-Functional Linguistics to Dialogic Syntax." *Cognitive Linguistics* 25, no. 3: 351–57. https://doi.org/10.1515/cog-2014-0023.

Du Bois, John W., and Elise Kärkkäinen. 2012. "Taking a Stance on Emotion: Affect, Sequence, and Intersubjectivity in Dialogic Interaction." *Text & Talk* 32, no. 4: 433–51.

Duffy, Richard, Mike Goldwater, and Jenny Pearce, dirs. 2015. *El Pasado No Es Historia: Memorias de Guerra y Revolución En Chalatenango, El Salvador*. https://vimeo.com/133053653.

References 191

Duranti, Alessandro. 1992. "Language and Bodies in Social Space: Samoan Ceremonial Greetings." *American Anthropologist* 94, no. 3: 657–91.

Duranti, Alessandro. 1994a. *From Grammar to Politics: Linguistic Anthropology in a Western Samoan Village.* Berkeley: University of California Press.

Duranti, Alessandro. 1994b. "Hierarchies in the Making: Space, Time, and Speaking in a Fono." In *From Grammar to Politics: Linguistic Anthropology in a Western Samoan Village.* Berkeley: University of California Press.

Duranti, Alessandro. 1997. "Universal and Culture-Specific Properties of Greetings." *Journal of Linguistic Anthropology* 7, no. 1: 63–97.

Duranti, Alessandro. 2009. "The Force of Language and Its Temporal Unfolding." In *Language in Life, and a Life in Language: Jacob Mey, a Festschrift,* edited by Bruce Fraser and Ken Turner, 63–72. Bingley, UK: Emerald Group. https://doi.org/10.1163/9789004253209_010.

Duranti, Alessandro, and Nicco A. La Mattina. 2022. "The Semiotics of Cooperation." *Annual Review of Anthropology* 51, no. 1: 85–101. https://doi.org/10.1146/annurev-anthro-041420-103556.

Dyrness, Andrea. 2012. "Contra Viento y Marea (Against Wind and Tide): Building Civic Identity among Children of Emigration in El Salvador." *Anthropology and Education Quarterly* 43: 41–60.

Dyrness, Andrea, and Enrique Sepúlveda III. 2015. "Education and the Production of Diasporic Citizens in El Salvador." *Harvard Educational Review* 85, no. 1: 108–31. https://doi.org/10.17763/haer.85.1.r6j5064448621r73.

Edwards, Derek, and David Middleton. 1986. "Joint Remembering: Constructing an Account of Shared Experience through Conversational Discourse." *Discourse Processes* 9, no. 4: 423–59.

Eley, Geoff, and Ronald Grigor Suny, eds. 1996. *Becoming National: A Reader.* New York: Oxford University Press.

Enchautegui, María E., and Cecilia Menjívar. 2015. "Paradoxes of Family Immigration Policy: Separation, Reorganization, and Reunification of Families under Current Immigration Laws." *Law & Policy* 37, no. 1–2: 32–60. https://doi.org/10.1111/lapo.12030.

Enfield, N. J. 2009. "Everyday Ritual in the Residential World." In *Ritual Communication,* edited by Gunter Senft and Ellen B. Basso, 51–80. Wenner-Gren International Symposium Series. New York: Berg [English ed.].

Englebretson, Robert, ed. 2007. *Stancetaking in Discourse: Subjectivity, Evaluation, Interaction.* Pragmatics & Beyond New Series, v. 164. Amsterdam: John Benjamins.

Erikson, Erik H. 1995. *A Way of Looking at Things: Selected Papers, 1930-1980.* Revised ed. New York: W. W. Norton.

Ervin-Tripp, Susan. 1976. "Is Sybil There? The Structure of Some American English Directives." *Language in Society* 5, no. 1: 25–66. https://doi.org/10.1017/S0047404500006849.

Escobar, Natalie. 2018. "Family Separation Isn't New." *The Atlantic.* August 14. https://www.theatlantic.com/family/archive/2018/08/us-immigration-policy-has-traumatized-children-for-nearly-100-years/567479/.ucu,

Fan, Yu-Kang, and Rhacel Salazar Parreñas. 2018. "Who Cares for the Children and the Elderly? Gender and Transnational Families." In *Childhood and Parenting in Transnational Settings,* edited by Viorela Ducu, Mihaela Nedelucu, and Aron Telegdi, 83–99. International Perspectives on Migration. Cham, Switzerland: Springer. https://doi.org/10.1007/978-3-319-90942-4_6.

Faraj, Samer, and Bijan Azad. 2012. "The Materiality of Technology: An Affordance Perspective." *Materiality and Organizing: Social Interaction in a Technological World,* edited by Paul M. Leonardi, Bonnie A. Nardi, and Jannis Kallinikos, 237–58. Online ed. Oxford Academic.

Faudree, Paja. 2013. *Singing for the Dead: The Politics of Indigenous Revival in Mexico.* Durham, NC: Duke University Press.

192 References

Faudree, Paja. 2015. "Singing for the Dead, on and off Line: Diversity, Migration, and Scale in Mexican Muertos Music." *Language & Communication* 44 (September): 31–43. https://doi.org/10.1016/j.langcom.2014.11.004.

Faudree, Paja. 2020. "'Making Medicine' with Salvia Divinorum: Competing Approaches and Their Implications." *Medical Anthropology* 39, no. 7: 582–96. https://doi.org/10.1080/01459740.2020.1814772.

Febres, Salomón Lerner. 2010. "La búsqueda de la memoria histórica en América Latina: reconciliación y democracia." *Hendu–Revista Latino-Americana de Direitos Humanos* 1, no. 1: 7. https://doi.org/10.18542/hendu.v1i1.367.

Feld, Steven. 2012. *Sound and Sentiment: Birds, Weeping, Poetics, and Song in Kaluli Expression.* 3rd ed. (30th anniversary ed. with a new introduction). Durham, NC: Duke University Press.

Félix-Brasdefer, J. César. 2005. "Indirectness and Politeness in Mexican Requests." In *Selected Proceedings of the 7th Hispanic Linguistics Symposium*, edited by David Eddington, 66–78. Somerville, MA: Cascadilla Proceedings Project. http://www.lingref.com/cpp/hls/7/paper1087.pdf.

Field, Margaret. 2001. "Triadic Directives in Navajo Language Socialization." *Language in Society* 30, no. 2: 249–63.

Firth, Raymond. 1972. "Verbal and Bodily Rituals of Greeting and Parting." In *The Interpretation of Ritual*, edited by J. S. La Fontaine, 1–38. London: Routledge.

Fisher, Berenice, and Joan Tronto. 1990. "Towards a Feminist Theory of Caring." In *Circles of Care: Work and Identity in Women's Lives*, edited by Emily K. Abel and Margaret K. Nelson, 35–62. Albany: State University of New York Press.

Fishman, Pamela M. 1978. "Interaction: The Work Women Do." *Social Problems* 25, no. 4: 397–406. https://doi.org/10.2307/800492.

Fivush, Robyn, and Judith A. Hudson, eds. 1990. *Knowing and Remembering in Young Children.* Emory Symposia in Cognition 3. New York: Cambridge University Press.

Flores, Andrea. 2018. "The Descendant Bargain: Latina Youth Remaking Kinship and Generation through Educational Sibcare in Nashville, Tennessee." *American Anthropologist* 120, no. 3: 474–86. https://doi.org/10.1111/aman.13052.

Flores, Andrea. 2021. *The Succeeders: How Immigrant Youth Are Transforming What It Means to Belong in America.* California Series in Public Anthropology 53. Oakland: University of California Press.

Flores, Nelson, Amelia Tseng, and Nicholas Subtirelu, eds. 2021. *Bilingualism for All? Raciolinguistic Perspectives on Dual Language Education in the United States.* Bilingual Education & Bilingualism 125. Bristol, UK: Multilingual Matters.

Folbre, Nancy. 2014. *Who Cares? A Feminist Critique of the Care Economy.* New York: Rosa Luxemburg Stiftung.

Fortier, Anne-Marie. 2000. *Migrant Belongings: Memory, Space, Identity.* Oxford: Berg.

Fox, Barbara. 2014. "On the Notion of Pre-Request." *Discourse Studies* 17, no. 1: 41–63.

Fraad, Harriet, Stephen A. Resnick, and Richard D. Wolff. 1994. *Bringing It All Back Home: Class, Gender and Power in the Modern Household.* New Directions/Rethinking Marxism. London: Pluto.

Frake, Charles O. 1975. "How to Enter a Yakan House." In *Sociocultural Dimensions of Language Use*, edited by Mary Sanches and Ben G. Blount, 25–40. Language, Thought, and Culture. New York: Academic Press.

Francisco-Menchavez, Valerie. 2015. "'The Internet Is Magic': Technology, Intimacy and Transnational Families." *Critical Sociology* 41, no. 1: 173–90. https://doi.org/10.1177/0896920513484602.

Francisco-Menchavez, Valerie. 2018. *The Labor of Care: Filipina Migrants and Transnational Families in the Digital Age.* Asian American Experience. Urbana: University of Illinois Press.

References **193**

Franklin, Sarah, and Susan McKinnon. 2000. "New Directions in Kinship Study: A Core Concept Revisited." *Current Anthropology* 41, no. 2: 275–79. https://doi.org/10.1086/300132.

Fraser, Nancy. 2017. "Crisis of Care? On the Social-Reproductive Contradictions of Contemporary Capitalism." In *Social Reproduction Theory: Remapping Class, Recentering Oppression*, edited by Tithi Bhattacharya, 21–36. Pluto Press. https://doi.org/10.2307/j.ctt 1vz494j.

French, Brigittine M. 2012. "The Semiotics of Collective Memories." *Annual Review of Anthropology* 41, no. 1: 337–53. https://doi.org/10.1146/annurev-anthro-081309-145936.

FUSADES. 2015. "Una Mirada a Las Familias Salvadoreñas: Sus Transformaciones y Desafios Desde La Óptica de Las Politicas Sociales Con Enfoque de Niñez." San Salvador, El Salvador: Fundación Salvadoreña para el Desarrollo Económico y Social.

Fussell, Elizabeth, and Alberto Palloni. 2004. "Persistent Marriage Regimes in Changing Times." *Journal of Marriage and Family* 66, no. 5: 1201–13.

Gal, S. 1989. "Language and Political Economy." *Annual Review of Anthropology* 18: 345–67.

Gal, Susan. 2002. "A Semiotics of the Public/Private Distinction." *Differences* 13, no. 1: 77–95. https://doi.org/10.1215/10407391-13-1-77.

Gálvez, Alyshia. 2011. *Patient Citizens, Immigrant Mothers: Mexican Women, Public Prenatal Care, and the Birth Weight Paradox*. Critical Issues in Health and Medicine. New Brunswick, NJ: Rutgers University Press.

Gamburd, Michele Ruth. 2000. *The Kitchen Spoon's Handle: Transnationalism and Sri Lanka's Migrant Housemaids*. Ithaca, NY: Cornell University Press.

Gamburd, Michele Ruth. 2004. "Breadwinners No More." In *Global Woman: Nannies, Maids, and Sex Workers in the New Economy*, edited by Barbara Ehrenreich and Arlie Russell Hochschild, 190–206. New York: Macmillan.

Gaonkar, Dilip Parameshwar. 2002. "Toward New Imaginaries: An Introduction." *Public Culture* 14, no. 1: 1–19.

García, Carmen. 1993. "Making a Request and Responding to It: A Case Study of Peruvian Spanish Speakers." *Journal of Pragmatics* 19, no. 2: 127–52.

García, Jessica. 2023. "Comisión resta importancia a estudio de Ley de Justicia Transicional." Noticias de El Salvador. December 11, 2023. https://www.elsalvador.com/noticias/nacional/obstruccion-a-la-justicia-ley-de-reconciliac ion-crimenes-lesa-humanidad-asamblea-legislativa/1109829/2023/.

García-Sánchez, Inmaculada M. 2018. "Children as Interactional Brokers of Care." *Annual Review of Anthropology* 47, no. 1: 167–84. https://doi.org/10.1146/annurev-anthro-102317-050050.

Gerson, Daniela, Chi Zhang, and Elizabeth Aguilera. 2021. "Shortcomings and Opportunities in U.S. Immigration Coverage." *Internews*. https://internews.org/wp-content/uploads/2021/08/MigratoryNotes_USImmigration_20210729.pdf.

Gibson-Graham, J. K. 2014. "Rethinking the Economy with Thick Description and Weak Theory." *Current Anthropology* 55, no. S9: S147–53. https://doi.org/10.1086/676646.

Gibson-Graham, J. K. 2020. "Reading for Economic Difference." In *The Handbook of Diverse Economies*, edited by J. Gibson-Graham and Kelly Dombroski, 476–85. London: Edward Elgar. https://doi.org/10.4337/9781788119962.00066.

Gill, Virginia Teas, Timothy Halkowski, and Felicia Roberts. 2001. "Accomplishing a Request without Making One: A Single Case Analysis of a Primary Care Visit." *Text–Interdisciplinary Journal for the Study of Discourse* 21, no. 1–2: 55–81.

Gilligan, Carol. 1982. *In a Different Voice: Psychological Theory and Women's Development*. Cambridge, MA: Harvard University Press.

Goldring, Luin. 1996. "Gendered Memory: Constructions of Rurality among Mexican Transnational Migrants." In *Creating the Countryside: The Politics of Rural and Environmental*

Discourse, edited by E. Melanie DuPuis and Peter Vandergeest, 303–29. Conflicts in Urban and Regional Development. Philadelphia, PA: Temple University Press.

Gomberg-Muñoz, Ruth. 2018. "The Complicit Anthropologist." *Journal for the Anthropology of North America* 21, no 1: 36–37. https://doi.org/10.1002/nad.12070.

Gómez, Réne, and Rosa María Pastrán. 2019. "Parte primer contingente de salvadoreños hacia EUA para trabajar con visas temporales." *La Prensa Gráfica*, December 19. https://www.laprensagrafica.com/elsalvador/Parte-primer-contingente-de-salvadorenos-hacia-EUA-para-trabajar-con-visas-temporales-20191219-0366.html.

Gonzalez, Carmen. 2020. "Migration As Reparation: Climate Change and the Disruption of Borders." *Loyola Law Review* 66 (January): 401–44.

Goodwin, Charles. 2018. *Co-Operative Action. Learning in Doing: Social, Cognitive and Computational Perspectives*. New York: Cambridge University Press.

Goodwin, Marjorie Harness. 1990. *He-Said-She-Said: Talk as Social Organization among Black Children*. Bloomington: Indiana University Press.

Goodwin, Marjorie Harness. 2006. "Participation, Affect, and Trajectory in Family Directive/Response Sequences." *Text & Talk* 26, no. 4–5: 515–43. https://doi.org/10.1515/TEXT.2006.021.

Goodwin, Marjorie Harness. 2015. "Care-Full Look at Language, Gender, and Embodied Intimacy." In *Shifting Visions: Gender and Discourses*, edited by Allyson Julé, 27–48. Newcastle upon Tyne, UK: Cambridge Scholars.

Goodwin, Marjorie Harness, and Asta Cekaite. 2018. *Embodied Family Choreography: Practices of Control, Care, and Mundane Creativity*. 1st ed. Directions in Ethnomethodology and Conversation Analysis. New York: Routledge.

Goodwin, Marjorie Harness, and Charles Goodwin. 1987. "Children's Arguing." In *Language, Gender, and Sex in Comparative Perspective*, edited by Susan Urmston Philips, Susan Steele, and Christine Tanz, 200–48. Studies in the Social and Cultural Foundations of Language, no. 4. Cambridge: Cambridge University Press.

Göransson, Kristina. 2013. "Reassessing the Intergenerational Contract." *Journal of Intergenerational Relationships* 11, no. 1: 62–75. https://doi.org/10.1080/15350770.2013.751832.

Gould, Jeffrey L., and Aldo Lauria-Santiago. 2008. *To Rise in Darkness: Revolution, Repression, and Memory in El Salvador, 1920-1932*. Durham, NC: Duke University Press.

Griffith, Laura. 2008. "Complaints, Sensitivities and Responsibility: An Ethnographic Investigation into the Debates Concerning the Care of Bangladeshi Mothers in the East End." *International Migration* 46, no. 5: 143–65. https://doi.org/10.1111/j.1468-2435.2008.00492.x.

Groes-Green, Christian. 2014. "Journeys of Patronage: Moral Economies of Transactional Sex, Kinship, and Female Migration from Mozambique to Europe." *Journal of the Royal Anthropological Institute* 20, no. 2: 237–55. https://doi.org/10.1111/1467-9655.12102.

Gumperz, John J. 1982. *Discourse Strategies*. Studies in Interactional Sociolinguistics 1. Cambridge [Cambridgeshire]: Cambridge University Press.

Guzmán, Jessica. 2019a. "Estos son los requisitos para salvadoreños que opten a visas de trabajo temporal en Estados Unidos." *elsalvador.com*, August 29. https://www.elsalvador.com/noticias/negocios/estos-son-los-requisitos-para-salvadorenos-que-opten-a-visas-de-trabajo-temporal-en-estados-unidos/635192/2019/.

Guzmán, Jessica. 2019b. "'Voy con la esperanza de sacar adelante a mi familia', la emotiva despedida de los salvadoreños que viajan a trabajar a EE.UU." *elsalvador.com*, December 19. https://www.elsalvador.com/noticias/negocios/voy-con-la-esperanza-de-sacar-adelante-a-mi-familia-salvadorenos-con-visas-de-trabajo-temporal-partieron-hacia-ee-uu/669927/2019/.

Guzmán, Jessica. 2019c. "25 salvadoreños viajan a EE.UU. a trabajar con visa temporal." *elsalvador.com*, December 20. https://www.elsalvador.com/eldiariodehoy/25-salvadorenos-viajan-a-ee-uu-a-trabajar-con-visa-temporal/670054/2019/.

References 195

Hagan, Jacqueline, Karl Eschbach, and Nestor Rodriguez. 2008. "U.S. Deportation Policy, Family Separation, and Circular Migration." *International Migration Review* 42, no. 1: 64–88. https://doi.org/10.1111/j.1747-7379.2007.00114.x.

Halilovich, Hariz. 2013. *Places of Pain: Forced Displacement, Popular Memory, and Trans-Local Identities in Bosnian War-Torn Communities*. Space and Place, v. 10. New York: Berghahn Books.

Hall, Kira. 1995. "Lip Service on the Fantasy Lines." In *Gender Articulated: Language and the Socially Constructed Self*, edited by Kira Hall and Mary Bucholtz, 183–216. New York: Routledge. https://doi.org/10.13140/2.1.4942.2402.

Hall, Stuart. 2017. "Racism and Reaction 1978." In *Selected Political Writings: The Great Moving Right Show and Other Essays*, edited by Sally Davison, David Featherstone, Michael Rustin, and Bill Schwarz, 142–57. Durham, NC: Duke University Press. https://doi.org/10.1215/9780822372943.

Hall, Stuart, Chas Critcher, Tony Jefferson, John Clarke, and Brian Roberts. 1978. *Policing the Crisis: Mugging, the State, and Law and Order*. Critical Social Studies. London: Macmillan.

Hallett, Miranda Cady. 2012. "'Better Than White Trash': Work Ethic, Latinidad and Whiteness in Rural Arkansas." *Latino Studies* 10, no. 1–2: 81–106. https://doi.org/10.1057/1st.2012.14.

Hallett, Miranda Cady. 2013. "Rooted/Uprooted: Place, Policy, and Salvadoran Transnational Identities in Rural Arkansas." In *Latin American Migrations to the U.S. Heartland: Changing Social Landscapes in Middle America*, edited by Linda Allegro and Andrew Grant Wood, 147–68. Chicago: University of Illinois Press. https://www.jstor.org/stable/10.5406/j.ctt2ttb7h.

Hallett, Miranda Cady. 2014. "Temporary Protection, Enduring Contradiction: The Contested and Contradictory Meanings of Temporary Immigration Status." *Law & Social Inquiry* 39, no. 3: 621–42.

Hallett, Miranda Cady. 2019. "Re/Imagined Community: Neoliberalism, Human Rights, and Officials' Accounts of the Salvadoran Transnation." *PoLAR: Political and Legal Anthropology Review* 42, no. 2: 298–316. https://doi.org/10.1111/plar.12311.

Hallett, Miranda Cady, and Lynnette Arnold. 2018. "Compounding the Crisis." NACLA. https://nacla.org/news/2018/07/24/compounding-crisis.

Hallett, Miranda Cady, and Beth Baker-Cristales. 2010. "Diasporic Suffrage: Rights Claims And State Agency In The Salvadoran Trans-Nation." *Urban Anthropology and Studies of Cultural Systems and World Economic Development* 39, no. 1/2: 175–211.

Hamilton, Nora, and Norma Stoltz Chinchilla. 1991. "Central American Migration: A Framework for Analysis." *Latin American Research Review* 26, no. 1: 75–110.

Hammock, John, María Elena Letona, Gilma Peréz, and Ana Isen Hammock. 2006. *Testimonios de Familias Migrantes Salvadoreñas: Pobreza y Trabajo*. Cambridge, MA: Centro Presente.

Han, Clara. 2012. *Life in Debt: Times of Care and Violence in Neoliberal Chile*. Berkeley: University of California Press.

Hanlon, Niall. 2012. *Masculinities, Care and Equality: Identity and Nurture in Men's Lives*. Genders and Sexualities in the Social Sciences. New York: Palgrave Macmillan.

Hannaford, Dinah. 2015. "Technologies of the Spouse: Intimate Surveillance in Senegalese Transnational Marriages." *Global Networks* 15, no. 1: 43–59. https://doi.org/10.1111/glob.12045.

Hannaford, Dinah. 2016. "Intimate Remittances: Marriage, Migration, and MoneyGram in Senegal." *Africa Today* 62, no. 3: 92–109.

Hansen, Thomas Blom, and Finn Stepputat. 2001. "INTRODUCTION: States of Imagination." In *States of Imagination*, edited by Thomas Blom Hansen and Finn Stepputat, 1–38. Ethnographic Explorations of the Postcolonial State. Durham, NC: Duke University Press. https://doi.org/10.2307/j.ctv11smxxj.4.

196   References

Hartigan, John. 2017. *Care of the Species: Races of Corn and the Science of Plant Biodiversity.* Minneapolis: University of Minnesota Press.

Harvey, David. 2005. *A Brief History of Neoliberalism.* New York: Oxford University Press.

Harvey, T. S. 2013. *Wellness beyond Words: Maya Compositions of Speech and Silence in Medical Care.* Albuquerque: University of New Mexico Press. https://ebookcentral.proquest.com/lib/uma/reader.action?docID=1112345.

Haviland, John B. 2009. "Little Rituals." In *Ritual Communication*, edited by Gunter Senft and Ellen B. Basso, 21–50. Wenner-Gren International Symposium Series. New York: Berg [English ed.].

Heidbrink, Lauren. 2019. "The Coercive Power of Debt: Migration and Deportation of Guatemalan Indigenous Youth." *The Journal of Latin American and Caribbean Anthropology* 24, no. 1: 263–81. https://doi.org/10.1111/jlca.12385.

Heidegger, Martin. 2008. *Being and Time.* Repr. ed. New York: Harper Perennial Modern Classics.

Heinemann, Trine. 2006. "'Will You or Can't You?': Displaying Entitlement in Interrogative Requests." *Journal of Pragmatics* 38, no. 7: 1081–1104. https://doi.org/10.1016/j.pragma.2005.09.013.

Hernández-Carretero, María. 2015. "Renegotiating Obligations through Migration: Senegalese Transnationalism and the Quest for the Right Distance." *Journal of Ethnic and Migration Studies* 41, no. 12: 2021–40. https://doi.org/10.1080/1369183X.2015.1045462.

Herrera, Jack. 2021. "Biden Brings Back Family Separation—This Time in Mexico." *POLITICO*, March 20. https://www.politico.com/news/magazine/2021/03/20/border-family-separation-mexico-biden-477309.

Herzfeld, Michael. 1997. *Cultural Intimacy: Social Poetics in the Nation-State.* New York: Routledge.

Hesson, Ted. 2023. "Close to 1,000 Migrant Children Separated by Trump yet to Be Reunited with Parents | Reuters." *Reuters*, February 2. https://www.reuters.com/world/us/close-1000-migrant-children-separated-by-trump-yet-be-reunited-with-parents-2023-02-02/.

Hirsch, Jennifer S. 2003. *A Courtship after Marriage: Sexuality and Love in Mexican Transnational Families.* Berkeley: University of California Press.

Hochschild, Arlie Russell. 2000. "Global Care Chains and Emotional Surplus Value." In *On the Edge: Globalization and the New Millennium*, edited by Anthony Giddens and Will Hutton, 130–46. London: Sage.

Hoey, Elliott. 2014. "Empathic Moments and the Calibration of Social Distance." UCLA Conference: International Conference for Conversation Analysis.

Holmstrom, Nancy. 1981. "'Women's Work,' the Family and Capitalism." *Science & Society* 45, no. 2: 186–211.

Holst-Warhaft, Gail. 2002. *Dangerous Voices: Women's Laments and Greek Literature.* 1st ed. Routledge.

Holt, Elizabeth, and Rebecca Clift. 2007. *Reporting Talk: Reported Speech in Interaction.* Cambridge: Cambridge University Press.

Horst, H. A. 2006. "The Blessings and Burdens of Communication: Cell Phones in Jamaican Transnational Social Fields." *Global Networks* 6, no. 2: 143–59.

Huntington, Patricia. 2016. "Asymmetrical Reciprocity and Practical Agency: Contemporary Dilemmas of Feminist Theory in Benhabib, Young, and Kristeva." In *Political Phenomenology: Essays in Memory of Petee Jung*, edited by Hwa Yol Jung and Lester Embree, 353–78. Contributions to Phenomenology. Cham, Switzerland: Springer International. https://doi.org/10.1007/978-3-319-27775-2_20.

Hutchby, Ian. 2001a. *Conversation and Technology: From the Telephone to the Internet.* Cambridge, UK: Polity Press.

References   197

Hutchby, Ian. 2001b. "Technologies, Texts and Affordances." *Sociology* 35, no. 2: 441–56. https://doi.org/10.1177/S0038038501000219.

Indigene Community. n.d. "Mutual Aid." Accessed December 13, 2021. https://sites.google.com/site/indigenecommunity/home/2-mutual-aid.

Indigenous Action. 2014. *Accomplices Not Allies: Abolishing the Ally Industrial Complex.* http://www.indigenousaction.org/accomplices-not-allies-abolishing-the-ally-industrial-complex/.

Ingold, Tim. 2011. *The Perception of the Environment: Essays on Livelihood, Dwelling and Skill.* London: Routledge.

International Organization for Migration. 2017. "Food Security and Emigration: Why People Flee and the Impact on Family Members Left behind in El Salvador, Guatemala and Honduras |." https://environmentalmigration.iom.int/food-security-and-emigration-why-people-flee-and-impact-family-members-left-behind-el-salvador.

International Telecommunication Union. 2014. "World Telecommunication Indicators Database." 2014. http://www.itu.int/en/ITU-D/Statistics/Pages/publications/wtid.aspx.

Irvine, Judith T. 1975. "Strategies of Status Manipulation in the Wolof Greeting." In *Explorations in the Ethnography of Speaking*, edited by Richard Bauman and Joel Scherzer, 167–91. New York: Cambridge University Press.

Irvine, Judith T. 1989. "When Talk Isn't Cheap: Language and Political Economy." *American Ethnologist* 16, no. 2: 248–67.

Irvine, Judith T. 1990. "Registering Affect: Heteroglossia in the Linguistic Expression of Emotion." In *Language and the Politics of Emotion*, edited by Catherine Lutz and Lila Abu-Lughod, 126–61. Studies in Emotion and Social Interaction. New York: Cambridge University Press.

ISDEMU. 2014. "El Salvador: Dónde y cómo estamos las mujeres. Compendio de estadisticas e indicadores de género 2009-2014." San Salvador, El Salvador: Instituto Salvadoreño para el desarollo de la mujer.

Iwamura, Susan Grohs. 1980. *The Verbal Games of Pre-School Children.* London: Croom Helm.

Jackson, Reagan. 2016. "Accomplices versus Allies." *The Seattle Globalist*, July 14, 2016. http://www.seattleglobalist.com/2016/07/14/accomplices-vs-allies/53654.

Jaffe, Alexandra M., ed. 2012. *Stance: Sociolinguistic Perspectives.* Oxford Studies in Sociolinguistics. Oxford: Oxford University Press.

Jakobson, Roman. 1960. "The Speech Event and the Functions of Language." In *On Language*, edited by Linda R. Waugh and Monique Monville-Burston, 69–79. Cambridge MA: Harvard University Press.

Jakobson, Roman. 1968. "Poetry of Grammar and Grammar of Poetry." *Lingua* 21: 587–609.

Jefferson, Gail. 1988. "On the Sequential Organization of Troubles-Talk in Ordinary Conversation." *Social Problems* 35: 418–41.

Johnson, Scott. 2014. "American-Born Gangs Helping Drive Immigrant Crisis at U.S. Border." *National Geographic*, July 23. http://news.nationalgeographic.com/news/2014/07/140723-immigration-minors-honduras-gang-violence-central-america/.

Justice Power. 2020. "Accompaniment." https://justicepower.org/accompaniment/.

Karimzad, Farzad, and Lydia Catedral. 2021. *Chronotopes and Migration: Language, Social Imagination, and Behavior.* Routledge Studies in Linguistics. New York: Routledge.

Katigbak, Evangeline O. 2015a. "Moralizing Emotional Remittances: Transnational Familyhood and Translocal Moral Economy in the Philippines' 'Little Italy.'" *Global Networks* 15, no. 4: 519–35. https://doi.org/10.1111/glob.12092.

Katigbak, Evangeline O. 2015b. "Emotional Ransom: Exploring Envy and Resentment among Filipino 'Hero-Migrants' and Their 'Left-Behind' Families." In *The Age of Asian Migration: Continuity, Diversity, and Susceptibility Volume 2*, edited by Yuk Wah Chan, Heidi

198 References

Fung, and Grażyna Szymańska-Matusiewicz, 93–107. Newcastle upon Tyne, UK: Cambridge Scholars.

KNOMAD. 2019. "Migration and Remittances: Recent Developments and Outlook." Migration and Development Brief 31. Global Knowledge Partnership on Migration and Development.

Kockelman, Paul. 2004. "Stance and Subjectivity." *Journal of Linguistic Anthropology* 14, no. 2: 127–50. https://doi.org/10.1525/jlin.2004.14.2.127.

Kofman, E. 2012. "Rethinking Care through Social Reproduction: Articulating Circuits of Migration." *Social Politics: International Studies in Gender, State & Society* 19, no. 1: 142–62. https://doi.org/10.1093/sp/jxr030.

Koike, Dale A. 1996. "Functions of the Adverbial Ya in Spanish Narrative Discourse." *Journal of Pragmatics* 25, no. 2: 267–79. https://doi.org/10.1016/0378-2166(94)00095-6.

Krause, Elizabeth L., and Massimo Bressan. 2018. "Circulating Children, Underwriting Capitalism: Chinese Global Households and Fast Fashion in Italy." *Current Anthropology* 59, no. 5: 572–95. https://doi.org/10.1086/699826.

Kroger, T. 2009. "Care Research and Disability Studies: Nothing in Common?" *Critical Social Policy* 29, no. 3: 398–420. https://doi.org/10.1177/0261018309105177.

Kuipers, Joel C. 1989. "'Medical Discourse' in Anthropological Context: Views of Language and Power." *Medical Anthropology Quarterly* 3, no. 2: 99–123. https://doi.org/10.1525/maq.1989.3.2.02a00010.

Kumar, Claire, Helen Dempster, Megan O'Donnell, and Cassandra Zimmer. 2022. *Migration and the Future of Care.* Washington, DC: Center for Global Development. https://cdn.odi.org/media/documents/Migration_and_the_future_of_care.pdf.

Labov, William. 1972. "The Transformation of Experience in Narrative Syntax." In *Language in the Inner City: Studies in the Black English Vernacular,* 354–96. Philadelphia: University of Pennsylvania Press.

Lai, Yingtong, and Eric Fong. 2022. "Support or Burden? Mental Health and Transnational Family Contact among Female Migrant Domestic Workers in Hong Kong." *Population, Space and Place* n.a.: e17. https://doi.org/10.1002/psp.2617.

Lakoff, Robin Tolmach. 2004. *Language and Woman's Place: Text and Commentaries.* Edited by Mary Bucholtz. Rev. and Expanded ed. Studies in Language and Gender. New York: Oxford University Press.

Landale, Nancy S., Jessica Halliday Hardie, R. S. Oropesa, and Marianne M. Hillemeier. 2015. "Behavioral Functioning among Mexican-Origin Children Does Parental Legal Status Matter?" *Journal of Health and Social Behavior* 56, no. 1: 2–18.

Landolt, Particia, Lilian Autler, and Sonia Baires. 1999. "From Hermano Lejano to Hermano Mayor: The Dialectics of Salvadoran Transnationalism." *Ethnic and Racial Studies* 22: 290–315.

Lara Martínez, Carlos Benjamín. 2018. *Memoria Histórica Del Movimiento Campesino de Chalatenango.* 1st ed. Colección Estructuras y Procesos, Volumen 50. San Salvador, El Salvador, Centroamérica: UCA Editores.

Lara Martínez, Carlos Benjamín. 2019. "Presentación del Dossier: Memoria Historica del conflicto político-militar de El Salvador." *Realidad: Revista de Ciencias Sociales y Humanidades* 153: 5–8.

Leinaweaver, Jessaca B. 2010. "Outsourcing Care: How Peruvian Migrants Meet Transnational Family Obligations." *Latin American Perspectives* 37, no. 5: 67–87. https://doi.org/10.1177/0094582X10380222.

Lempert, Michael. 2012. "Indirectness." In *The Handbook of Intercultural Discourse and Communication,* edited by Scott Kiesling, Christina Bratt Paulston, and Elizabeth S. Rangel, 180–204. New York: John Wiley.

References 199

Lempert, Michael, and Sabina Perrino. 2007. "Entextualization and the Ends of Temporality." *Language & Communication* 27, no. 3: 205–11. https://doi.org/10.1016/j.langcom.2007.01.005.

LeoGrande, William M. 1998. *Our Own Back Yard: The United States in Central America, 1977-1992*. Chapel Hill: University of North Carolina.

Lerner, Gene H. 1992. "Assisted Storytelling: Deploying Shared Knowledge as a Practical Matter." *Qualitative Sociology* 15: 247–71.

Levitt, P. 1998. "Social Remittances: Migration Driven Local-Level Forms of Cultural Diffusion." *International Migration Review* 32, no. 4: 926–48.

Lindo-Fuentes, Héctor, Erik Ching, and Rafael A. Lara-Martínez. 2007. *Remembering a Massacre in El Salvador: The Insurrection of 1932, Roque Dalton, and the Politics of Historical Memory*. Albuquerque: University of New Mexico Press.

Lindström, Anna. 2005. "Language as Social Action: A Study of How Senior Citizens Request Assistance with Practical Tasks in the Swedish Home Help Service." In *Syntax and Lexis in Conversation*, edited by Auli Hakulinen and Margret Selting, 209–30. Amsterdam: John Benjamins.

Locher, Miriam A., and Richard J. Watts. 2005. "Politeness Theory and Relational Work." *Journal of Politeness Research. Language, Behaviour, Culture* 1, no. 1: 9–33. https://doi.org/10.1515/jplr.2005.1.1.9.

Locher, Miriam A., and Richard J. Watts. 2008. "Relational Work and Impoliteness: Negotiating Norms of Linguistic Behaviour." In *Impoliteness in Language*, edited by Derek Bousfield and Miriam A. Locher, 77–99. Berlin: Mouton de Gruyter.

Lohmuller, Michael. 2014. "US State Dept Report Shows Central America Still Main Cocaine Corridor." *Insight Crime*, March 4. http://www.insightcrime.org/news-briefs/us-state-dept-report-shows-central-america-still-main-cocaine-corridor.

López Vigil, María. 2000. *Oscar Romero: Memories in Mosaic*. Washington, DC: EPICA.

Lovato, Roberto. 2020. *Unforgetting: A Memoir of Family, Migration, Gangs, and Revolution in the Americas*. New York: Harper.

Madianou, Mirca. 2012. "Migration and the Accentuated Ambivalence of Motherhood: The Role of ICTs in Filipino Transnational Families." *Global Networks* 12, no. 3: 277–95. https://doi.org/10.1111/j.1471-0374.2012.00352.x.

Madianou, Mirca, and Daniel Miller. 2011a. "Mobile Phone Parenting: Reconfiguring Relationships between Filipina Migrant Mothers and Their Left-behind Children." *New Media & Society* 13, no. 3: 457–70. https://doi.org/10.1177/1461444810393903.

Madianou, Mirca, and Daniel Miller. 2011b. "Crafting Love: Letters and Cassette Tapes in Transnational Filipino Family Communication." *South East Asia Research* 19, no. 2: 249–72. https://doi.org/10.5367/sear.2011.0043.

Madianou, Mirca, and Daniel Miller. 2012a. *Migration and New Media: Transnational Families and Polymedia*. New York: Routledge.

Madianou, Mirca, and Daniel Miller. 2012b. "Polymedia: Towards a New Theory of Digital Media in Interpersonal Communication." *International Journal of Cultural Studies* 16, no. 2: 169–87. https://doi.org/10.1177/1367877912452486.

Mahler, Sarah J. 1999. "Engendering Transnational Migration: A Case Study of Salvadorans." *The American Behavioral Scientist* 42: 690–719.

Mahler, Sarah J. 2001. "Transnational Relationships: The Struggle to Communicate across Borders." *Identities* 7: 583–619.

Maj, Anna, and Daniel Riha, eds. 2009. *The Globytal: Towards an Understanding of Globalised Memories in the Digital Age*. Oxford: Inter-Disciplinary Press.

Malinowski, Bronislaw. 1923. "The Problem of Meaning in Primitive Languages." In *The Meaning of Meaning: A Study of the Influence of Language upon Thought and of the Science*

200 References

of Symbolism, edited by C. K. Ogden and I. A. Richards, 296–336. San Diego, CA: Harcourt Brace Jovanovich.

Malkin, Elisabeth, and Gene Palumbo. 2016. "Salvadoran Court Overturns Wartime Amnesty, Paving Way for Prosecutions." *The New York Times*, July 14, sec. World. https://www.nyti mes.com/2016/07/15/world/americas/salvadoran-court-overturns-wartime-amnesty-pav ing-way-for-prosecutions.html.

Maltz, Daniel N., and Ruth A. Borker. 1983. "A Cultural Approach to Male–Female Miscommunication." In *Language and Social Identity*, edited by John J. Gumperz, 196–216. Studies in Interactional Sociolinguistics. Cambridge: Cambridge University Press. https://doi.org/10.1017/CBO9780511620836.013.

Mangual Figueroa, Ariana. 2012. "'I Have Papers So I Can Go Anywhere!': Everyday Talk about Citizenship in a Mixed-Status Mexican Family." *Journal of Language, Identity & Education* 11, no. 5: 291–311. https://doi.org/10.1080/15348458.2012.722894.

Marcus, George E. 1995. "Ethnography in/of the World System: The Emergence of Multi-Sited Ethnography." *Annual Review of Anthropology* 24, no. 1: 95–117.

Marroquín Parducci, Amparo. 2008. "Crónica de La Prensa Salvadoreña: Imaginarios Que Migran." *Encuentro* 80 (Migrantes transformando Centroamérica): 23–43.

Marroquín Parducci, Amparo. 2009. "El Salvador, Un País, Muchas Narrativas: Contrapunta y Fuga de la Patria Chica." In *Entre saberes desechables y saberes indispensables: Agendas de país desde la comunicación*, edited by Jesús Martín Barbero, 71–98. Bogotá, Colombia: Centro de Competencia en Comunicación para América Latina, Frierich Ebert Stiftung.

Marroquín Parducci, Amparo. 2019. "Comunicación y migración: Pedagogías lingüísticas y resistencias de la narrativa sobre migración internacional." *Chasqui. Revista Latinoamericana de Comunicación* 141 (November): 161–76. https://doi.org/10.16921/chasqui.v0i141.4079.

Marsilli-Vargas, Xochitl. 2016. "The Offline and Online Mediatization of Psychoanalysis in Buenos Aires." *Signs and Society* 4, no. 1: 135–53. https://doi.org/10.1086/685822.

Martel, Roxana. 2006. "Las Maras Salvadoreñas: Nuevas Formas de Espanto y Control Social." *Estudios Centroamericanos* 61, no. 696: 957–79.

Martel, Roxana, and Amparo Marroquín Parducci. 2007. "Crónica de Fronteras: La Música Popular y La Identidad Salvadoreña Migrante." *Istmo*. http://istmo.denison.edu/n14/articu los/cronica.html.

Martínez Franzoni, Juliana. 2008. *Domesticar La Incertidumbre En América Latina: Mercado Laboral, Política Social y Familias*. San José: Editorial Universidad de Costa Rica.

Mattingly, Cheryl. 1998. *Healing Dramas and Clinical Plots: The Narrative Structure of Experience*. Cambridge: Cambridge University Press.

Mattingly, Cheryl. 2010. *The Paradox of Hope: Journeys through a Clinical Borderland*. Berkeley: University of California Press.

Maynard, Douglas W., and John Heritage. 2005. "Conversation Analysis, Doctor–Patient Interaction and Medical Communication." *Medical Education* 39, no. 4: 428–35. https://doi.org/10.1111/j.1365-2929.2005.02111.x.

McClintock, Anne. 1996. "'No Longer a Future Heaven': Nationalism, Gender, and Race." In *Becoming National: A Reader*, edited by Geoff Eley and Ronald Grigor Suny, 260–85. New York: Oxford University Press.

McElhinny, Bonnie. 2010. "The Audacity of Affect: Gender, Race, and History in Linguistic Accounts of Legitimacy and Belonging." *Annual Review of Anthropology* 39, no. 1: 309–28. https://doi.org/10.1146/annurev-anthro-091908-164358.

MCIES. 2020. "Cuatro Años Sin Ley de Amnistía En El Salvador: Escasos Avances En Justicia, Verdad, y Reparación Para Las Víctimas Del Conflicto Armado." https://drive.google.com/file/d/1MjoBjrEeJjQkVtH8CNdubleePOWIV0K7/view?usp=embed_facebook.

References 201

McIntosh, Janet. 2005. "Liminal Meanings: Sexually Charged Giriama Funerary Ritual and Unsettled Participant Frameworks." *Language & Communication* 25, no. 1: 39–60. https://doi.org/10.1016/j.langcom.2004.03.002.

McKay, Deirdre. 2007. "'Sending Dollars Shows Feeling'—Emotions and Economies in Filipino Migration." *Mobilities* 2, no. 2: 175–94. https://doi.org/10.1080/17450100701381532.

McLaren, Anne E. 2000. "The Grievance Rhetoric of Chinese Women: From Lamentation to Revolution." *Intersections* 4. http://intersections.anu.edu.au/issue4/mclaren.html.

Mendoza-Denton, Norma. 2008a. *Homegirls: Language and Cultural Practice among Latina Youth Gangs*. New Directions in Ethnography 2. Malden, MA: Blackwell.

Mendoza-Denton, Norma. 2008b. "Smile Now, Cry Later: Memorializing Practices Linking Language, Materiality, and Embodiment." In *Homegirls: Language and Cultural Practice among Latina Youth Gangs*, 176–206. Malden, MA: Blackwell.

Menjívar, Cecilia. 2000. *Fragmented Ties: Salvadoran Immigrant Networks in America*. Berkeley: University of California Press.

Menjívar, Cecilia. 2006. "Liminal Legality: Salvadoran and Guatemalan Immigrants' Lives in the United States." *American Journal of Sociology* 111, no. 4: 999–1037. https://doi.org/10.1086/499509.

Menjívar, Cecilia, and Leisy J. Abrego. 2012. "Legal Violence: Immigration Law and the Lives of Central American Immigrants." *American Journal of Sociology* 117, no. 5: 1380–1421. https://doi.org/10.1086/663575.

Menjívar, Cecilia, and Andrea Gómez Cervantes. 2018. "El Salvador: Civil War, Natural Disasters, and Gang Violence Drive Migration." Migrationpolicy.Org, August 27. https://www.migrationpolicy.org/article/el-salvador-civil-war-natural-disasters-and-gang-violence-drive-migration.

Menjívar, Cecilia, and Néstor Rodriguez, eds. 2005. *When States Kill: Latin America, the U.S., and Technologies of Terror*. 1st ed. Austin: University of Texas Press.

Merla, Laura. 2012. "Salvadoran Transnational Families, Distance and Eldercare: Understanding Transnational Care Practices in Australia and Belgium." In *Migration, Familie Und Soziale Lage*, edited by Thomas Geisen, Tobias Studer, and Erol Yildiz, 295–312. Wiesbaden, Germany: VS Verlag für Sozialwissenschaften.

Merla, Laura. 2015. "Salvadoran Migrants in Australia: An Analysis of Transnational Families' Capability to Care across Borders." *International Migration* 53, no. 6: 153–65. https://doi.org/10.1111/imig.12024.

Middleton, David. 1997. "The Social Organization of Conversational Remembering: Experience as Individual and Collective Concerns." *Mind, Culture, and Activity* 4, no. 2: 71–85. https://doi.org/10.1207/s15327884mca0402_2.

Middleton, David, and Derek Edwards, eds. 1990. *Collective Remembering. Inquiries in Social Construction*. Newbury Park, CA: Sage.

Migration Policy Institute. 2015. "The Salvadoran Diaspora in the United States." https://www.migrationpolicy.org/research/select-diaspora-populations-united-states.

Milton, Kay. 1982. "Meaning and Context: The Interpretation of Greetings in Kasigau." In *Semantic Anthropology*, edited by D. Parkin, 261–77. London: Academic Press.

Ministerio de Trabajo de El Salvador, dir. 2019a. "Estado salvadoreño brinda apoyo total a compatriotas que viajan a través de Visa H-2A." December 20, 2019. https://www.mtps.gob.sv/noticias/estado-salvadoreno-brinda-apoyo-total-compatriotas-viajan-traves-visa-h-2a/.

Ministerio de Trabajo de El Salvador, dir. 2019b. *Requisitos Para Aplicar a La Programa de Visas H2-A*. https://www.facebook.com/watch/?v=2395627783862335.

Ministero de Relaciones Exteriores. 2010. "Oportunidades y Desafíos de La Migración Internacional: El Caso de El Salvador." http://www.cepal.org/celade/noticias/paginas/4/37384/JJGarcia.pdf.

202 References

Mittermaier, Amira. 2011. *Dreams That Matter: Egyptian Landscapes of the Imagination.* Berkeley: University of California Press.

Miyares, Ines M., Richard Wright, Alison Mountz, Adrian J. Bailey, and Jennifer Jonak. 2003. "The Interrupted Circle: Truncated Transnationalism and the Salvadoran Experience." *Journal of Latin American Geography* 2: 74–86.

Mizielińska, Joanna, Jacqui Gabb, and Agata Stasińska. 2018. "Editorial Introduction to Special Issue: Queer Kinship and Relationships." *Sexualities* 21, no. 7: 975–82. https://doi.org/10.1177/1363460717718511.

Mol, Annemarie, Ingunn Moser, and Jeannette Pols, eds. 2010a. *Care in Practice: On Tinkering in Clinics, Homes and Farms.* 1. Aufl. VerKörperungen 8. Bielefeld, Germany: Transcript-Verl.

Mol, Annemarie, Ingunn Moser, and Jeannette Pols, eds. 2010b. "Care: Putting Practice into Theory." In *Care in Practice: On Tinkering in Clinics, Homes and Farms*, edited by Annemarie Mol, Ingunn Moser, and Jeanette Pols, 7–26. Bielefeld, Germany: Transcript.

Molina, Karen. 2023. "Envío de Remesas Cerró 2022 Con Cifra Más Alta Desde 2017—Noticias de El Salvador," January 22. https://www.elsalvador.com/noticias/nacional/remesas-familia res-estados-unidos-bcr-diaspora-salvadorena-/1033926/2023/.

Montes, Veronica. 2013. "The Role of Emotions in the Construction of Masculinity: Guatemalan Migrant Men, Transnational Migration, and Family Relations." *Gender & Society* 27, no. 4: 469–90. https://doi.org/10.1177/0891243212470491.

Moodie, Ellen. 2010. *El Salvador in the Aftermath of Peace: Crime, Uncertainty, and the Transition to Democracy.* Philadelphia: University of Pennsylvania Press.

Moore, Leslie. 2012. "Language Socialization and Repetition." In *The Handbook of Language Socialization*, edited by Alessandro Duranti, Elinor Ochs, and Bambi B. Schieffelin, 209–26. Malden, MA: Wiley-Blackwell.

Moreno, Raúl. 2004. "La Globalización Neoliberal En El Salvador." Barcelona, Spain: Fundación Món-3. http://mon-3.org/pdf/elsalvador.pdf.

Morgan, Lynn M., and Elizabeth F.S. Roberts. 2012. "Reproductive Governance in Latin America." *Anthropology & Medicine* 19, no. 2: 241–54. https://doi.org/10.1080/13648 470.2012.675046.

Morgan, Lynn M. 2019. "Reproductive Governance, Redux." *Medical Anthropology* 38, no. 2: 113–17. https://doi.org/10.1080/01459740.2018.1555829.

Moslimani, Mohamad, Luis Noe-Bustamante, and Sono Shah. 2021. "Facts on Hispanics of Salvadoran Origin in the United States, 2021." *Pew Research Center's Hispanic Trends Project* (blog). https://www.pewresearch.org/hispanic/fact-sheet/us-hispanics-facts-on-salvadoran- origin-latinos/.

Mountz, Alison, Richard Wright, Ines Miyares, and Adrian J. Bailey. 2002. "Lives in Limbo: Temporary Protected Status and Immigrant Identities." *Global Networks* 2: 335–56.

Mulla, Sameena. 2014. *The Violence of Care: Rape Victims, Forensic Nurses, and Sexual Assault Intervention.* New York: New York University Press.

Mullings, Leith. 1996. *On Our Own Terms: Race, Class, and Gender in the Lives of African- American Women.* New York: Routledge.

Mullings, Leith. 2005. "Resistance and Resilience: The Sojourner Syndrome and the Social Context of Reproduction in Cenral Harlem." *Transforming Anthropology* 13, no. 2: 79–91. https://doi.org/10.1525/tran.2005.13.2.79.

Mullings, Leith. 2021. "The Necropolitics of Reproduction." In *The Routledge Handbook of Anthropology and Reproduction*, 1st ed., by Sallie Han and Cecília Tomori, 106–22. London: Routledge. https://doi.org/10.4324/9781003216452-9.

Mullings, Leith, Jada Benn Torres, Agustín Fuentes, Clarence C.

Gravlee, Dorothy Roberts, and Zaneta Thayer. 2021. "The Biology of Racism." *American Anthropologist* 123, no. 3: 671–80. https://doi.org/10.1111/aman.13630.

Nakano Glenn, Evelyn. 2010. *Forced to Care: Coercion and Caregiving in America*. Cambridge, MA: Harvard University Press.

Ochs, Elinor. 1988. *Culture and Language Development: Language Acquisition and Language Socialization in a Samoan Village*. Studies in the Social and Cultural Foundations of Language, no. 6. Cambridge: Cambridge University Press.

Ochs, Elinor. 1990. "Indexicality and Socialization." In *Cultural Psychology: Essays on Comparative Human Development*, edited by James W. Stigler, Richard A. Schweder, and Gilbert Herdt, 287–308. Cambridge: Cambridge University Press.

Ochs, Elinor. 2012. "Experiencing Language." *Anthropological Theory* 12, no. 2: 142–60. https://doi.org/10.1177/1463499612454088.

Ochs, Elinor, and Lisa Capps. 1996. "Narrating the Self." *Annual Review of Anthropology* 25: 19–43.

Ochs, Elinor, and Bambi Schieffelin. 1989. "Language Has a Heart." *Text* 9: 7–25.

Okin, Susan Moller. 1989. *Justice, Gender, and the Family*. New York: Basic Books.

Olthuis, Gert, Helen Kohlen, Jorma Heier, and Joan C Tronto. 2014. *Moral Boundaries Redrawn: The Significance of Joan Tronto's Argument for Political Theory, Professional Ethics, and Care as Practice*. Leuven, Belgium: Peeters.

Ong, Aihwa. 1999. *Flexible Citizenship: The Cultural Logics of Transnationality*. Durham, NC: Duke University Press.

Ong, Aihwa. 2006. "Introduction: Neoliberalism as Exception, Exception to Neoliberalism." In *Neoliberalism as Exception: Mutations in Citizenship and Sovereignty*, 1–27. Durham: Duke University Press. https://read.dukeupress.edu/books/book/1050/chapter/150789/Introd uctionNeoliberalism-as-Exception-Exception.

Orellana, Marjorie Faulstich. 2001. "The Work Kids Do: Mexican and Central American Immigrant Children's Contributions to Households and Schools in California." *Harvard Educational Review* 71, no. 3: 366–90.

Orellana, Marjorie Faulstich. 2009. *Translating Childhoods: Immigrant Youth, Language, and Culture*. The Rutgers Series in Childhood Studies. New Brunswick, NJ: Rutgers University Press.

Osuna, Steven. 2020. "Transnational Moral Panic: Neoliberalism and the Spectre of MS-13." *Race & Class* 61, no. 4: 3–28. https://doi.org/10.1177/0306396820904304.

Osuna, Steven, and Leisy J. Abrego. 2022. "The State of Exception: Gangs as a Neoliberal Scapegoat in El Salvador." *Brown Journal of World Affairs* XXIX, no. 1: 59–73. https://www.academia.edu/95631169/The_State_of_Exception_Gangs_as_a_Neoliberal_Scapegoat_in_El_Salvador.

"Our Parents' Bones | About the Campaign." 2014. https://ourparentsbones.com/about-the-campaign/.

Padilla, Yajaira M. 2012. *Changing Women, Changing Nation: Female Agency, Nationhood, and Identity in Trans-Salvadoran Narratives*. Albany: State University of New York Press.

Paris, Django, and H. Samy Alim. 2017. *Culturally Sustaining Pedagogies: Teaching and Learning for Justice in a Changing World*. New York: Teachers College Press.

Parkin, David. 2013. "Medical Crises and Therapeutic Talk." *Anthropology and Medicine* 20, no. 2: 124–41.

Parreñas, Rhacel Salazar. 2001. *Servants of Globalization: Women, Migration and Domestic Work*. Stanford, CA: Stanford University Press.

Parreñas, Rhacel Salazar. 2005. *Children of Global Migration: Transnational Families and Gendered Woes*. Stanford, CA: Stanford University Press.

Parsons, Talcott. 1951. *The Social System*. New Orleans, LA: Quid Pro Books.

Passel, Jeffrey S., and D'Vera Cohn. 2015. "Share of Unauthorized Immigrant Workers in Production, Construction Jobs Falls Since 2007." Pew Hispanic Research Center. http://

204 References

www.pewhispanic.org/2015/03/26/share-of-unauthorized-immigrant-workers-in-product ion-construction-jobs-falls-since-2007/.

Patel, Ian Sanjay. 2021. *We're Here Because You Were There: Immigration and the End of Empire*. London: Verso.

Pauli, Julia, and Franziska Bedorf. 2018. "Retiring Home? House Construction, Age Inscriptions, and the Building of Belonging among Mexican Migrants and Their Families in Chicago and Rural Mexico." *Anthropology & Aging* 39, no. 1: 48–65. https://doi.org/10.5195/aa.2018.173.

Paz, Alejandro I. 2016. "Speaking like a Citizen: Biopolitics and Public Opinion in Recognizing Non-Citizen Children in Israel." *Language & Communication* 48 (May): 18–27. https://doi.org/10.1016/j.langcom.2016.01.002.

Paz, Alejandro I. 2018. *Latinos in Israel: Language and Unexpected Citizenship*. Public Cultures of the Middle East and North Africa. Bloomington: Indiana University Press.

Pedersen, David. 2013. *American Value: Migrants, Money, and Meaning in El Salvador and the United States*. Chicago Studies in Practices of Meaning. Chicago: University of Chicago Press.

Peña, Elaine A. 2011. *Performing Piety: Making Space Sacred with the Virgin of Guadalupe*. Berkeley: University of California Press.

Pérez, Ramona Lee. 2014. "*Las Fronteras Del Sabor*: Taste as Consciousness, Kinship, and Space in the Mexico-U.S. Borderlands: Consciousness, Kinship, and Space in the Mexico-U.S. Borderlands." *The Journal of Latin American and Caribbean Anthropology* 19, no. 2: 310–30. https://doi.org/10.1111/jlca.12094.

Perrino, Sabina. 2011. "Chronotopes of Story and Storytelling Event in Interviews." *Language in Society* 40, no. 1: 91–103. https://doi.org/10.1017/S0047404510000916.

Perrino, Sabina. 2020. *Narrating Migration: Intimacies of Exclusion in Northern Italy*. Routledge Studies in Linguistic Anthropology 4. New York: Routledge.

Perrino, Sabina, and Gregory Kohler. 2020. "Chronotopic Identities: Narrating Made in Italy across Spatiotemporal Scales." *Language & Communication* 70 (January): 94–106. https://doi.org/10.1016/j.langcom.2019.01.003.

Perrino, Sabina, and Sonya Pritzker. 2019. "Language and Intimate Relations." In *The Oxford Handbook of Language and Sexuality*, edited by Kira Hall and Rusty Barrett. Online. Oxford Academic. https://doi.org/10.1093/oxfordhb/9780190212926.013.58.

Perrino, Sabina, and Stanton Wortham. 2018. "Discursive Struggles over Migration." *Language & Communication* 59 (March): 1–3. https://doi.org/10.1016/j.langcom.2017.03.002.

Pfeiler, Bárbara. 2007. "'Lo Oye, Lo Repite y Lo Piensa.' The Contribution of Prompting to the Socialization and Language Acquisition in Yukatek Maya Toddlers." *Learning Indigenous Languages: Child Language Acquisition in Mesoamerica* 33: 183–202.

Philips, Susan U. 2014. "The Power of Gender Ideologies in Discourse." In *The Handbook of Language, Gender, and Sexuality*, edited by Susan Ehrlich, Miriam Meyerhoff, and Janet Holmes, 2nd ed., 297–315. Malden MA: Wiley Blackwell.

PNUD El Salvador. 2005. "Informe sobre el Desarollo Humano El Salvador. Una mirada al nuevo nosotros: El impacto de las migraciones." San Salvador: PNUD El Salvador: Consejo Nacional para el Desarrollo Sostenible.

Povinelli, Elizabeth A. 2002. *The Cunning of Recognition: Indigenous Alterities and the Making of Australian Multiculturalism*. Politics, History, and Culture. Durham, NC: Duke University Press.

Pratt, Mary Louise. 1994. "Women, Literature, and National Brotherhood." *Nineteenth-Century Contexts* 18, no. 1: 27–47. https://doi.org/10.1080/08905499408583379.

Prensa Latina. 2023. "Denuncian en El Salvador demora en juicio por masacre de El Mozote" March 11. https://www.prensa-latina.cu/2023/03/11/denuncian-en-el-salvador-demora-en-juicio-por-masacre-de-el-mozote.

Pribilsky, Jason. 2012. "Consumption Dilemmas: Tracking Masculinity, Money and Transnational Fatherhood Between the Ecuadorian Andes and New York City." *Journal of Ethnic and Migration Studies* 38, no. 2: 323–43. https://doi.org/10.1080/13691 83X.2012.646429.

Pritzker, Sonya E. 2014. *Living Translation: Language and the Search for Resonance in U.S. Chinese Medicine.* New York: Berghahn Books.

Pritzker, Sonya E., and Sabina Perrino. 2021. "Culture inside: Scale, Intimacy, and Chronotopic Stance in Situated Narratives." *Language in Society* 50, no. 3: 365–87. https://doi.org/10.1017/S0047404520000342.

Quan, Adán. 2005. "Through the Looking Glass: U.S. Aid to El Salvador and the Politics of National Identity." *American Ethnologist* 32, no. 2: 276–93.

Quintana, Angel Arnaiz. 2007. *Tierras Pagadas a Precio de Sangre: Testimonios y Retratos Del Bajo Lempa Usuluteca, El Salvador, CA.* San Salvador, El Salvador: Impresos el Rosario.

Radcliffe, Sarah A., and Sallie Westwood. 1996. *Remaking the Nation: Place, Identity and Politics in Latin America.* London: Routledge.

Ragland, Cathy. 2003. "Mexican Deejays and the Transnational Space of Youth Dances in New York and New Jersey." *Ethnomusicology* 47, no. 3: 338. https://doi.org/10.2307/3113938.

Raia, Federica. 2020. "The Temporality of Becoming: Care as an Activity to Support the Being and Becoming of the Other." *Mind, Culture, and Activity* 27, no. 3: 292–312. https://doi.org/10.1080/10749039.2020.1745846.

Rao, Sonya. 2021. "Linguistic Lives as Working Lives: Conducting Lingual Life Histories for the Labor Movement." *Journal of Anthropological Research* 77, no. 1: 52–66. https://doi.org/10.1086/712281.

Rapp, Rayna. 1978. "Family and Class in Contemporary America: Notes Toward an Understanding of Ideology." *Science & Society* 42, no. 3: 278–300. https://doi.org/10.4324/9780203724491-18.

Reynolds, Jennifer F., and Marjorie Faulstich Orellana. 2009. "New Immigrant Youth Interpreting in White Public Space." *American Anthropologist* 111, no. 2: 211–23.

Richards, Fayana. 2021. "'Stepping in the Gap to Make Family': Care Calculation and Grandparent Caregiving in Detroit, Michigan." *Journal for the Anthropology of North America* 24, no. 1: 4–15. https://doi.org/10.1002/nad.12140.

Richman, Karen E. 2005. *Migration and Vodou.* 1st ed. Gainesville: University Press of Florida.

Ricoeur, Paul. 2011. "Memory-History-Forgetting." In *The Collective Memory Reader*, edited by Jeffrey K. Olick, Vered Vinitzky-Seroussi, and Daniel Levy, 475–80. New York: Oxford University Press.

Rivas, Cecilia M. 2014. *Salvadoran Imaginaries: Mediated Identities and Cultures of Consumption.* Latinidad: Transnational Cultures in the United States. New Brunswick, NJ: Rutgers University Press.

Rivas Hernández, Annette Georgina. 2016. "Cartografía de la memoria: actores, lugares, prácticas en El Salvador de posguerra (1992-2015)." PhD diss., Universidad Autonoma de Madrid. https://repositorio.uam.es/handle/10486/672117.

Rivera-Mills, Susana V. 2011. "Use of Voseo and Latino Identity: An Intergenerational Study of Hondurans and Salvadorans in the Western Region of the U.S." In *Selected Proceedings of the 13th Hispanic Linguistics Symposium*, edited by Luis A. Ortiz-López, 94–106. Somerville, MA: Cascadilla Proceedings Project.

RM, Carlos. 2009. *Monumento a La Memoria y La Verdad.* Photo. https://www.flickr.com/photos/camaro27/4880271289/.

Roca, Ana, and John M. Lipski. 2011. *Spanish in the United States: Linguistic Contact and Diversity.* Berlin: Walter de Gruyter.

206 References

Rocha, José Luis. 2018. *La desobediencia de las masas: la migración no autorizada de centroamericanos a Estados Unidos como desobediencia civil*. 1st ed. Colección Estructuras y Procesos, vol. 44. San Salvador, El Salvador: UCA Editores.

Rodríguez, Ana Patricia. 2005. "'Departamento 15': Cultural Narratives of Salvadoran Transnational Migration." *Latino Studies* 3, no. 1: 19–41. https://doi.org/10.1057/palgrave.lst.8600120.

Rodriguez, Leila. 2022. "From Quantitative Fact to Discursive Practice: Techniques for Asserting the Reliability of Anthropological Knowledge in Expert Testimony." *Annals of Anthropological Practice* 46, no. 1: 107–11. https://doi.org/10.1111/napa.12186.

Ros, Adela, Elisabeth González, Antoni Marín, and Papa Sow. 2007. "Migration and Information Flows: A New Lens for the Study of Contemporary International Migration" (Working Paper IN3). Barcelona: Universitat Oberta de Catalunya.

Rosa, Jonathan, and Nelson Flores. 2017. "Unsettling Race and Language: Toward a Raciolinguistic Perspective." *Language in Society* 46, no. 5: 621–47. https://doi.org/10.1017/S0047404517000562.

Rossi, Giovanni. 2012. "Bilateral and Unilateral Requests: The Use of Imperatives and *Mi X?* Interrogatives in Italian." *Discourse Processes* 49, no. 5: 426–58. https://doi.org/10.1080/0163853X.2012.684136.

Rossi-Landi, Ferruccio. 1983. *Language as Work & Trade: A Semiotic Homology for Linguistics & Economics*. South Hadley, MA: Bergin & Garvey.

Ruzickova, Elena. 2007. "Strong and Mild Requestive Hints and Positive-Face Redress in Cuban Spanish." *Journal of Pragmatics* 39, no. 6: 1170–1202. https://doi.org/10.1016/j.pragma.2006.06.005.

Sacks, Harvey. 1975. "Everyone Has to Lie." In *Sociocultural Dimensions of Language Use*, edited by Mary Sanches and Ben G. Blount, 57–80. Language, Thought, and Culture. New York: Academic Press.

Sacks, Harvey, Emanuel A. Schegloff, and Gail Jefferson. 1974. "A Simplest Systematics for the Organization of Turn-Taking for Conversation." *Language* 50, no. 4: 696–735.

Sadruddin, Aalyia Feroz Ali. 2020. "The Care of 'Small Things': Aging and Dignity in Rwanda." *Medical Anthropology* 39, no. 1: 83–95. https://doi.org/10.1080/01459740.2019.1643852.

Safri, Maliha, and Julie Graham. 2010. "The Global Household: Toward a Feminist Postcapitalist International Political Economy." *Signs: Journal of Women in Culture and Society* 36, no. 1: 99–125. https://doi.org/10.1086/652913.

Sahlins, Marshall David. 2013. *What Kinship Is - and Is Not*. Chicago: University of Chicago Press.

Salazar, Noel B. 2011. "The Power of Imagination in Transnational Mobilities." *Identities* 18, no. 6: 576–98. https://doi.org/10.1080/1070289X.2011.672859.

Salazar, Noel B. 2013. *Envisioning Eden: Mobilizing Imaginaries in Tourism and Beyond*. New York: Berghahn Books.

Salmond, Anne. 1974. "Rituals of Encounter among the Maori: Sociolinguistic Study of a Scene." In *Explorations in the Ethnography of Speaking*, edited by Richard Bauman and Joel Sherzer, 192–212. Studies in the Social and Cultural Foundations of Language 8. New York: Cambridge University Press.

Santana Cardoso, Ciro Flamarion. 1975. "Historia Económica Del Café En Centroamérica (Siglo XIX): Estudio Comparativo." *Estudios Sociales Centroamericanos* 4, no. 10: 9–55.

Savelsberg, Joachim, and Ryan D. King. 2007. "Law and Collective Memory." *Annual Review of Law and Social Science* 3: 189–211.

Schegloff, Emanuel A. 2005. "On Complainability." *Social Problems* 52, no. 4: 449–76. https://doi.org/10.1525/sp.2005.52.4.449.

Schegloff, Emanuel A. 2007. *Sequence Organization in Interaction: A Primer in Conversation Analysis, Volume 1*. Cambridge: Cambridge University Press.

Schegloff, Emanuel A., and Harvey Sacks. 1973. "Opening up Closings." *Semiotica* 8, no. 4: 289–327.

Schieffelin, Bambi B. 1990. *The Give and Take of Everyday Life: Language Socialization of Kaluli Children*. Tucson, AZ: Fenestra Books.

Schieffelin, Bambi B., and Elinor Ochs. 1986. "Language Socialization." *Annual Review of Anthropology* 15, no. 1: 163–91. https://doi.org/10.1146/annurev.anthro.15.1.163.

Schmidt Camacho, Alicia R. 2008. *Migrant Imaginaries: Latino Cultural Politics in the U.S.-Mexico Borderlands*. Nation of Newcomers. New York: New York University Press.

Schneider, David. 1984. *A Critique of the Study of Kinship*. Ann Arbor: University of Michigan Press. https://doi.org/10.3998/mpub.7203.

Shankar, Shalini, and Jillian Cavanaugh. 2012. "Language and Materiality in Global Capitalism." *Annual Review of Anthropology* 41, no. 1: 355–69. https://doi.org/10.1146/annurev-anthro-092611-145811.

Shohet, Merav. 2007. "Narrating Anorexia: 'Full' and 'Struggling' Genres of Recovery." *Ethos* 35, no. 3: 344–82.

Shohet, Merav. 2013. "Everyday Sacrifice and Language Socialization in Vietnam: The Power of a Respect Particle." *American Anthropologist* 115, no. 2: 203–17. https://doi.org/10.1111/aman.12004.

Shohet, Merav. 2018. "Two Deaths and a Funeral: Ritual Inscriptions' Affordances for Mourning and Moral Personhood in Vietnam." *American Ethnologist* 45, no. 1: 60–73. https://doi.org/10.1111/amet.12599.

Silber, Irina Carlota. 2011. *Everyday Revolutionaries: Gender, Violence, and Disillusionment in Postwar El Salvador*. Genocide, Political Violence, Human Rights Series. New Brunswick, NJ: Rutgers University Press.

Silber, Irina Carlota. 2022. *After Stories: Transnational Intimacies of Postwar El Salvador*. Stanford, CA: Stanford University Press.

Silver, Lauren J. 2020. "Queering Reproductive Justice: Memories, Mistakes, and Motivations to Transform Kinship." *Feminist Anthropology* 1, no. 2: 217–30. https://doi.org/10.1002/fea2.12019.

Silverstein, Michael. 1984. "On The Pragmatic 'Poetry' of Prose: Parallelism, Repetition, and Cohesive Structure in the Time Course of Dyadic Conversation." In *Meaning, Form, and Use in Context: Linguistic Applications*, edited by Deborah Schiffin, 181–99. Washington, DC: Georgetown University Press.

Silverstein, Michael. 2004. "'Cultural' Concepts and the Language-Culture Nexus." *Current Anthropology* 45, no. 5: 621–52. https://doi.org/10.1086/423971.

Silverstein, Michael. 2005. "Axes of Evals: Token versus Type Interdiscursivity." *Journal of Linguistic Anthropology* 15, no. 1: 6–22.

Skurski, Julie. 1996. "The Ambiguities of Authenticity in Latin America: Dona Barbara and the Construction of National Identity." In *Becoming National: A Reader*, edited by Geoff Eley and Ronald Grigor Suny, 371–402. New York: Oxford University Press.

Slembrouck, Stef, and Mieke Vandenbroucke. 2019. "Scale." In *The Routledge Handbook of Linguistic Ethnography*, edited by Karen Tusting, 70–83. New York: Routledge.

Smalls, Krystal A. 2020. "Race, Signs, and the Body: Towards a Theory of Racial Semiotics." In *The Oxford Handbook of Language and Race*, edited by H. Samy Alim, Angela Reyes, and Paul V. Kroskrity, 231–60. Oxford University Press. https://doi.org/10.1093/oxfordhb/9780190845995.013.15.

Smith, Benjamin. 2012. "Language and the Frontiers of the Human: Aymara Animal-Oriented Interjections and the Mediation of Mind." *American Ethnologist* 39, no. 2: 313–24. https://doi.org/10.1111/j.1548-1425.2012.01366.x.

Smith, Christian. 1996. *Resisting Reagan: The U.S. Central America Peace Movement*. Chicago: University of Chicago Press.

References

Smith, Robert C. 2006. *Mexican New York: Transnational Lives of New Immigrants*. Berkeley: University of California Press.

Soltero, Jose, and Romeo Saravia. 2000. "Politics, Networks, and Circular Migration." *Journal of Poverty* 4, no. 1–2: 109–30. https://doi.org/10.1300/J134v04n01_05.

Sommer, Doris. 1993. *Foundational Fictions: The National Romances of Latin America*. 1st ed. (paperback print). Latin American Literature and Culture 8. Berkeley: University of California Press.

Southern Poverty Law Center. 2020. "Family Separation under the Trump Administration – a Timeline." Southern Poverty Law Center. June 17. https://www.splcenter.org/news/2020/06/17/family-separation-under-trump-administration-timeline.

Spade, Dean. 2020. *Mutual Aid: Building Solidarity during This Crisis (and the Next)*. London: Verso.

Stack, Carol B. 1975. *All Our Kin: Strategies for Survival in a Black Community*. Repr., Harper Torchbook 1982. New York: Harper & Row.

Stack, Carol B., and Linda M. Burton. 1993. "Kinscripts." *Journal of Comparative Family Studies* 24, no. 2: 157–70.

Stack, Trevor. 2012. "Beyond the State? Civil Sociality and Other Notions of Citizenship." *Citizenship Studies* 16, no. 7: 871–85. https://doi.org/10.1080/13621025.2012.716197.

Stepan, Nancy. 1991. *The Hour of Eugenics: Race, Gender, and Nation in Latin America*. Ithaca, NY: Cornell University Press.

Stephen, Lynn. 2007. *Transborder Lives: Indigenous Oaxacans in Mexico, California, and Oregon*. Durham, NC: Duke University Press.

Stevanovic, Melisa, and Anssi Peräkylä. 2012. "Deontic Authority in Interaction: The Right to Announce, Propose, and Decide." *Research on Language & Social Interaction* 45, no. 3: 297–321. https://doi.org/10.1080/08351813.2012.699260.

Suárez-Orozco, Carola, Hirokazu Yoshikawa, Robert T. Teranishi, and Marcelo M. Suárez-Orozco. 2011. "Growing up in the Shadows: The Developmental Implications of Unauthorized Status." *Harvard Educational Review* 81, no. 3: 438–73.

Svendsen, Mette N., Laura E. Navne, Iben M. Gjødsbøl, and Mie S. Dam. 2018. "A Life Worth Living: Temporality, Care, and Personhood in the Danish Welfare State." *American Ethnologist* 45, no. 1: 20–33. https://doi.org/10.1111/amet.12596.

Taleghani-Nikazm, Carmen. 2006. *Request Sequences: The Intersection of Grammar, Interaction and Social Context*. Studies in Discourse and Grammar, v. 19. Amsterdam: John Benjamins.

Tannen, Deborah. 1987. "Repetition in Conversation: Toward a Poetics of Talk." *Language* 63, no. 3: 574–605. https://doi.org/10.2307/415006.

Tannen, Deborah. 1989. "'Oh Talking Voice That Is so Sweet': Constructing Dialogue in Conversation." In *Talking Voices: Repetition, Dialogue, and Imagery in Conversational Discourse*, 102–32. Cambridge: Cambridge University Press.

Taylor, Charles. 1985. "The Person." In *The Category of the Person: Anthropology, Philosophy, History*, edited by Michael Carrithers, Steven Collins, and Steven Lukes, 257–81. Cambridge: Cambridge University Press.

Tazanu, Primus Mbeanwoah. 2015. "On the Liveness of Mobile Phone Mediation: Youth Expectations of Remittances and Narratives of Discontent in the Cameroonian Transnational Family." *Mobile Media & Communication* 3, no. 1: 20–35.

Tazanu, Primus Mbeanwoah. 2018. "Communication Technologies and Legitimate Consumption: Making Sense of Healthcare Remittances in Cameroonian Transnational Relationships." *Africa* 88, no. 2: 385–403. https://doi.org/10.1017/S0001972017000961.

Tazanu, Primus Mbeanwoah. 2012. *Being Available and Reachable. New Media and Cameroonian Transnational Sociality*. Mankon, Bamenda: Langaa RPCIG.

Thelen, Tatjana, and Cati Coe. 2017. "Political Belonging through Elderly Care: Temporalities, Representations and Mutuality." *Anthropological Theory* 19 (December): 279–99. https://doi.org/10.1177/1463499617742833.

Ticktin, Miriam. 2019. "From the Human to the Planetary: Speculative Futures of Care." *Medicine Anthropology Theory | An Open-Access Journal in the Anthropology of Health, Illness, and Medicine* 6, no. 3. https://doi.org/10.17157/mat.6.3.666.

Ticktin, Miriam Iris. 2011. *Casualties of Care: Immigration and the Politics of Humanitarianism in France*. Berkeley: University of California Press.

Todd, Molly. 2010. *Beyond Displacement: Campesinos, Refugees, and Collective Action in the Salvadoran Civil War*. Critical Human Rights. Madison: University of Wisconsin Press.

Toerien, Merran, and Celia Kitzinger. 2007. "Emotional Labour in Action: Navigating Multiple Involvements in the Beauty Salon." *Sociology* 41: 645–62.

Tomlinson, Barbara, and George Lipsitz. 2013. "American Studies as Accompaniment." *American Quarterly* 65, no. 1: 1–30. https://doi.org/10.1353/aq.2013.0009.

Tronto, Joan C. 1993. *Moral Boundaries: A Political Argument for an Ethic of Care*. New York: Routledge.

Trouillot, Michel-Rolph. 1991. "Anthropology and the Savage Slot: The Poetics and Politics of Otherness." In *Recapturing Anthropology: Working in the Present*, edited by Richard G. Fox, 17–44. Santa Fe, NM: School of American Research Press.

UNIVISION, dir. 2016a. *7o. ANIVERSARIO HERMANO LEJANO Con Berta Luz Campos PARTE 2*. https://www.youtube.com/watch?v=xpofKwsGLIY.

UNIVISION, dir. 2016b. *Reencuentros Hermano Lejano Con Berta Luz Campos: Mauricio Saravia*. https://www.youtube.com/watch?v=XH4_yVXIRt0&list=WL&index=8.

UNIVISION, Berta Luz, dir. 2018. *Reencuentros Hermano Lejano Con Berta Luz Campos: Mayvery Hernandez*. https://www.youtube.com/watch?v=EvtVnyVkcyw&list=WL&index=26.

Urciuoli, Bonnie. 1995. "Language and Borders." *Annual Review of Anthropology* 24: 525–46.

Uy-Tioco, Cecilia. 2007. "Overseas Filipino Workers and Text Messaging: Reinventing Transnational Mothering." *Continuum* 21, no. 2: 253–65. https://doi.org/10.1080/10304310701269081.

Van Vleet, Krista E. 2008. *Performing Kinship: Narrative, Gender, and the Intimacies of Power in the Andes*. Austin: University of Texas Press.

Vargas, Miguel Angel. 2006. "Epistolary Communication between Migrant Workers and Their Families." In *Letters across Borders: The Epistolary Practices of International Migrants*, edited by Bruce S. Elliott, David A. Gerber, and Suzanne M. Sinke, 124–38. Cham, Switzerland: Springer.

Velasquez Carillo, Carlos. 2011. "La Consolidación Oligárquica Neoliberal En El Salvador y Los Retos Para El Gobierno Del FMLN." *Revista América Latina* 10: 161–202.

Velásquez, Eugenia. 2021. "Se Frustra Ratificación de La Ley de Reconciliación Nacional y 9F Como El Día Del 'Golpe de Estado Fallido Nunca Más.'" *Noticias de El Salvador - Elsalvador. Com* (blog). April 27. https://www.elsalvador.com/noticias/nacional/ley-de-reconciliacion-nacional-justicia-transicional-asamblea-veto-bukele/831797/2021/.

Vélez-Ibáñez, Carlos, and James T. Greenberg. 1992. "Formation and Transformation of Funds of Knowledge among US-Mexican Households." *Anthropology & Education Quarterly* 13, no. 4: 313–35.

Voloshinov, Valentin N. 1929. *Marxism and the Philosophy of Language*. Cambridge, MA: Harvard University Press.

Vora, Kalindi. 2015. *Life Support: Biocapital and the New History of Outsourced Labor*. Difference Incorporated. Minneapolis: University of Minnesota Press.

Watkins, John F. 1999. "Life Course and Spatial Experience: A Personal Narrative Approach in Migration Studies." In *Migration and Restructuring in the United States: A Geographic*

210 References

Perspective, edited by Kavita Pandit and Suzanne Davies Withers, 294–312. Lanham, MD: Rowman & Littlefield.

Warner, Michael. 2002. "Publics and Counterpublics." *Public Culture* 14 (1): 49–90.

Watts, Richard J. 1997. "Silence and the Acquisition of Status in Verbal Interaction." In *Silence: Interdisciplinary Perspectives*, edited by Adam Jaworski, 87–116. Studies in Anthropological Linguistics 10. Berlin: Mouton de Gruyter.

Wertsch, James V. 2009. "Collective Remembering." *Semiotica* 173: 233–47. https://doi.org/10.1515/SEMI.2009.009.

Wilce, James M. 1998. *Eloquence in Trouble: The Poetics and Politics of Complaint in Rural Bangladesh*. Oxford Studies in Anthropological Linguistics 21. New York: Oxford University Press.

Wilce, James M. 2005. "Traditional Laments and Postmodern Regrets." *Journal of Linguistic Anthropology* 15, no. 1: 60–71. https://doi.org/10.1525/jlin.2005.15.1.60.

Wilce, James M. 2006. "Magical Laments and Anthropological Reflections: The Production and Circulation of Anthropological Text as Ritual Activity." *Current Anthropology* 47, no. 6: 891–914. https://doi.org/10.1086/507195.

Wilce, James M. 2009. *Crying Shame: Metaculture, Modernity, and the Exaggerated Death of Lament*. Malden, MA: Wiley-Blackwell.

Williams, Raymond. 1977. *Marxism and Literature*. Oxford: Oxford University Press.

Wilson Gilmore, Ruth. 2022. *Abolition Geography: Essays towards Liberation*. Edited by Brenna Bhandar and Alberto Toscano. London: Verso.

Wiltberger, Joseph. 2014. "Beyond Remittances: Contesting El Salvador's Developmentalist Migration Politics." *The Journal of Latin American and Caribbean Anthropology* 19, no. 1: 41–62. https://doi.org/10.1111/jlca.12065.

Woods, Michael M. L., and Susana V. Rivera-Mills. 2012. "El Tú Como Un 'Mask': Voseo and Salvadoran and Honduran Identity in the United States." *Studies in Hispanic and Lusophone Linguistics* 5, no. 1: 191–216.

Woolard, Kathryn A. 1985. "Language Variation and Cultural Hegemony: Toward an Integration of Sociolinguistic and Social Theory." *American Ethnologist* 12: 738–48.

World Bank Group. 2016. "Migration and Remittances Factbook 2016." https://siteresources.worldbank.org/INTPROSPECTS/Resources/334934-1199807908806/4549025-145045 5807487/Factbookpart1.pdf.

Yanagisako, S. J. 1979. "Family and Household: The Analysis of Domestic Groups." *Annual Review of Anthropology* 8, no. 1: 161–205. https://doi.org/10.1146/annurev.an.08.100 179.001113.

Yarris, Kristin Elizabeth. 2017. *Care across Generations: Solidarity and Sacrifice in Transnational Families*. Stanford, CA: Stanford University Press.

Yoon-Hendricks, Alexandra, and Zoe Greenberg. 2018. "Protests across U.S. Call for End to Migrant Family Separations." *The New York Times*, June 30, sec. U.S. https://www.nytimes.com/2018/06/30/us/politics/trump-protests-family-separation.html.

Young, Iris Marion. 1997. "Asymmetrical Reciprocity: On Moral Respect, Wonder, and Enlarged Thought." *Constellations* 3, no. 3: 340–63. https://doi.org/10.1111/j.1467-8675.1997.tb00064.x.

Yuval-Davis, Nira, Floya Anthias, and Jo Campling, eds. 1989. *Woman, Nation, State*. Houndmills, UK: Macmillan.

Zentella, Ana Celia. 2018. "LatinUs and Linguistics: Complaints, Conflicts, and Contradictions - The Anthro-Political Linguistics Solution." In *Questioning Theoretical Primitives in Linguistic Inquiry: Papers in Honor of Ricardo Otheguy*, edited by Naomi L. Shin and Daniel Erker, 76:189–207. Amsterdam: John Benjamins. https://doi.org/10.1075/sfsl.76.

Zentgraf, Kristine M. 2002. "Immigration and Women's Empowerment: Salvadorans in Los Angeles." *Gender & Society* 16: 625–46.

Zigon, Jarrett. 2010. "Moral and Ethical Assemblages." *Anthropological Theory* 10, no. 1–2: 3–15. https://doi.org/10.1177/1463499610370520.

Zigon, Jarrett, and C. Jason Throop. 2014. "Moral Experience: Introduction." *Ethos* 42, no. 1: 1–15. https://doi.org/10.1111/etho.12035.

Zilberg, Elana. 2004. "Fools Banished from the Kingdom: Remapping Geographies of Gang Violence between the Americas (Los Angeles and San Salvador)." *American Quarterly* 56, no. 3: 759–79. https://doi.org/10.1353/aq.2004.0048.

Zilberg, Elana. 2007. "Gangster in Guerilla Face: A Transnational Mirror of Production between the USA and El Salvador." *Anthropological Theory* 7, no. 1: 37–57. https://doi.org/10.1177/1463499607074289.

Zilberg, Elana. 2011. *Space of Detention: The Making of a Transnational Gang Crisis between Los Angeles and San Salvador*. Durham, NC: Duke University Press.

Zimmerman, Mary K., Jacquelyn S. Litt, and Christine E. Bose, eds. 2006. *Global Dimensions of Gender and Carework*. Stanford, CA: Stanford Social Sciences.

Index

For the benefit of digital users, indexed terms that span two pages (e.g., 52–53) may, on occasion, appear on only one of those pages.

abandonment of family by migrants, fear of, 49–51, 102–3
abolition, 172–74
accompaniment, for collective social transformation, 169–74
accompliceship, 169–74
address, forms of, 60–62, 98
adjacency pairs, 122, 124, 134–35
affective communicative labor, 87–89, 97, 119–20, 152
affordances, communicative, 75–76
age, care expectations related to, 38–39, 40, 70–71, 79–80, 108, 113
alignment (of stance), 151–52, 156–57
allyship. *See* accompliceship
ambassadors. *See* working ambassador *(embajador laboral)*
asylum, granted by US, 9
asymmetrical care practices
    asymmetrical reciprocity, 65–66, 70–71, 108, 113
    gendered, 40, 70–72, 113, 120
    generational, 40, 70–71, 79–80, 108, 113
    migrant *vs.* nonmigrant relatives, 102–3, 108–10, 116–17, 119–20, 136
    transnational phone calls, 66–67, 79–80, 82, 106–9, 119–20

bilingual education, 171

Campos, Berta Luz (television show host), 49
Cantón El Río (village pseudonym), 9–12, 142–43
care
    and communication, 6–7, 18–24, 162–67
    co-optation under neoliberal capitalism, 18, 23, 37–38
    definitions of, 14–16
    gendered, 40, 70–72
    as a generational responsibility, 40, 79–80

role in reproducing social inequities, 15, 21, 68–69, 83–84, 110, 164–66
    understood as unidirectional, 33, 41–42, 52–53, 166–67
    as a verb *(cuidar)*, 6
care calculation, 17
care labor. *See* care work
care practices
    asymmetrical care engagements, 57–58, 66–67, 88, 108–10, 119–20
    asymmetrical reciprocity, 65–66, 70–71, 108, 113
    in enacting *convivencia*, 5–6, 16, 87, 111, 153–54, 165
    mobilized in support of neoliberal projects, 55 (*see also* neoliberalism)
    mutual care obligations, 62–63, 169–70, 173–74
    as producing inequities, 15, 21, 83–84, 164
care work
    distribution of, 42, 71–72, 79–80, 113
    gendering of, 21, 39–41, 51, 57–58, 69–72, 120
    as relied upon by capitalism, 18, 23, 37–38
care, cross-border. *See* cross-border care
cellphone technology and access, 74, 77–78, 80, 170–71
Central America, US intervention in, 5, 9
Central American migrants, negative depictions of, 3, 32
children, socialization of, 129
    migrant *vs.* nonmigrant relatives, 102–5
civil disobedience, 13–14
civil war, Salvadoran, 9–10, 37, 140–42, 143–44
climate change, 11
collective care, 5–6, 58, 67–68, 163
collective forgetting, 141–42, 148–49
collective memory, 139–40, 142–43, 146–49, 159–60

214 Index

communication. *See also* cross-border communication
  as care work, 6–7, 18, 19–21, 79–80, 162–63
  digital technologies for, 18–19, 74, 75–78, 86–87, 170–71 (*see also* digital technologies for communication)
  as transformative resource, 81–82, 83, 165–69, 173–74
communication technologies. *See also* digital technologies for communication
  arrival of in El Salvador, 74
  video *saludos* (greetings), 86–88, 93
communication, cross-border. *See* cross-border communication
communication, everyday, 166–69
  as vital care practice, 6–7, 18–19, 20–21, 135–36
communication, phatic, 89–90, 110
communicative action, requests, 121–22, 123–25, 126, 128, 130, 158–59
communicative affordances, 75–76
communicative care, 19–22, 27, 156–57
  humor used in, 133–35, 138–39, 158–59
  as resistance, 166–67
communicative labor, 19, 79–80, 82–83, 148–49
  affective, 87–89, 97, 119–20, 152
  remittances, 116–17, 119–20
communicative memory practices, 140, 142, 143–45, 146–47, 159–60
community engagement model of accompaniment, 169–74
complaints as indirect requests, 123–25, 126, 128, 130
  intensified with reported speech, 126–28, 130, 133
consumption, legitimate, 115–16
contract, intergenerational, 66, 67–68, 108
conversational temporality, 113–14, 122–23, 126, 132–35, 136–37, 167–69
convivencia (living-together), 2, 88–89, 111, 153–54, 159–60
  children of migrants *vs.* nonmigrants, 103–5
  conversational, 159–60
  idealization of, 153
  and remittances, 33, 119
  transnational, 5–6, 23, 58
  video *saludos* (greetings), 87, 93
corrupting influence of US on migrants, imagined, 48–50, 139

criminalized deportee (figure of migrant personhood), 44–46, 54
cross-border care
  asymmetrical, migrant *vs.* nonmigrant, 22–23, 72–74, 108–10, 116–17, 119–20, 136
  communication, 2–3, 18–19, 27–29, 59, 156–57, 164–67
  multigenerational, 16–17, 40, 65–68, 113
  phone calls, 25–26, 66–67, 75, 77–81, 106–9
  rituals of remembering, 146–48
cross-border communication, 2–3, 18–19, 22–23, 59–60, 164–67
  about remittances, 112, 115–16, 121, 129–30, 136, 158–59
  as diagnostic of migrants' sense of family obligation, 48, 50
  imagined togetherness, 155–57
  in maintaining transnational *convivencia*, 16, 111, 150–52, 153–54
  migrants *vs.* nonmigrants, 72–74, 82–83, 102–3
  phone calls, 66–67, 75, 77–81, 106–9
  remembering, joint, 28–29, 138–40, 149–50, 152, 153–54, 159–60
  requests, 121–22, 123–25, 126, 128, 130
  video calls, 78, 170–71
  video *saludos* (greetings), 28, 86–88, 93, 97–99
cross-border mobility, 161–62

data
  open-ended interviews, 25
  participant observation, 25, 26
  transnational phone calls, 25–26, 74–75, 77–78, 112
  video *saludos* (greetings), 91–92
Day of the Dead (Día de los Difuntos), 146–49
decolonial perspectives on migration, 13–14
dehumanization, 44–46
Departamento 15 (the 15th department) Salvadoran diaspora, 34–35
deportation
  criminalized deportee (figure of migrant personhood), 44–46
  as a worry, 12–13, 49–50, 112–13
Día de los Difuntos (Day of the Dead), 146–49
dialogic syntax, 157, 158–59

Index 215

dialogism, 156–57, 158–59
digital technologies for communication, 18–
19, 74, 170–71
access, 18–19, 74, 77–78, 170–71
affordances, 74, 75–76
Facebook, 75–78, 161–62
phone calls, 77–79
video calls, 74, 78, 170–71
video *saludos* (greetings), 86–88, 93
direct requests, 121–22, 125
discourses of migration and family. *See also*
state-endorsed migration discourse
resistance to, 157, 166–67, 171–72
disintegration of family, as caused by
migration, 49, 53–54
distant brother. See *hermano lejano*
distribution of (care) labor, 42, 71–72, 79–
80, 116–17
gendered norms, 69–70, 71–72, 113, 120

El Salvador. *See also* state-endorsed
migration discourse
communication technologies, 74, 77–78
historical context, 8–12, 140–42
neoliberal restructuring, 37, 55
embajador laboral (working ambassador),
30–31, 36t, 41–42
enactment and signification, simultaneity of,
59–60, 84, 110–11, 165–67
entrepreneurial returnee (figure of migrant
personhood), 36t
ethico-moral personhood, 41–43, 54–55
moral imaginaries, 27, 39–40, 68–71,
73, 83–84
ethico-morality, 22
ethico-moral evaluations, 21, 69
ethico-moral figurations of
personhood, 33–35
ethico-moral meanings, 21, 39–41, 69–70,
73–74, 163
ethico-moral personhood, 41–43, 54–55
ethnographic research, 24–25
evidence of remittance spending, 115–16,
119, 147–48
extended households, multigenerational, 65,
67–68, 71

Facebook, 75–78, 161–62
failed migrants (as scapegoats), 35, 44–46, 54
family abandonment by migrants, fear of,
49–51, 102–3

family disintegration, as caused by migration,
49, 53–54
family separation, 1–2, 4–5, 49, 172
family, imaginaries of, 83–84, 97–99, 103,
105, 110–11, 171–72
femininity, 71–72, 77
figures of migrant personhood. *See* migrant
figures of personhood
FMLN (Farabundo Martí National
Liberation Front), 9–10, 123
forgetting. *See also* remembering
collective and intergenerational, 141
institutional, 140–42, 148–49
resistance to, 139–40, 141–42, 145, 148–
49, 154

gender ideologies, 72, 113
gender norms, 1, 71–72
sacrifice, 42–43
transnational remittances, 113, 120
gendering of care work, 21, 39–41, 51, 57–
58, 69–72
resistance to, 79–82, 127
gendering of migrant figures, 38–39, 40–
42, 51
generational understanding of kin care, 40–
41, 70–71, 108, 113
generational understanding of migrant
figures, 38–39, 40, 41–42
geopolitical borders, mapped onto kin ties,
99, 108–10, 164
global households, 67
macroeconomic role of, 112
global inequality as driver of migration,
164–65, 172
global North and South
inequities between, 2–3, 82–83, 105, 110–
11, 115–16, 172
inequities entangled with family and political
economies, 84, 94, 115–16, 164–65
glosses, 14
governance, reproductive, 4
gracious personhood, 70–74, 75–76, 77–78
grammars, relational, 61–63, 95, 97–99
greetings, 93, 110–11. *See also* mandar
saludos (genre of greeting)
importance of, 89–90, 165
indirect, 90–91, 108–9
grievance, rhetorics of, 124–25, 127

habitus, embodied and linguistic, 69

216 Index

health, conversations about, 1, 14, 132, 134
hermano lejano (distant brother)
  figure of migrant personhood, 35–37,
    36*t*, 38–44
  postwar monument, 30
  television show, 49
heroic figures of migrant personhood, 35–44
heteronormative masculinity, 40–41
heteronormative understandings of kin and
  kin care, 39, 43–44, 54–55, 69–70
hierarchies, 66
  based on social difference, 39–40, 65–
    66, 88, 89
  entangled with political-economic
    inequities, 22–23, 82–83, 84, 88,
    136, 164–65
  interpersonal relationships, 61–62, 88
  of kinship, 84, 97–99, 165–66
  patriarchal ideas of, 39–40, 42, 69–70
  scalar, 8
historical memory *(memoria histórica)*, 140,
  141–45, 148–49
households
  extended, multigenerational, 65, 71
  global, 67, 112
humor used in care, 133–35, 138–39, 158–59

ideologies
  of gender, 113 (*see also* gender norms)
  of language socialization, 100–1
  neoliberal, 11, 43–44 (*see also*
    neoliberalism)
  of transnational families, 53–54, 83–84
imaginaries
  definition of, 34–35
  of family, 83–84, 97–99, 103, 105, 110–
    11, 171–72
  of migration, 34–35, 38, 41–44, 154
  moral, 27–28, 68–71, 73, 83–84
  national imaginaries, 37–38, 39–40, 43–
    44, 54–56
imagined togetherness, 155–57, 158–59
immigration policy, 4–5, 11–12, 32, 105, 161
  mixed-status families, uneven
    protection of, 66
  temporary agricultural work visas, 30–
    31, 41
  temporary status, 12–13
indirect greetings, 90–91, 108–9. *See also*
  mandar saludos (genre of greeting)
indirect requests, 123–25, 126, 128, 130, 133

inequities between global North and South,
  2–3, 82–83, 105, 110–11, 115–16, 172
  as driver of migration, 164–65, 172
inequities, gendered, 21, 71–72, 113, 127, 164
inequities, reproduced by care, 15, 21, 68–69,
  83–84, 110, 164–66
institutional forgetting, 140–42
  resistance to, 141–42, 145, 148–49
institutional silence, 140–41, 142–45
interactional timescales, 113–14, 122–23,
  134–35, 136–37, 168
interdiscursivity, 126, 127, 129–30, 132–33,
  156–57, 167–68
intergenerational (care) contract, 66, 67–
  68, 108
intergenerational care, 70–71, 113
  remittances, 40–41, 108, 113
intergenerational forgetting, 141
intermediary used for sending greetings. *See*
  indirect greetings
internet, accessibility of, 74, 170–71
intersubjective attunement, 134
intersubjective relations, 151–52
intertextuality. *See* interdiscursivity
intimacy, 17–18, 56, 78–79
  as a methodological stance, 24–25

joint remembering, 28–29, 138–40, 149–50,
  152, 153–54, 159–60
  imagined togetherness, 155–57, 158–59

kin care
  asymmetrical, gendered, 40, 70–72,
    113, 120
  asymmetrical, migrant *vs.* nonmigrant,
    102–3, 108–10, 116–17, 119–20, 136
  intergenerational, 40–41, 70–71, 108, 113
  as transformative work, 18, 83, 165–69
kinship
  based on ancestry rather than marriage, 71
  as emerging from care practices, 17, 18–19
  geopolitical borders mapped onto kin ties,
    99, 108–10, 164
  hierarchies, 84, 97–99, 165–66
  imaginaries of transnational kin ties, 97–
    99, 105
  patriarchal ideas of, 39–40, 69–70
kinship, transnational, and global inequity,
  84, 104–5, 108–10, 116–17

lament, ritual, 124–25

Index **217**

language
and care, 162–69
as crucial to emergence of moral
imaginaries, 69
as a material phenomenon, 16, 164
multifunctionality of, 59–60, 165–67
role of language in care, 19–22, 27
and transnational *convivencia*, 16, 59, 88–
89, 111, 153–54
language brokering, 20
language education policy, 171
language proficiency of children of
migrants, 103
language socialization, 99–101, 129, 131–32
prompting, 100–1
legitimate consumption, 115–16
linguistic anthropology, 7–8
imaginaries, 34–35
and medical anthropology, 14
methods, 26

mandar saludos (genre of greeting), 87, 88–
89, 97, 110–11
indirect greetings, 90–91
language socialization, 99–103
phone calls, 106–9
video *saludos*, 28, 86–88, 93, 97–99
masculinity, 40–41, 72, 113
Matanza, La (The Slaughter)
(1932), 140–41
memoria histórica (historical memory), 140,
141–45, 148–49
memory. *See* remembering
memory work, 28–29, 147–48
methodology
ethnographic research, 24–25
linguistic anthropology, 26
multisited ethnography, 6–7, 24–25
participant observation, 25, 26
transnational phone calls, 25–26
migrant experience. *See also* migrant *vs.*
nonmigrant relatives
of family abandonment worries, 52
migrant figures of personhood, 33–35, 36*t*
criminalized deportee, 44–46, 54
failed migrants, 35, 44–46, 54
heroic migrants, 35–44
migrante desobligado (the selfish migrant
figure), 46–53, 139, 154
migrant remittances. *See* remittances
migrant voting rights, from overseas, 55

migrant *vs.* nonmigrant relatives
asymmetrical care practices, 102–3, 108–
10, 116–17, 119–20, 136
children's socialization, 102–5
cross-border communication, 2–3, 18–19,
22–23, 72–74, 82–83, 164–67
geopolitical borders mapped onto kin
ties, 164
national imaginaries of, 41–42, 43–
44, 54–56
normative care roles, 21, 47, 82–83
transnational kin care, 72–74, 116–
17, 119–20
migrante desobligado (the selfish migrant
figure), 46–53, 139, 154
migrants, undocumented, 5, 12, 105, 161
migration
driven by global inequality, 164–65, 172
driven by violence, 11–12, 141
from El Salvador, 10–12, 104–5
imaginaries of, 34–35, 38, 41–44, 154
motivated by intergenerational
contract, 66
as a political act, 13–14
migration discourse, state-endorsed. *See*
state-endorsed migration discourse
migration rates
among women, 10–11
of Salvadorans, 12
mixed-status families, uneven protection
under US immigration law, 66
mobility, cross-border, 161–62
Monumento a la Memoria y la Verdad
(Monument to Memory and
Truth), 143–44
moral corruption, fear of, 48–53
moral imaginaries, 27, 68–71, 73, 83–84
of care and gracious personhood, 39–40,
68–71, 83–84
of family, 83–84, 103, 105, 110–11, 171–72
moral panics, transnational, 44–46
morality. *See* ethico-morality
multidirectional care, 58, 77–78, 83–84, 111
multigenerational care, 16–17, 40, 65–68, 113
multigenerational families
migrant families in the US, 82–83
multigenerational extended households,
65, 67–68, 71
music, migration discourse in, 38–39
mutual aid, 173–74
mutual care obligations, 62–63, 169–70

218 Index

naming the victims of violence, 143–45
narratives, complaints embedded within, 126, 128
nation as family, 32–33, 36*t*, 38–40, 43–44
national imaginaries, 39–40, 43–44
  of migration, 37–38, 41–44, 54–56, 154
national reputation, 41
neoliberalism, 11, 43–44
  co-optation of family ties, 23, 33, 37–38, 55, 108, 170
  and Salvadoran state discourses, 43–44, 55
  structural adjustment programs in El Salvador, 37
nonmigrants
  obligations of, 102–3, 108–10
  travel to US, 161–62
  understandings of, 41–42, 72–74

Our Parents' Bones (organization), 142–43

personhood. *See also* migrant figures of personhood
  ethico-moral, 41–43, 54–55
  gracious, 70–74, 75–76, 77–78
phatic communication, 89–90, 110
phone calls, transnational, 66–67, 75, 77–81, 106–9
policy, immigration, 4–5, 11–12, 32, 161
political-economic forces, as driver of migration, 164–65
postwar monuments, San Salvador, 30, 143–44
privacy of communication, 77–78
privatization, 37. *See also* neoliberalism

raciolinguistics, 168–69
radio greetings, 90–91
reciprocity, asymmetrical, 65–66, 70–71, 108, 113
relational grammars, 61–63, 95, 97–99
remembering, 138–40, 141–42
  as care, 148–49
  and forgetting, 139–40
  imagined togetherness, 155–57, 158–59
  joint remembering, 28–29, 138–40, 149–50, 152, 153–54, 159–60
  memoria histórica (historical memory), 140, 141–45, 148–49
  naming the victims of violence, 143–45
  as resistance, 139, 141–42, 145, 148–49, 154, 159–60

rituals of, 144–45, 146–49
  understanding of, 28–29
reminiscence, shared, 138–39, 149–54
remittances, 10–11, 112–13, 115–16
  asymmetrical care practices, 66–67, 113, 116–17, 119–20, 128
  communication about, 121, 123–25, 126–28, 129–30, 136, 158–59
  emotional/affective communicative labor, 116–17, 119–20
  evidence of spending, 115–16, 119, 147–48
  gendered distributions of care work, 40, 41–42, 113, 120
  as generational reciprocity, 40–41, 108, 113
  from the heroic migrant figure, 35–38, 40–42
  requests for, 130, 133, 158–59
  for rituals of remembering, 147
  role in sustaining economies, 23, 37–38, 112
  as topic of transnational phone conversations, 112, 115–16
reported speech, 126, 127, 133
reproductive governance, 4
requests
  as form of communicative action, 121–22, 123–25, 126, 128, 130, 158–59
  indirect, through complaints, 123–25, 126–28, 130
resistance, 154
  to capitalism, 23, 108, 170
  to dominant discourses of migration and family, 157, 166–67, 171–72
  to gendered care work, 79–82, 127
  to institutional forgetting, 141–42, 145, 148–49
  mutual aid, 173–74
  to narratives of migrant forgetting, 139, 154
resistance, collective, 13–14, 141–42, 145
rhetorics of grievance, 124–25, 127
ritual lament, 124–25
rituals of remembering, 144–45, 146–49
Romero, Óscar (Salvadoran Archbishop), 169

sacrifice, gendered conceptualization of, 42–43
Salvadoran civil war, 9–10, 37, 140–42, 143–44
Salvadoran diaspora, labeled *Departamento 15* (the 15th department), 34–35

San Salvador postwar monuments, 30, 143–44

scale (theoretical concept), 7–8, 167–69

scapegoating
   of failed migrants, 35, 44–46, 54
   of transnational families, 54

selfish migrant figure (*migrante desobligado*), 46–53, 139

separation, family, 1–2, 4–5, 49, 172

sequence organization (conversation analysis), 113–14

signification and enactment, simultaneity of, 59–60, 84, 110–11, 165–67

silence, institutional, 140–41, 142–45

smartphones, 74

social change work, 173–74

socialization of children, 129
   migrant *vs.* nonmigrant relatives, 102–5

speech, reported, 126, 127, 133

stance alignment, 151–52, 156–57

state-endorsed migration discourse, 27, 31–32, 111
   failed migrants as scapegoats, 35, 44–46, 54
   figures of migrant personhood, 33–35, 36*t*
   hermano lejano television show, 49
   migrant remittances, 37–38
   and neoliberalism, 32–33, 37–38, 43–44, 55
   in popular music, 38–39
   transnational families as scapegoats, 54
   understandings of nonmigrants, 41–42

technologically mediated communication, 18–19, 74, 170–71
   access, 18–19, 74, 77–78, 170–71
   affordances, 74, 75–76
   Facebook, 75–78, 161–62
   phone calls, 77–79
   radio greetings, 90–91
   video calls, 74, 78, 170–71
   video *saludos* (greetings), 86–88, 93, 97–99

television, *hermano lejano* show, 49

temporality, 150–51, 158–59
   ahorita (right now), 127–28
   conversational, 113–14, 122–23, 126, 132–35, 136–37, 167–69
   ya (adverb), 47–48

temporary status (immigration policy), 12–13

temporary work visa program, 30–31, 41

timescales, interactional and interdiscursive, 113–14, 167–69

togetherness, imagined, 155–57, 158–59

transformative work, 18, 165–69, 173–74
   using communication as resource, 81–82, 83

transnational care
   asymmetrical, migrant *vs.* nonmigrant, 22–23, 72–74, 108–10, 116–17, 119–20, 136
   communication, 2–3, 18–19, 27–29, 59, 156–57, 164–67
   multigenerational, 16–17, 40, 65–68, 113
   phone calls, 25–26, 66–67, 75, 77–81, 106–9
   rituals of remembering, 146–48

transnational *convivencia*, 5–6, 23, 57–58, 83–84, 88–89, 111
   and children, 103, 105
   enacted to bridge separation, 150–52, 153–54, 159–60
   as resistance, 8, 13–14, 23, 111, 139, 153–54

transnational families, 5
   communicative care, 6–7, 74–75, 160, 166–69
   ideologies of, 53–54, 83–84, 171–72
   remittances, 10–11, 112–14, 119–20
   as scapegoats, 54
   socialization into, 101–5, 129, 131–32

transnational remembrance, 139, 146–47, 159–60

Trump administration
   immigration policy, 4–5, 32
   rhetoric, 32, 45–46

undocumented migrants, 5, 12, 105, 161

unidirectional understanding of care, 33, 41–42, 52–53, 166–67

United States as corrupting influence, 48–50, 139

US immigration policy, 4–5, 11–12, 32, 105, 161
   family separation caused by, 4–5, 172
   mixed-status families, uneven protection for, 66
   temporary agricultural work visas, 30–31
   temporary status, 12–13

US intervention in Central America, 5, 9

US intervention in El Salvador, 141
   neoliberal restructuring, 37, 55

220 Index

victimized migrant (figure of migrant personhood), 36*t*
video calls, transnational, 78, 170–71
video *saludos* (greetings), 28, 86–88, 93, 97–99
violence
  as driver of migration, 11–12, 141
  naming the victims of, 143–45
  wartime, 140–42, 144–45
visa application process, 161–62
vos (informal second-person pronoun), 60–62
voting rights for overseas migrants, 55

war crimes, 140–42
women
  gendering of care work, 40, 42–43, 57–58, 69–72, 79–82 (*see also* gender ideologies; gender norms)
  migration rates of, 10–11, 38–39
  subordination of, 39–40
  transnational remittances, 42–43, 113, 120
working ambassador (*embajador laboral*), 30–31, 36*t*, 41–42

ya (adverb), 47–48

The manufacturer's authorised representative in the EU for product safety is Oxford
University Press España S.A. of El Parque Empresarial San Fernando de Henares,
Avenida de Castilla, 2 – 28830 Madrid (www.oup.es/en or product.safety@oup.com).
OUP España S.A. also acts as importer into Spain of products made by the manufacturer.

Printed in the USA/Agawam, MA
August 15, 2025

892047.008